COMIBAM 1984-2000:

HISTORICAL ANALYSIS OF A MAJORITY WORLD MISSIONARY NETWORK

by

Julio S. Guarneri

BOB GARRETT, Ph.D., Faculty Chair

STEPHEN M. STOOKEY, Ph.D., Committee Member

SUZANNE KAVLI, Ph.D., Committee Member

Adam Wright, Ph. D., Dean, Gary Cook School of Leadership

A Dissertation Presented in Partial Fulfillment

Of the Requirements for the Degree

Doctor of Philosophy

Dallas Baptist University

November 11, 2013

© 2017 EMS Press
All rights reserved. No part of this work may be reproduced or transmitted in any form or by any means, electronics or mechanical, including photocopying and recording, without the prior permission of the publisher. The only exceptions are brief quotations in printed reviews.

Published by EMS Press
5511 SE Hawthorne Blvd., Portland, OR 97215
www.emsweb.org

COMIBAM 1984-2000:
Historical Analysis of a Majority World Missionary Network
By Julio Guarneri

ISBN: 978-1945607035

We hereby recommend that the submitted Dissertation

Title: **COMIBAM 1984-2000: HISTORICAL ANALYSIS OF A MAJORITY WORLD MISSIONARY NETWORK**

By: Julio S. Guarneri

Be accepted in partial fulfillment of the requirements for the Degree of:

Doctor of Philosophy in Leadership Studies

Jeremy Dutschke, Ph.D., Program Director	Date

Dissertation Committee

Bob Garrett, Ph.D., Committee Chair	Date
Suzanne Kavli, Ph.D., Committee Member	Date
Stephen M. Stookey, Ph.D., Committee Member	Date

Dean, Gary Cook School of Leadership

Adam Wright, Ph.D.	Date

Abstract

This dissertation provides a historical analysis of the *Cooperación Misionera Ibero Americana* [Ibero American[1] Missionary Cooperation] (COMIBAM). This historical analysis consists of COMIBAM's first sixteen years (1984-2000). The purpose is to tell the story of this important network and its missionary advance and to provide the baseline for further research on the topic. The thesis posits that COMIBAM as a missionary network from the Majority World represents an indigenous movement that has made a significant impact on the global missionary advance. Visionary indigenous leadership, a context of ecumenism, missionary fervor and changes in the Latin American landscape have given COMIBAM International the impetus of a movement. This is a case study of the right leadership in the right context producing an effective missionary network. The research method consisted of first reviewing the body of secondary source literature. Secondly, the primary sources were examined. The third step consisted of interviews with COMIBAM leaders, missionaries and other Latin American evangelicals and the examination of the COMIBAM/Bertuzzi archive in order to obtain further data, validation of written documentation and complementation of differing perspectives. The dissertation was written using a humanities paradigm. The study has demonstrated that COMIBAM International was a successful missionary network in the twentieth century

---

[1] In the controversy regarding hyphenation of compound nationalities, some have suggested that the hyphen may indicate bias. Since the *Chicago Manual of Style* (16th ed.) in section 8:38 indicates that the hyphen does not aid in the comprehension of such terms, this dissertation will avoid the use of the hyphen for the terms Ibero America and Ibero American.

in regard to the broadening scope of its outreach, the increased number of missionaries sent, the growth in number of missionary training and sending agencies that were formed, and the longevity of the organization. The study of COMIBAM as a missionary network from the Majority World yields practical insights for the advancement of mission in the twenty-first century. These implications include the impact of missionary sending from the Majority World on the global church, the need for the church in the northern hemisphere and the church in the southern hemisphere to partner in order to effectively fulfill the Great Commission, the urgency of reexamining the mobilization of Hispanic evangelicals in the United States, and the need for the continued development of a Latin American missiology in the twenty-first century.

Keywords: COMIBAM, *Cooperación Misionera Ibero Americana,* Ibero American Missionary Cooperation, missionary network, Majority World, indigenous movement, global missions, evangelical church in Latin America, *Fraternidad Teológica Latinoamericana,* FTL, Latin American Theological Fraternity, leadership, missionary sending, global church, mobilization, Hispanic evangelicals, Latin American missiology, CLADE, CONELA, *Misión Integral,* Integral Mission, Luis Bush, David Ruiz, Rudy Girón, Jonathan Lewis, Federico Bertuzzi, Bertil Ekström, Carlos Scott, Jesús Londoño, Samuel Escobar, René Padilla, Ralph Winter, UPGs, 10/40 Window.

Dedication

To my wife, Monica Soria Guarneri, who gave me continuous moral and emotional support throughout this eight-year journey, encouraged me constantly, protected my time countless times, sacrificed dates and vacation times on multiple occasions, and never doubted my ability to get it done. I could not have done it without you! I love you!

To my children, Joshua, Rachel, Mia and Stevan, whose support, encouragement and sacrifice will forever be appreciated. I love you all with all my heart!

In memory of Bro. Leo Jimenez, who lit a fire under me, sponsored me financially through the seminar phase, encouraged me to the end, and championed my cause every chance he had, and his dear wife, Sulema "Sule" Jimenez, for her steadfast love. They have treated me like a son. I am indebted to them both.

Acknowledgments

The completion of a doctoral dissertation is a feat that cannot be accomplished by an individual without the significant support and guidance of multiple people and entities. I am deeply grateful for each individual and organization that made the completion of my journey possible.

I am thankful for my extended family's love and support. My father Carlo Guarneri and my mother Elizabeth M. Guarneri prayed for me and believed in me. My father and mother-in-law, Jose Isaac and Diana Soria, who never stopped praying and who frequently encouraged me with their words.

Cohort I of the Ph.D. program at DBU was a source of encouragement throughout the eight-year journey, especially my friend Sergio A. Ramos, who also became an accountability partner in this process.

I thank God for Dallas Baptist University and the Gary Cook Graduate School of Leadership and for the servant-leadership and personal encouragement I received from many in the administration and faculty, including Dr. Gary Cook, President of DBU; Dr. Karen Bullock, first Director of the Ph.D. program; and Dr. Jeremy Dutschke, current director of the Ph.D. program.

My dissertation committee offered me helpful guidance, challenged me, and encouraged me. Dr. Bob "Roberto" Garrett incessantly worked with me with great enthusiasm, believing in the value of this project, and spending countless hours on phone calls, emails, text messages, revisions and face-to-face conversations. Dr. Garrett was instrumental in my connecting with key COMIBAM leaders and in the publishing of a seminal seminar paper in an EMS journal.

Dr. Justice "Justo" Anderson also shared in the enthusiasm of this project and offered to help me. The Lord called Dr. Anderson to his heavenly home before I finished the dissertation but his smile and great example as a passionate missions scholar and practitioner motivated me.

I am thankful for Texas Baptists (the Baptist General Convention of Texas) and to the DBU ministerial scholarship office led by Dr. Joe Mosley for the ministerial grant received during the dissertation phase. I treasure the prayers, support and sacrificial patience of Iglesia Bautista Getsemani in Fort Worth, Texas, where I served as Senior Pastor from 1993 to 2010 and where I completed the seminar phase. The congregation, the deacon body, and the staff were a constant source of strength for me. The prayerful support and constant encouragement of Calvary Baptist Church in McAllen, Texas where I have served as Lead Pastor from 2010 to the present, has been invaluable. The deacon body, the personnel committee, the wonderful staff and the entire congregation held my arms up during the dissertation phase.

I am indebted to those who, like Karen Hatley, connected me with COMIBAM leaders and with COMIBAM leaders including, José de Dios, Daniel Bianchi, David Ruiz, Luis Bush, Rudy Girón, Carlos Scott, Jesús Londoño, Decio DeCarvalho, Jonathan Lewis, Ted Limpic and Federico Bertuzzi, who shared valuable information with me . I am especially grateful to Jesús Londoño who agreed to include me in the "by-invitation-only" Fourth General Assembly of COMIBAM in Bogota (2009) which proved to be a very fruitful trip, and to Federico Bertuzzi who, while living in Granada, Spain, agreed to meet me in Santa Fe, Buenos Aires, giving me full access to his vast COMIBAM archive room, and making a classic Argentine "asado" for me at his house. I'll never forget it!

Table of Contents

Acknowledgments...v

List of Tables..xii

List of Figures..xiii

CHAPTER 1. INTRODUCTION..1

    Introduction to the Research Question..1

    Purpose and Scope of the Study...2

    Rationale, Significance of the Study and Research Questions...................4

    Method...5

    Background of the Study...9

    Assumptions and Limitations..13

    Definition of Terms...13

CHAPTER 2. PRECURSORS TO THE FORMATION OF COMIBAM............18

    Introduction..18

    Congresses on World Evangelization..18

        The Edinburgh Missionary Conference...21

        Congreso de Acción Misionera en América Latina, Panama..........23

        Iglesia y Sociedad en América Latina...23

        Congress for World Evangelization, Berlin....................................24

        Congreso Latinoamericano de Evangelización, Bogota.................24

        International Congress for World Evangelization, Lausanne............25

    The Latin American Context..28

        Socio-Economic Context..29

Political Context..31

Religious Context..33

Fraternidad Teológica Latinoamericana..36

An Alternative Missiology for Latin America...37

Emergence of a New and Proactive Indigenous Leadership................40

René Padilla Advocates *Misión Integral*..41

National Mission Movements..44

Three Important National Movements...45

El Salvador...46

Argentina...47

Evangelical Organizations that Contributed to COMIBAM.........................50

World Evangelical Fellowship...50

Operation Mobilization...52

Congreso Latinoamericano de Evangelización..................................53

Confraternidad Evangélica Latinoamericana....................................54

Misión Mundial Books...55

Summary and Conclusions..61

CHAPTER 3. COMIBAM '87: THE BIRTH OF A MISSIONS MOVEMENT...........64

Introduction..64

The First Congress..65

The Process for the Conceptualization of the Congress.....................66

The Proposed Scope of the Congress..70

Plenary Sessions: Topics and Personalities..81

viii

The Congress Becomes a *Cooperación*: COMIBAM International.................84

Leadership Theory and COMIBAM Leaders...85

National Mission Movements: The Network's First Level.........................89

Leaders and Leadership at the Continental Level....................................100

    Leadership through Communicating the Vision............................100

    Coordinating Committee and Administrative Staff........................104

    Connecting with the Rest of the World and Theological Conference....106

    Leadership Transition after the First Congress..............................108

Missiological Reflection at the Onset of the Movement...........................112

    Missiological Dialogue before COMIBAM '87............................114

    Plenary Sessions: Missiological Observations.............................124

Summary and Conclusions..132

CHAPTER 4. COMIBAM II: A MISSIONS NETWORK CONSOLIDATES..........136

Introduction..136

Missiological Currents in Latin America..138

    Post-Imperial Missiology...139

    Managerial Missiology..140

    Holistic Missiology...141

Missiological Currents of the *Fraternidad Teológica Latinoamericana* and

    COMIBAM...141

The Second Congress..143

    Numerical Status of Ibero American Missionary Sending................144

    Congress Presenters..147

    Topics of Discussion at the Second Congress..............................148

    Missionary Testimonies and National Consultation Reports...............149

    Publications Surrounding the Second COMIBAM Congress..............151

    COMIBAM Publications from the Acapulco Congress Forward.........165

National Mission Movements..168

    Cooperation between Churches and Missionary Agencies................169

    Comprehensive Missionary Training..170

    Enlistment and Screening of Missionary Candidates............... 170

    The More Advanced National Mission Movements........................171

    The Less Mature National Mission Movements............................173

COMIBAM Meetings between Congresses...175

    CLADE IV...176

    First COMIBAM Consultation on the Pastoral Care of Missionaries....181

    First COMIBAM General Assembly..181

    Reach-a-People-Group Committee Strategy Meeting......................186

Leaders and Leadership...189

    Organizational Development by Leaders....................................190

    Luis Bush: Leadership from COMIBAM to AD2000.....................191

    Partnership with Local Churches and Pastors..............................195

Other Missiological Issues...196

COMIBAM Missionaries..200

    Ibero American Missionaries: Identity and Geography....................201

    Ibero American Missionaries: The Challenges They Faced..............203

x

       COMIBAM, The Majority World and the World Christian

              Movement……………………………………………………....203

    Summary and Conclusions…………………………………………..…208

CHAPTER 5. CONCLUSION…………………………………………………...210

    Introduction……………………………………………………………..210

    Assessment of COMIBAM in the Twentieth Century………………………211

        Remarkable Success and Nominal Challenges……………………211

        COMIBAM 2006 Research Project………………………………..217

        Contributing Factors to the Success of COMIBAM……….………218

    Implications of the Study……………………………………………….222

        COMIBAM and Missionary Sending from the Majority World……..222

        The Church in the Northern Hemisphere and Majority World

              Sending……………………………………………………....223

        Mobilization of Hispanic Evangelicals in the United States…………...225

        Development of a Latin American/Majority World Missiology………226

    Recommendations for Future Research…………………………………228

        National and Regional Missionary Movements……………………...228

        A Thirty-Five Year Assessment……………………………………...229

        Organizational Developments from Inception to Present Day………...229

        Missionary Training Organizations in Latin America…………………230

        A History of Latin American Missionaries…………………………...230

    Conclusion……………………………………………………………...230

List of Tables

Table 1. Twentieth century conferences leading to COMIBAM..........................20

Table 2. COMIBAM operations budget summary (Aug. 1985-Dec. 1987)...............79

Table 3. Ibero American National Mission Movements by country......................97

Table 4. Antigua Theological Conference topics and presenters........................120

Table 5. Publications from the Acapulco Congress forward.............................165

Table 6. Development of COMIBAM's "Adopt-a-People-Group".......................187

Table 7. Projection of missionary sending shift from North to South...................204

Table 8. Christian foreign missionaries in A.D. 2000 according to Barrett.............205

Table 9. Protestant, Independent, and Anglican missionaries in A.D. 2000............206

Table 10. Protestant/PIA foreign missionaries in A.D. 1990 and 2000...................207

Table 11. Organization of COMIBAM/Bertuzzi Archive, Santa Fe, Argentina.........282

Table 12. National Missions Conferences and Congresses...............................293

Table 13. Assignment of people per Ibero American Countries..........................308

List of Figures

Figure 1. Photo of the COMIBAM '87s first coordinating committee......................71

Figure 2. Collins' (2001) "Good-to-Great matrix of creative discipline"...................86

Figure 3. Photos of file drawers and cardboard boxes in Bertuzzi archive room.........281

Figure 4. Catalog of file folders compiled by Bertuzzi......................................288

Figure 5. Catalog of cardboard boxes compiled by Bertuzzi...............................289

CHAPTER 1. INTRODUCTION

Missions conferences and publications have recently given significant attention to the growth and the global participation of the Latin American church, especially that of the evangelical segment. This new development is a part of the larger initiative about missionary sending from the Majority World, namely Africa, Asia, and Latin America. These portions of the world at one point were considered to be mission fields because of the small percentage of Christians and because of the extensive material poverty. Yet, today the evangelical church in the Majority World represents a significant mission-sending force. The study of COMIBAM (Spanish acronym for Ibero American Missionary Cooperation) as a Majority World missionary network offers a helpful analysis of the recent evangelical movement in Latin America. Such a study holds significance not only for the Latin American church, but also for the global church (Guarneri, 2009, p. 222).

Introduction to the Research Question

The current study provides a historical analysis of the *Cooperación Misionera Ibero Americana* [Ibero American Missionary Cooperation] known by its acronym COMIBAM. The birth, growth and development of this organization demonstrate vividly the manner in which the church in Latin America and the Iberian Peninsula has risen to the challenge of becoming a global missionary force. COMIBAM is a network that has mobilized the church in Latin America and Spain for global missions (Ruiz, 2007, p. 5; Taylor, 2007, p. 4). Its self-reported success and its longevity establishes

COMIBAM as a significant force among Latin American and Iberian evangelicals.[1] COMIBAM leaders and participants have published several documents. These documents, which are listed in Appendix A, shed light on the nature and work of this network. COMIBAM International has also published and distributed at least twenty-one books. Appendix B lists the COMIBAM International publications. No less than twenty-four books and periodical articles on the subject of missions from the Majority World refer specifically to COMIBAM. Appendix C consists of the list of books and articles that refer to COMIBAM. There is, however, no academic publication that examines the history of the organization. The current study provides a historical analysis of COMIBAM during its first sixteen years (1984-2000). The purpose is to tell the story of this important network and its missionary advance and to provide the baseline for further research on the topic. Such a historical analysis of a strategic new organization has value for the fields of missiology and leadership studies.

Purpose and Scope of the Study

The growth of the number of missionaries in the field from Latin America and the corresponding growth of sending organizations indigenous to Ibero America are parallel developments to the growth and influence of COMIBAM as a network. This legitimizes the significance of writing a chronicle of the first sixteen years of the organization's history.

---

[1] The entire issue of *Connections: The Journal of the WEA Missions Commission*, April-May, 6, 2007 is dedicated to COMIBAM. (The WEA is the World Evangelical Alliance).

The thesis of the current study is that COMIBAM, as a missionary network from the Majority World, represents an indigenous movement that has made a significant impact on the global missionary advance. Visionary indigenous leadership, a context of ecumenism, missionary fervor, and changes in the Latin American landscape have given COMIBAM International the impetus of a movement. The current study is a case study of the right leadership in the right context producing an effective missionary network.

The documents that relate the birth and development of COMIBAM International treat the themes of visionary indigenous leadership, a context of ecumenism, missionary fervor and changes in the Latin American landscape. These themes have also surfaced in conversations this researcher has had with COMIBAM leaders since the presentation of the COMIBAM paper at the 2008 EMS meeting in Colorado (J. Londoño, phone interview, September 25, 2008; D. Ruiz, personal interview, September 26, 2008; J. De Dios, personal interview, April 28, 2009; D. Bianchi, personal interview, May 8, 2009 and various conversations at the IV International Assembly in Bogota, October 29-November 1, 2009). This historical treatment of COMIBAM observed that indigenous leadership and missionary fervor intersected with one another and how they have contributed to COMIBAM International.

The current study limited the scope of research to the activities of COMIBAM International as an official organization. This implies that while background information on the growth of missionary enthusiasm among Spanish and Portuguese speaking evangelicals was at times included to complete a broader panorama, nevertheless this broader analysis remains beyond the purview of the dissertation. In addition, the current study examined only a sixteen-year period of history in the life of the organization, namely 1984 to 2000. The sixteen years chosen are of interest because of the 1984 meeting in Mexico to plan the first congress and the various international meetings that took place in 2000 as follow-up initiatives to the Acapulco Congress. These year-2000 meetings included the Fourth *Congreso Latinoamericano de Evangelización* [Latin American Evangelization Congress] (CLADE) in Quito, the First COMIBAM Consultation on the Pastoral Care of Missionaries in Lima, the First COMIBAM General Assembly also in Lima, and the "Reach-a-People-Group" Committee Strategy Meeting in Guatemala. Taking the first congress, which met in 1987, the second congress, which met in 1997, and the 2000 follow-up meetings as major markers in the life of the organization, this sixteen-year study provides a thorough historical analysis and evaluation of the organization. Limiting the study of this organization to these sixteen years provides a clear marking of the parameters with which the study was conducted. Yet, the sixteen-year period is sufficient to chronicle the birth and maturation of COMIBAM.

Rationale, Significance of the Study and Research Questions

A historical analysis of COMIBAM has missiological value. COMIBAM's birth and development relate to shifts in the global missionary sending force. The evangelical church in Africa, Asia and Latin America has grown numerically in a significant way (Escobar, 1999; Escobar 2003; Jenkins, 2002). Various authors have recently observed that the missionary sending force is shifting to the Majority World (Ruiz, 2002; Scott, 2007; Thomas, 2007). How has COMIBAM contributed to this surge in missionary sending? Is COMIBAM simply a network, or is it also a movement? If so, what are the characteristics of such a movement? The answers to these questions are relevant for other indigenous missionary sending initiatives from the Majority World. Additionally, COMIBAM's contributions and development have implications for missionary sending models and practices in the rest of the world (Dowsett, 2007; Rajendran, 2007; Ruiz, 2007; Thomas; van Laar, 2007).

> This COMIBAM study is significant to the story of missionary work in Latin America and the Iberian Peninsula. As such it is a sure sign of maturity for the Latin American church. It is also significant to the global church because of the increased importance of Christianity's shift to the southern hemisphere.
> (Guarneri, 2009, p. 245)

A historical analysis of COMIBAM also contributes to the discipline of leadership studies. If indeed COMIBAM is a movement and a grassroots network, what kind of leadership has characterized it? How has its leadership understood and interacted with its context? How has its leadership shaped the movement? How has its leadership transitioned and developed other leaders? These questions are relevant to the study of leadership in ministry, specifically missionary leadership.

The other closely related area is that of organizational leadership. COMIBAM is a network. What aspects of this network are institutional and what aspects are a grassroots movement? Why was the network model chosen for this initiative? Has this organizational model evolved with the organization? If so, how? How has it been effective? What are the possible implications of this for other mission sending networks?

Method

The researcher's interest in COMIBAM began with a doctoral seminar paper presented at the Evangelical Missiological Society's (EMS) regional and national meetings in Houston, Texas and Denver, Colorado, respectively, and which was subsequently published in the EMS journal (Wan, 2009). The encouragement received from knowledgeable missiologists, researchers, and key leaders of COMIBAM suggested that the topic was worthy of a fuller treatment in a dissertation.

The research combined written sources and personal interviews. Primary sources were subdivided into two types: papers, articles and books written by COMIBAM as an organization and by COMIBAM leaders, which are listed in Appendix A; and archives of historical documents of the organization, which are listed in Appendix D. Many of the documents in the first grouping were initially available in Spanish, English or Portuguese from the organization's website: www.comibam.org[2]. Subsequently, COMIBAM published some of these documents in booklet form. Appendix B lists these booklets published by COMIBAM. (The researcher has a proficient level of skill in both the English and Spanish languages. Most documents in Portuguese are available in either English or Spanish also). The secondary sources consisted of all book chapters, articles and papers written about COMIBAM. A list of these secondary sources is provided in Appendix C. The interviews provided the third research approach to this current study. The researcher interviewed twenty leaders and individuals who related to the movement or the COMIBAM organization at different stages of the sixteen-year scope covered in this historical investigation. Appendix E lists the individuals interviewed. In summary, the three methodological approaches consisted of a review of primary and secondary

---

[2] The organization's website has been reorganized and these documents are no longer available at that URL. The researcher downloaded and has maintained hard copies of these documents.

written documents, a review of the COMIBAM/Bertuzzi historical archive, and interviews of individuals who have related to COMIBAM in various ways.

The sequence of the research consisted of first reviewing the body of secondary source literature. Secondly, the primary sources, excluding the COMIBAM/Bertuzzi archive, were examined. The third step consisted of personal interviews with COMIBAM leaders, missionaries and other Latin American evangelicals and the examination of the COMIBAM/Bertuzzi archive in order to obtain further data, validation of written documentation and complementation of differing perspectives. In order to achieve this the researcher identified the precursor events to the formation of COMIBAM, the context in which it was formed, its leaders, its organizational components, its philosophy of missions, objectives, a chronology of its activity, and the results of its work.

Preliminary contacts were made with COMIBAM leaders in 2008 and 2009 in order to identify sources of data and other key individuals who could provide important information (J. Londoño, phone interview, September 25, 2008; D. Ruiz, personal interview, September 26, 2008; J. De Dios, personal interview, April 28, 2009; D. Bianchi, personal interview, May 8, 2009). During these encounters two important research elements emerged. The first element was the identification of Federico Bertuzzi as the point person for historical documents. The second element was the information about the upcoming COMIBAM General Assembly in Bogota, Colombia in October 2009. The researcher requested an invitation to attend this closed assembly for research purposes and it was granted.

The researcher traveled to Bogota, Colombia for the Fourth General Assembly of COMIBAM in October 2009. During this meeting the researcher met several of the COMIBAM leaders and participants, including Rudy Girón, Ted Limpic, Jonathan Lewis, Carlos Scott, and Jesús Londoño, conducted interviews and gathered contact information to conduct subsequent interviews with others. One of the key leaders the researcher met at this gathering was Federico Bertuzzi who had archived all of the COMIBAM documents from its inception. Bertuzzi offered the researcher access to these archives. However, the archives were stored in Santa Fe, Argentina and Bertuzzi was residing in Granada, Spain. Travel arrangements were made for the researcher and Bertuzzi to meet in Santa Fe, Argentina in May 2010.

During the Argentina trip, the researcher interviewed key Argentine leaders in the missionary movement such as Edgardo Surenian, Pablo Bongarrá and Pablo Deíros in Buenos Aires. The researcher then spent four days, May 28-31, in the archive room in the city of Santa Fe and scanned electronically as many relevant documents as possible within that time frame. The result was 888 electronic documents in PDF format (1.41 GB). Appendix D provides a description and inventory list of the COMIBAM/Bertuzzi archive.

Current and former leaders of COMIBAM were contacted to request an interview with them. The selection represented a cross-section of leaders. The interviews consisted of open-ended questions related to the same areas sought in the literature which are mentioned previously. Appendix F contains the list of interview questions. Interviews were conducted either in person, via Skype, or by telephone.

The purpose of the interviews was to obtain narrative data that would supplement the data found in written sources. The assumption was that there are stories that may not be told in the written documents. The interview instrument served as a guide to the dialogue seeking to discover the individual's personal feelings, thoughts and experiences with COMIBAM or with the activity that COMIBAM purports to facilitate. The researcher's command of the Spanish language and high level of identification with the Ibero American culture facilitated a significant level of interpersonal dialogue, thus yielding information and nuances which might not have been available otherwise.

All of the guidelines for the protection of human subjects established by Dallas Baptist University were followed. The digital recordings of the interviews were transcribed. Standard interview research methods in keeping with Dallas Baptist University's guidelines were employed.

The current study was written using a humanities paradigm to present a history of an emerging movement among Spanish and Portuguese speaking evangelicals. The data collected from interviews and document reviews was used throughout the current study to support the argumentation. Additionally, appendices with relevant information were included as needed in the end matter of the dissertation.

Background of the Study

Two spheres of research provided the background for the study of COMIBAM as a Majority World missionary network. The first sphere consists of the developments of mission mobilization in the global evangelical community of the twentieth century. The second sphere encompasses the particular developments of the evangelical church in Latin America toward the end of the twentieth century.

COMIBAM launched a movement from the platform of a missionary congress. Thus, the study of this missionary network is conducted against the backdrop of various important twentieth century worldwide and regional missionary conferences. Some of the significant world evangelization conferences of the twentieth century include the 1910 World Missionary Conference in Edinburgh, Scotland; the 1916 Congress on Christian Work in Latin America in Panama City, Panama; the 1966 World Congress on Evangelism in West Berlin, Germany; and the 1974 International Congress on World Evangelization in Lausanne, Switzerland (Guarneri, 2009). The 1910 Edinburgh conference set the tone for ecumenical cooperation in the accomplishment of the Great Commission. The 1916 Panama conference brought the conversation of world evangelization to Latin America. The 1966 Berlin conference called for the involvement of evangelicals, some of whom otherwise would not be a part of the ecumenical movement, in the task of world evangelization and secured the involvement of Latin Americans in the process. The 1974 Lausanne conference refined the work of the Berlin conference, addressed issues of holistic mission and helped in the formation of specific cooperative initiatives in Latin America. These missionary conferences shared in common the spirit of cooperation, the missionary fervor and the concern for a contextualized missiology with the first COMIBAM congress.

The developments in theological reflection and missionary advance in Latin America toward the end of the twentieth century also provide an important background to the study of COMIBAM. Of particular interest are the missiological developments of the CLADE conference and the birth of the Latin American Theological Fraternity (FTL). In particular Samuel Escobar and René Padilla emerge as spokespersons for a theological Latin American perspective on missions.

The significance of CLADE for the Latin American missionary movement was its appeal to the more conservative segment of the evangelical community and the theological discussions that eventually resulted in the development of an indigenous missiology. In a similar shift from Protestant Ecumenism to Evangelical Cross-Denominational Cooperation, CLADE organized as an alternative to the *Conferencia Evangélica Latinoamericana* [Latin American Evangelical Conference] (CELA) (Escobar, 1987; Plou, 2004; Ruiz, 2007). CELA related to the World Council of Churches, and thus to the mainline Protestant ecumenical movement. On a global scale, the Berlin congress in 1966, sponsored by the Billy Graham Evangelistic Association, provided the conservative evangelical alternative to the more liberal mainline Protestant World Council of Churches missionary conferences. Soon after Berlin, the first CLADE convened in 1969 in Bogotá (Escobar, 1987). CLADE I attempted to combine the interest in the evangelization of Latin America with the concern for social action as part of the church's mission discussed at the Berlin Conference (Escobar, 1987; Plou, 2004). However, some of the Latin American Evangelical leaders felt like CLADE I had too much influence from North American fundamentalism and saw the need to develop a more indigenous theology and missiology (Plou, 2004).

The perceived need to develop a more indigenous missiology coincided with the formation of the FTL (Escobar, 1987; Plou, 2004; Salinas, 2005). The imminent dangers for the advance of the integral mission in Latin America were two-fold. On the one side, identification with liberation theology and liberalism posed the threat of alienating the more conservative portion of evangelical leaders and participants. On the other extreme, Latin Americans did not want a wholesale adoption of North American fundamentalism, which seemed too individualistic and failed to give proper attention to the social concerns (Escobar, 1987; Plou, 2004). A holistic gospel based on biblical authority did not necessarily fit the existing Protestant Anglo-Saxon categories of liberal and conservative (Escobar, 1987).

In 1970, at Cochamba, Bolivia, during the first CLADE consultation, Latin American evangelical leaders drafted the Cochamba statement and the guidelines that essentially constituted the formation of the FTL (Coy, 1999; Escobar, 1999; Salinas, 2005). The formation of the FTL shortly after CLADE I insured an indigenous agenda and leadership for CLADE II (Plou, 2004). The leaders' discernment and ability to do this successfully in a brief period of time proved to be critical. CLADE I and the formation of the FTL took place between the Berlin Conference and the Lausanne Congress on World Evangelization. By 1974, the year of Lausanne's Congress, the FTL had formulated and articulated its theological and missiological positions, thus allowing Latin Americans a platform from which to influence the Lausanne movement (Guarneri, 2009).

Latin American Leaders such as Samuel Escobar, René Padilla, Orlando Costas, Emilio Nuñez, Peter Savage, Andrew Kirk and others organized the FTL to develop theological reflection that would be conservative, evangelistic and holistic in its missiology (Escobar, 1987; Smith, 1983). The FTL was in large measure a product of missiological concern, namely the need to advance a holistic mission in Latin America. The FTL perceived itself to be living in a *kairos* moment of history and their swift actions demonstrated such a conviction. The FTL, and later COMIBAM, pursued indigenous theological reflection and displayed a keen sense of the changing times. Furthermore, the resulting missiological theology produced by the FTL both influenced and challenged the Latin American missionary movement.

The study of COMIBAM is thus conducted against the backdrop of world missionary advance in the twentieth century and developments in the evangelical community of Latin America toward the end of the same century. The manner in which these contextual events and organizations affected COMIBAM has been considered. In what sense COMIBAM was unique and made its own and new contributions has also been examined.

Assumptions and Limitations

The researcher assumes that the evangelical distinctives, including the authority of Scripture, salvation in Christ by faith, the need for personal conversion and the mandate of the church to make followers of Christ are valid and beneficial.

Since COMIBAM is an international network of regional and national networks, this study is limited to characteristics of the movement at the macro level. This study refers to national networks only as they shed light on the international movement. The particular expressions of COMIBAM in each country and region would eventually necessitate a separate study of each.

Definition of Terms

Several of the terms utilized in the current study require definition in order to provide clarity about their meaning in the context of this study.

Church. The term church is used in several ways throughout the current study. Church may mean the local body of believers who gather for worship and service. When capitalized, the term may indicate a particular denomination such as the Roman Catholic Church or the Presbyterian Church. Often it refers to the grouping of a particular segment of Christianity, although not a formal organism, such as the evangelical church, the Latin American church, or the Pentecostal church, and it may include local churches, individuals and para-church organizations within that segment. In this last sense, it usually infers that this segment of Christianity crosses denominational boundaries. COMIBAM uses the term in the singular to refer to both the expression of the body of Christ in a global sense and to local congregations (COMIBAM International, 2006a).

Cross-cultural missionary. According to COMIBAM, this is the individual who crosses a language or cultural barrier in order to fulfill the Great Commission. COMIBAM includes in this group those who go to another country of the same language and similar culture but have crossed national geopolitical barriers (COMIBAM International, 2006a).

Evangelical. This term is used in the current study to refer to the element of Protestant Christianity that emphasizes biblical authority, salvation by faith in Christ alone, personal conversion, and the mandate to evangelize the world. Although these emphases may cut across the three larger branches of the church in Latin America: Roman Catholic, Protestant and Pentecostal, the term evangelical is most often associated with Free Churches.

Hispanic. This is the term used to refer to individuals who live in the United States of America and who either come from Latin America/Spain or whose ancestors came from Latin America/Spain. It often includes those whose ancestors lived in regions of the Southwest United States that formerly belonged to Mexico. COMIBAM limits this term to U.S. citizens whose mother tongue is either Spanish or Portuguese (COMIBAM International, 2006a). However, this usage of the term is limited since it excludes millions of Hispanics who are resident aliens or undocumented immigrants (Gonzalez, 2002). It also could omit those who by ethnicity are Hispanics but whose mother tongue is English. Thus in the current study, the researcher's definition of the term Hispanic refers to an individual living in the United States whose ethnic or linguistic heritage can be traced to either Spain or Latin America.

Ibero America. A conglomerate of countries which share affinity either because of language or ethnicity, consisting of South America, Central America, Mexico, the Caribbean, Spain, Portugal, and Hispanics in the United States and Canada. COMIBAM uses this designation because it includes the Iberian Peninsula and Latin America in one word. The term roughly subsumes most of the one-sixth of the world population that speaks Spanish or Portuguese. Leaders from these various regions of the world collaborated together in theological reflection and world evangelization strategies before the formation of COMIBAM (Padilla, 2007).

Integral Mission (*Misión Integral*). Rene Padilla coined this term to refer to the church's mission of evangelizing the world by taking a careful reading of the cultural context in which mission is done and by participating in both evangelism and social action, such as addressing poverty and social injustice (Padilla, 2006).

International/Global Church. This term refers to the sum of Christians around the world. Occasionally the term alludes to nothing more than a demographic designation. More often the descriptor assumes a spiritual or missional connection across denominational lines. It does not necessarily imply classic ecumenism or an organizational unity. Justice Anderson used the global church term in a more specific way to refer to the church of the third millennium. Anderson (2005) argued that in the first millennium, the Eastern church was the leader and it was associated with Christendom; in the second millennium, the Western church was the leader and was associated with World Christianity; in the third millennium, the Southern church will be the leader and it will be associated with Global Christianity.

Latin American. For the purposes of the current study, this term refers to people who either live in, or come from South America, Central America, Mexico or the Caribbean. It includes Brazil because of its affinity with South America in geography, in Latin-based language, and in culture.

Latino. This term refers to both Latin Americans and Hispanics. Consequently, it is sometimes used interchangeably for either of these two terms.

Mission(s). In this study the term mission(s) generally refers to the church's activity in the world as it accomplishes the purposes of God. It includes world evangelization, sending missionaries to other countries, and to social action in the community. It often relates the mission of the church, or to the *Missio Dei*, namely the mission of God. Missiologists often use the term in the singular mission to refer to all that the church does, while they use the plural missions to refer to all human activities where the church presents a gospel witness beyond itself to a lost world (Knell, 2006; Porter, 2007).

Missionaries. This term often refers to all who cross some boundary and share the gospel with unbelievers. However, COMIBAM limits this term to long-term vocational missionaries for the purposes of research and statistics. (COMIBAM International, 2006a). While the inclusion of non-professional missionaries and short-term assignments must be part of a twenty-first century strategy for world evangelization, (Escobar, 1999), it makes sense that for the purposes of reporting missionary sending statistics, COMIBAM would apply this term in its stricter sense. Such use is less cumbersome in the process of gathering data, and it allows for a consistent tracking of the categories. Nevertheless, some provision needs to be made to track the explosive numerical growth of those who serve in one-through-three-years terms, those who participate in projects ranging from one week to one semester, and those whose job-related travel and/or migration allows them to make missionary contributions even if they have not been sent by a church or agency. The initial definition of this term by COMIBAM in 1986 was, "A missionary is a disciple called by God and sent by Him through the local church, crossing geographical and/or cultural barriers, in order to communicate the whole gospel either for the establishment of the church or for its holistic growth" (Ruiz, 2000).

Visionary Leadership. For the purposes of the current study, visionary leadership consists of the demonstrated ability to assess accurately the present context and lead change that meets the objectives of a group in a way that impacts the future positively.

This brief glossary should help the reader understand with consistency how these terms are used in the current study.

CHAPTER 2. PRECURSORS TO THE FORMATION OF COMIBAM

The birth, growth, and development of COMIBAM is a fascinating example of the manner in which Latin America has risen to the challenge of becoming a global missionary force. COMIBAM is a network that seeks to mobilize the church in Latin America and Spain for global missions (Ruiz, 2007; Taylor, 2007). COMIBAM's sustained success established this entity as a significant mission sending force among Ibero American evangelicals (Taylor, 2007). COMIBAM's development parallels changes in the global missionary sending force. As noted in chapter 1, the majority world is fast becoming a missionary sending force (Bush, 2002; Dick, 2011; Ruiz, 2002). The growth of the evangelical church in the same regions of the world accompanies this shift (Anderson, 2005; Escobar, 1999; Escobar, 2003; Jenkins, 2002).

A study of COMIBAM necessitates a consideration of the events and people that preceded its formation. These precursors help in understanding the nature of COMIBAM and the timeliness of such an enterprise. Of significance are congresses on world evangelization, the Latin American cultural and ecclesiological context, the FTL, the *movimientos misioneros nacionales* [national missions movements] (MMN), and other evangelical organizations that directly contributed to the formation of COMIBAM. This chapter will examine each of the precursor events and organizations and the way in which they contributed directly or indirectly to the formation of COMIBAM.

Congresses on World Evangelization

Visionary leadership in a ripe Latin American helped to stimulate the rise of COMIBAM International (Ruiz, n.d.). One particular type of event that served as a precursor for the emergence of movements like COMIBAM was congresses on world evangelization. These congresses can be traced back as early as the beginning of the twentieth century.

Referring to these twentieth century events, Bush (2002) rightly argued that global mission conferences have a lasting impact on world evangelization. Mark Noll (2000) organized his brief overview of the history of Christianity around turning points. He listed the Edinburg Missionary Conference in 1910 as the turning point of the 20th century. The formation of COMIBAM International at the end of the same century is in some ways a ripple effect of the Edinburg Conference (Ruiz, 2003). The Edinburg Conference was followed by numerous conferences and congresses of a similar nature. Several of these world evangelization congresses paved the way for the formation of COMIBAM.

Some of the more significant missionary and world evangelization conferences that contributed to the eventual formation of COMIBAM are the 1910 World Missionary Conference in Edinburgh, Scotland; the 1916 Congress on Christian Work in Latin America in Panama City, Panama; the 1966 World Congress on Evangelism in West Berlin, Germany; and the 1974 International Congress on World Evangelization in Lausanne, Switzerland. Table 1 provides a list of these congresses along with other similar ones in order to provide a chronological context. These are referred to as the Edinburgh, Panama, Berlin and Lausanne conferences, respectively. In his analysis of multiple twentieth century global mission conferences, Bush (2002) identified Edinburgh 1910 and Lausanne 1974 as the most important ones (p. 91). The significance of these conferences and congresses is mentioned in Table 1.

Table 1

Twentieth century conferences leading to COMIBAM

Year	Conference	Sponsor	Place
1910	The Edinburgh Missionary Conference		Edinburgh, Scotland
1916	*Congreso de Acción Cristiana en América Latina* [Christian Action in Latin America Congress]		Panama City, Panama
1949	CELA I *Conferencia Evangélica Latinoamericana* [Latin American Evangelical Conference]	World Council of Churches (WCC)	Buenos Aires, Argentina
1961	CELA II *Conferencia Evangélica Latinoamericana* [Latin American Evangelical Conference]	World Council of Churches (WCC)	Lima, Peru
1962	Establishment of ISAL *Iglesia y Sociedad en América Latina* [Church and Society in Latin America]	World Council of Churches (WCC)	Sao Paulo, Brazil
1966	Congress for World Evangelization	Billy Graham Evangelistic Association (BGEA)	Berlin, Germany
1969	CELA III *Conferencia Evangélica Latinoamericana* [Latin American Evangelical Conference]	World Council of Churches (WCC)	Buenos Aires, Argentina
1969	CLADE I *Congreso Latinoamericano de Evangelización* [Latin American Congress for Evangelization]	Billy Graham Evangelistic Association (BGEA)	Bogota, Colombia
1970	CLADE's *Congreso Latinoamericano de Evangelización* [Latin American Congress for Evangelization] first international consultation and formation of the FTL *Fraternidad Teológica Latinoamericana* [Latin American Theological Fraternity]		Cochabamba, Bolivia

Year	Conference	Sponsor	Place
1973	Workshop on Evangelicals and Social Concern		Chicago, USA
1974	International Congress On World Evangelization (ICOWE)	Billy Graham Evangelistic Association (BGEA)	Lausanne, Switzerland
1976	*Congreso Misionero de Curitiba* [Curitiba Missionary Congress]		Quito, Ecuador
1978	Consultation on "Gospel and Culture" of the ICOWE (International Congress on World Evangelization)	Billy Graham Evangelistic Association (BGEA)	Willowbank, Bermuda
1982[3]	CONELA *Confraternidad Evangélica Latinoamericana* [Latin American Evangelical Fellowship]	Billy Graham Evangelistic Association (BGEA), World Evangelical Fellowship (WEF) and the Luis Palau Evangelistic Association	Panama City, Panama
1987	COMIBAM *Congreso Misionero Ibero Americano* [Ibero American Missionary Congress]		Sao Paulo, Brazil

The Edinburgh Missionary Conference

The Edinburgh Missionary Conference in 1910 did not have direct influence on COMIBAM but it was significant in providing a landscape of a worldwide ecumenical

---

[3] Ruiz, 2007. Luis Bush (personal communication, January 26, 2011) challenged this date in an e-mail to the researcher, believing it to be 1983. The 1982 date will be used since this date is found in published documents.

mission for the church. The Edinburgh conference, considered by Noll (2000) a major turning point in the history of the church, set the tone for ecumenical cooperation in the accomplishment of the Great Commission (Bosch, 1991; Escobar, 2003). The Edinburgh Conference led to the establishment of the International Missionary Conference and the Universal Christian Conference on Life and Work and the World Conference on Faith and Order, resulting eventually in the creation of the World Council of Churches in 1948 (Noll, 2000). Subsequently the Edinburgh Conference also contributed to the formation of CELA, and the *Iglesia y Sociedad en América Latina* [Church and Society in Latin America] (ISAL) organization (Escobar, 2003; Plou, 2004). Thus the significance of the conference was dual: its ecumenical appeal and its focus on the worldwide mission of the church. Ironically, the idea of evangelizing Latin America was dismissed by the conference (Ruiz, 2003).

An important leader in the Student Volunteer Movement for Foreign Missions at the turn of the 20th century catalyzed the organization of a congress in Latin America. John Mott was a Methodist layman born in 1865 in New York and also played a significant role in the leadership of the International Missionary Council and the World's Students Christian Federation (John R. Mott: The noble peace price 1946; Biography). Surprised by the Edinburgh Conference's neglect of Latin America and concerned for its evangelization, Mott, in cooperation with Robert Speer and Samuel Guy Inman, organized the *Congreso de Acción Misionera en América Latina* [Christian Action in Latin America Congress] which took place in Panama City, Panama in 1916 (Escobar, 1987; Ruiz, 2003). This attention to Latin America bore fruit in subsequent years.

Congreso de Acción Misionera en América Latina, Panama

The Panama Congress brought the conversation of world evangelization to Latin America since it had been ignored at the Edinburgh Conference (Padilla, n.d.). The Panama Congress was the first organized effort across denominational lines to consider the evangelization of Latin America (Plou, 2004). While the focus of COMBIAM years later would be evangelization from, not of, Latin America, the Panama Congress was significant because it pioneered the formation of other similar conferences. The organization of CELA, which met in 1949, 1961 and 1969, was direct influence of the Panama Congress (Escobar 2003, p. 49). The World Council of Churches sponsored all these conferences, linking them with the mainline ecumenical movement (Plou, 2004, p. 1). The CELA conference that met in Lima, Peru in 1961 paved the way for the establishment of a significant organization the following year.

Iglesia y Sociedad en América Latina

The establishment of ISAL took place in Sao Paulo, Brazil in 1962. This was initially a think-tank of mainly Protestant theologians, such as Julio de Santa Ana, Julio Barreiro, Jose Míguez-Bonino and Ruben Alves, that consequently incorporated liberation theology (Avila, 1996; Padilla, n.d.). Eventually liberation theology became more represented by Roman Catholic theologians such as Gustavo Gutierrez, Juan Luis Segundo, Pablo Richard, Enrique Dussell, Jose Miranda, Leonardo Boff, Clodovis Boff, Ignacio Ellacuria and Jon Sobrino (Padilla, n.d.). In some ways, it was the first formal expression of a social-theological awakening among Latin American theologians, both Catholic and evangelical (Moreno, 2001). ISAL contributed significantly to the development of the church in Latin America. Interestingly the developments that led to the formation of COMIBAM were often reactions to the direction of ISAL.

Congress for World Evangelization, Berlin

The Edinburgh Conference, the Panama Congress and the CELA conferences were all related to the World Council of Churches. In the meantime, the Billy Graham Evangelistic Association organized a Congress for World Evangelization. This congress would take place in Berlin, Germany in 1966. The Berlin Congress called for the involvement of evangelicals in the task of world evangelization (Bosch, 1991; Bush, 2002) and secured the involvement of Latin Americans in the process (Ekström, 2006; Padilla, 1986; Bertuzzi, 2006). The Congress for World Evangelization marked a shift in the direction of missionary conferences as it provided evangelicals with an option to the ecumenical conferences related to the WCC. The concept of cooperation across denominational lines for the sake of evangelism, rather than for the sake of organic unity, would eventually become part of the fabric of movements among evangelicals such as the International Congress on World Evangelization (ICOWE), which initially met in Lausanne, and later, COMIBAM. Additionally, the Berlin Congress dealt with the social responsibility of the church in the context of world evangelization (Bush, 2002). The participation of Latin American leaders and the concern for social responsibility paved the way for CLADE and, eventually, the FTL.

Congreso Latinoamericano de Evangelización, Bogotá

Another product of the initiatives led by the Billy Graham Evangelistic Assocation was the *Congreso Latinoamericano de Evangelización* [Latin American Congress for Evangelization] (CLADE). CLADE was significant because it appealed to the more conservative segment of the evangelical community in Latin America and because of the eventual development of an indigenous missiology (Saracco, 2000). "The first meeting of CLADE took place in Bogotá in 1969. The FTL was organized as an evangelical response not only to the ISAL movement, but also as a response to the dominant North American evangelical conservatism that was uninterested in social questions" (Moreno, 2001, p. 3). CLADE organized itself as an alternative to CELA opting for evangelical cross-denominational interactions instead of the classic Protestant ecumenism (Escobar, 1987; Plou, 2004; Ruiz, 2007). Taking its cue from the Berlin Conference, CLADE combined the interest in the evangelization of Latin America with the concern for social action as essential elements of the church's mission (Escobar, 1987; Plou, 2004). However, some Latin American evangelical leaders felt like CLADE was unduly influenced by North American fundamentalism and thus they sought to develop a more indigenous missiology (Plou, 2004). CLADE influenced the eventual formation of COMIBAM.

International Congress for World Evangelization, Lausanne

The International Congress for World Evangelization at Lausanne in 1974, was the fruit of the Berlin Congress. Convened by Billy Graham and drawing approximately 2,700 people from 150 countries, the Lausanne Congress produced important documents, marked significant shifts in world evangelization, and launched a movement (Bush, 2002). Two of the most significant documents were the Lausanne Covenant, which listed the necessity and goals of world evangelization (Lausanne), and A Call to Radical Discipleship, which demanded a greater emphasis on addressing the social needs of those who would be evangelized (Lausanne, 1974).

The Lausanne conference refined the work of the Berlin conference, addressed issues of holistic mission, and helped in the formation of specific cooperative initiatives in Latin America (Ekström, 2006; Taylor, 2000). Presenters such as Samuel Escobar, Rene Padilla and John Stott supported this holistic emphasis. Escobar presented a paper in a plenary session entitled, Evangelism and Man's Search for Freedom, Justice and Fulfillment, where he argued that biblical and effective evangelism must be accompanied by social action. He was one of the leading editors of A Call to Radical Discipleship (Smith, 1983). René Padilla introduced the concept of *Misión Integral* [Integral Mission] (Escobar, 2003). Escobar and Padilla were both members of the FTL (Latin American Theological Fraternity). Bush (2002) proposed that the leading influence on Stott in this regard was Orlando Costas, whom he also credited with pioneering the concept of holistic evangelism. Alvaro Fernandez, a leader in COMIMEX, the COMIBAM expression in Mexico, stated, "Lausanne was a breakthrough event that contributed directly to the creation of COMIBAM and the attention to the social responsibility in the mission of the church" (A. Fernandez, personal communication, February 18, 2011).

The Berlin and Lausanne Congresses struggled with the relation of the social responsibility of the church and its evangelism task. Billy Graham explicitly included the social dimension within evangelism at the Berlin Congress and John Stott continued the discussion at the Lausanne Congress (Bosch, 1991; Bush, 2002). The theme of the Second International Congress for World Evangelization, which met in Manila, in 1989, namely, Calling the Whole Church to Take the Whole Gospel to the Whole World, demonstrated that integral mission would not be dismissed easily (Lausanne II, 1989).

Although Lausanne came short of taking the holistic gospel concept to its full implications, significant progress was made in the evangelical approach to world evangelization. Another significant outcome of Lausanne was the shift in missionary paradigm advanced by Ralph Winter from a focus on political nation states to people groups (Bush, 2002; Eshleman, 2010; A. Fernandez, personal communication, February 9, 2011; Lewis, 1990; Parks & Scott, 2010). A series of congresses and consultations have continued to meet over the years as a result of Lausanne. Evangelicals in different parts of the world now owned the global evangelization fervor, the spirit of cooperation across denominations, the emphasis on people groups, and the focus on a holistic gospel. Jonathan Lewis, a missionary to Latin America who has worked within the COMIBAM organization in the areas of publication and training, noted a characteristic that distinguished COMIBAM from Lausanne. Lewis (personal communication, November 1, 2009), pointed out that while Lausanne was an event-oriented movement of individuals, COMIBAM became an association of institutions: agencies, churches, and training centers.

These series of conferences and congresses on world evangelization throughout the twentieth century had a systemic impact on the advancement of the church's mission and, consequently, on the rise of movements like COMIBAM. "By the early 1980s, then, it seemed that a new spirit was establishing itself in mainstream evangelicalism. Regional evangelical groupings followed suit" (Bosch, 1991). The proliferation of these conferences in Latin America was a sign of maturity according to COMIBAM's first president, Luis Bush (L. Bush personal communication, February 9, 2011). There were many other conferences but these are the most significant in relation to the mission sending movement in Latin America. Ralph Winter pointed out that the Pioneer Missions World Conference in Edinburg in 1980 was one of the largest in history because of the large number of representatives sent by mission agencies (Winter, 1981, p. 155). He also credited this conference with producing student movements. Nevertheless there is little mention of this conference in materials related to the development of COMIBAM or Latin American missiology.

The Latin American Context

The Latin American context in which COMIBAM emerged merits a brief treatment. The socio-cultural precursors to the formation of COMIBAM International included: the rise and decline of multiple revolutionary movements and radical political changes in Latin America; the developing stages of liberation theologies and the reactions to it; the growth of the evangelical church in Latin America; and the migration of Latin Americans to other parts of the world (Ruiz, 2002; Plou, 2004; Padilla, n.d.; Escobar, 1999). These factors were accompanied by unprecedented theological and missiological reflection, by ecumenical Protestantism and evangelicalism. The socio-economic, political, and religious realities of the 1960s, 1970s and 1980s shaped the theological and missiological developments in Latin America.

The COMIBAM movement was not purely a product of its context but it was certainly affected by it. In fact, COMIBAM leaders were eager to represent the unique contributions Ibero Americans could make t world missions efforts. COMIBAM's first congress took place in 1987. During this time many changes were taking place: the globalization phenomenon, the invention and widespread use of the Internet, the accessibility of travel by air, and e-commerce (Lewis, 2003; Tinsley, 2005). Latin

America in particular was experiencing demographic explosion, migration, and the growth of Protestantism, Roman Catholicism and Pentecostalism. The drastic changes in the decades of the 1960s, 1970s and 1980s gave way to the rise of movements that sought to change the world from Latin American soil.

Socio-Economic Context

The socio-economic context in the Latin America of the second half of the twentieth century changed first by the awareness of the conditions and the drive to do something about it. Marxism and revolutionary ideas would find fertile ground in Latin America as early as the 1950s.

> It was not until the 1950s that new "indigenous" approaches to the social reality emerged in Latin America. While a Marxist analysis was present in Latin America, especially after the triumph of the Russian revolution, it became prominent and more influential in academic circles during the 1960s. Since the beginning, two basic options were followed, namely, reform or revolution…The Cuban revolution, consummated in the year 1959, became a paradigm and inspired numerous revolutionary movements in Latin America. (Avila, 1996, pp. 18, 20)

While political reform may have been the option for some, revolution became the more viable alternative for many. The masses of those who felt oppressed and the multitudes of university students open to new ideologies gave way to protests, riots and guerrilla warfare in various regions of Latin America. A Latin American theologian affirmed this assessment of the tumultuous situation during this time,

> The Latin American situation beginning in the 1960s may be described as a revolutionary situation. The growth of poverty, exacerbated by the problems resulting from increasing urbanization and industrialization and closely related to both internal corruption and international exploitation, was fertile soil for the seed of a socialist revolution. Encouraged by the triumph of the Cuban revolution in 1959, labor and student movements considered that the time was ripe to overthrow U.S. imperialism and to change the socioeconomic and political structures through a Marxist revolution. With this idea in mind, convinced of the inevitability of violence, many young people, including university students, joined guerrilla groups in several countries. (Padilla, n.d.)

The response of the church to these revolutionary movements would cover the spectrum from opposition to support. Many groups sought to distance themselves from the controversy of these issues. Nevertheless, the same socio-economic realities that gave way to revolutionary movements would bring about theological and missiological reform in the Latin American context. Bosch (1991) stated, "To a significant extent, theologies of liberation, particularly the classical Latin American variety, evolved in protest against the inability of the Western church and missionary circles, both Catholic and Protestant, to grapple with the problems of systemic injustice" (pp. 432-433). Even for those segments of the church that did not embrace liberation theologies, the socio-economic context lent itself for theological reflection about its meaning. Padilla (n.d.) argued that while the preoccupation of Protestant theology in Latin America since the colonial period had been primarily religious freedom, in the 1960s it shifted to reflection on the meaning of the Christian faith in a revolutionary context.

Political Context

Closely related to the socio-economic context, the political context in Latin America during the last half of the twentieth century was also in a state of flux. Dictatorships that resulted from or reacted to revolutionary movements eventually gave way to relative democracy in some countries while others saw the installation of military regimes. Avila (1996) wrote,

> (The 1970s) was characterized by a prominent search for liberation, growth of nationalism and militarism, emergence of weak democracies and a considerable increase of the external debt of most Latin American nations....In the decade of the 1980s....there was a considerable growth of dependence and of hegemonies—also of poverty and oppression. The revolutionary climate of the previous decade was substituted by the installation of military regimes in many countries (for example, Chile, Argentina, Brazil and Ecuador). (pp. 20-21)

These political situations presented new challenges to the church in Latin America. The political context was often oppressive of the church. Yet, the oppression and instability of Latin American governments resulted in growth and expansion for the evangelical church. Luis Bush (2001) argued that the civil strife in El Salvador produced a spiritual hunger in the nation (pp. 13-14). Furthermore, he stated that the curfew instituted in the country forced the church to meet in small groups, which in turn led to missionary fervor (L. Bush, personal communication, February 9, 2011). Pablo Deíros (personal communication, May 31, 2010), president of the Baptist Seminary in Buenos Aires, Argentina and also a leader in the missions movement in Argentina, also believed that the political context in the Latin America of the 1970s and 1980s forced many to leave their countries as political refugees. This fact, Deíros argued, led local churches to view cross-cultural missions in a different way. The migration of evangelicals from their countries of origin opened up new missionary opportunities for the Latin American churches.

The socio-economic and political situation in Latin America led to philosophical and theological reflection. Avila (1996) argued, "The interpretation of Latin American reality was controlled until the middle of this century by European and North American historical, economical, and sociological theories" (p. 16). He further stated that this interpretation,

> depended until the end of the 1980s, in different degrees (consciously or not, critically or naively), on two basic paradigms: modernization theory and dependency theory. There was a conscious effort in the FTL to articulate a socio-historical analysis of Latin America in a critical dialogue with these basic paradigms (which informed political ideologies and were in open conflict in the continent), but also informed by and faithful to the Scriptures. (p. 15)

The effort at contextualized reflection evidenced a Latin American church that was reaching a new level of maturity. This coming of age had the potential of producing contextualized theology and indigenous missionary movements.

By the decade of the 1980s, the church in Latin America became stronger in spite of its political context. Bill Taylor (2000) wrote, "The social and political context changed completely in the 1980s. The Communist bloc disintegrated, Latin American dictatorships weakened and started to disappear, and the church in the continent was strengthened and growing with unusual energy" (p. 364). The emergence of a stronger church in the context of socio-economic and political instability demonstrated that religion in Latin America was not dead. On the contrary it was thriving and evolving. While the church may have felt itself to be in survival mode, it produced reflection, growth, renewal and expansion in its Catholic, Protestant and Pentecostal expressions.

Religious Context

Marxism, revolution, dictatorships, military governments and political instability did not quench the fires of religion in Latin America. The Christian church in its various expressions experienced growth and renewal. In Roman Catholic, Pentecostal and Evangelical streams there were significant developments. Noll (2000) noted that the rise of Pentecostalism around the world and the developments of the Second Vatican Council had direct influence on the Latin American landscape.

Pentecostalism did not only grow in its traditional form but also through evangelical churches. A resurgence of the charismatic movement across Latin America, often referred to as renewal, brought about church growth to many churches in the 1980s (Anderson, 2005; P. Deíros, personal communication, May 31, 2010). A case-in-point of this phenomenon was the situation in Argentina. Bongarrá, an Argentine pastor, noted that the evangelical church in Argentina experienced a charismatic renewal at the end of the 1960s (personal communication, May 26, 2010). According to Bongarrá, while those who were a part of it perceived this as a blessing, it also proved to be divisive. Churches and denominations in Argentina divided over this issue and remained distanced and closed to cooperation with each other. Juan Pablo Bongarrá and Luis Palau promoted unity among evangelicals in Buenos Aires through evangelistic crusades in 1977 and 1979, eventually resulting in the formation of the *Misión Evangélica Iberoamericana*

(MEI), from whence the emergence of the *Misiones Mundiales* [World Missions] national movement would come (J. Bongarrá, personal communication, May 26, 2010).

Another significant development in the decades preceding COMIBAM was a shift in the Roman Catholic Church. The Vatican Council II sparked Roman Catholic renewal in Latin America during the 1960s (Anderson, 2005; Moreno, 2001). One of the primary outcomes of Vatican II reforms in the Latin American landscape was the development of liberation theologies. "Christians became conscious of the situation of oppression and exploitation that Latin America suffers and of the role that the Church has played in it" (Avila, 1996, p. 24). Moreno (2001) positioned this shift in the context of five centuries: "During the 1960s, a growing social awareness and theological reflection among certain Catholic theologians developed regarding the backwardness and lack of social and economic development that had persisted in Latin America for 500 years" (p. 2).

The event that formalized this paradigm change for the Roman Catholic Church in Latin America was the *Consejo Episcopal Latinoamericano* [Latin American Bishop's Council] (CELAM). "In 1968 the Latin American Catholic Bishop's Conference (CELAM) met in Medellín, Colombia, and offered pastoral guidelines along the lines of Liberation Theologies" (Avila, 1996, p. 22). The socio-economic context and the religious reforms were contributing factors for the production of a contextualized theology in the Roman Catholic Church. Vatican II certainly prepared the way for the development of liberation theologies in the Latin American context. However, there were other changes that would result from Vatican II. These changes included a biblical revival, ecclesiastical renewal, prominence, at least numerically, of Latin American bishops among the world's Catholics, and the empowering of the Catholic laity through base communities (Anderson, 2005).

Both in its Pentecostal and Roman Catholic expressions, the church in Latin America experienced renewal. The evangelical church also underwent changes during this period. After World War II, the missionary advance from Europe and the U.S. to Latin America included a new element, namely that of the independent evangelical missionaries (Escobar, 1987). This development was a shift from the traditional Protestant denominational missionaries. The increase of independent evangelical missionaries mirrored the growth of evangelicalism in the United States. The Billy Graham Evangelistic Association, the publication of the *Christianity Today* magazine and the establishment of conservative evangelical seminaries were all contributing factors to the advance of independent evangelical missionaries (Ruiz, 2003). It was in this context that the BGEA, prompted by *Christianity Today*'s editor, Carl F. H. Henry, held the Berlin World Congress on Evangelism in 1966 (Winter, 1995). The proliferation of independent missionaries meant a strong presence of evangelicals in Latin America. It also imported a missiology that would eventually be challenged by some Latin American evangelicals. Some of the aspects of such an imported missiology were its agency orientation, its focus on personal evangelism, and church growth. Members of the FTL offered a more church-centered and holistic alternative.

Evangelical thinkers were also challenged by the new hermeneutical approaches to Scripture developed among liberation theologians and Bible scholars (Avila, 1996). This need for reflection produced movements that contextualized theology and missiology for evangelical churches in Latin America.

Fraternidad Teológica Latinoamericana

The contributions of several theologians and missiological thinkers are significant as precursors to the COMIBAM movement. "There emerged in these movements of ISAL and the FTL a number of Latin American Baptist leaders such as René Padilla, Samuel Escobar, Rolando Gutierrez, Orlando Costas, Oscar Pereira, Pablo Deíros, Jorge Pixley, and Samuel Silva Gotay" (Moreno, 2001, p. 3). Some of these Latin American leaders were influenced by John Mott, John Mackay, and John Stott. John Mott, who was a leader of the Student Volunteer Movement, and the Edinburgh and Panama conferences, would be an inspirational leadership model for Luis Bush and other Latin American missionary leaders. Bush dedicated an entire chapter in his doctoral dissertation to the life and work of John Mott (Bush, 2002). John Mackay, a Scottish missionary to Mexico, who wrote *The Other Spanish Christ: A Study in the Spiritual History of Spain and South America* (1933), influenced the Christology of Latin American evangelicals (Escobar, 1998; Padilla, n.d.). From Padilla's (n.d.) perspective, Mackay's (1933) book suggested that Latin American Christianity did not need a replica of the Protestantism from Anglo-Saxon countries. John Stott, English pastor and teacher, was an influential leader in the Berlin and Lausanne conferences and was instrumental in facilitating the dialogue about holistic mission at these venues (Padilla, 1986). Samuel Escobar, a Peruvian missiologist, made several contributions to the development of an indigenous missiology and theology among evangelicals in Latin America, including his leadership of the FTL. René Padilla, another Latin American leader in the FTL who had studied under F.F. Bruce, is credited with articulating the holistic mission ideology (Padilla, 1986; Taylor, 2000). These individuals provided inspiration, reflection and leadership for a new sense of mission by evangelicals in Latin America, and eventually the development of a missionary spirit among them.

An Alternative Missiology for Latin America

Like COMIBAM, the FTL was established as an organization in the context of the congresses for world evangelization. The FTL did not directly contribute to the formation of COMIBAM. Instead, the FTL provided theological and missiological reflection while COMIBAM mobilized the church for cross-cultural mission within the conservative evangelical segment of the Latin American church. Both organizations are examples of the emergence of indigenous leadership among evangelicals in Latin America. While independent these two organizations exerted strong influence on each other.

Rudy Girón, the Guatemalan who served as COMIBAM's second president, noted that Samuel Escobar and the FTL were not perceived initially as supportive of COMIBAM's strategy and missiology (R. Girón, personal communication, October 31, 2009). In fact, the FTL and COMIBAM were at odds until both entities were convened in Miami on April, 1995 to discuss their commonalities and their differences (*Comunicado de Prensa* [Press Release] April 26, 1995. COMIBAM/Bertuzzi Archive file 201). Present at that meeting were Federico Bertuzzi, Miguel Angel de Marco, Carlos Del Pino, Rudy Girón, Manfred Grellert, Daniel R. Guerrero, Timoteo Halls, Luciano Jaramillo, Jonathan Lewis, Moisés López, Emilio Nuñez, Patricio Paredes, Edison Queiroz, Victor Rey, Valdir Steuernagel, Hernán Zapata, Israel Ortíz and Tito Paredes (Timoteo Halls Memo, May 10, 1995).

The competing paradigms were the missiologies of the FTL and Ralph Winter. Jonathan Lewis (personal communication, October 31, 2009) described Ralph Winter's paradigm as agency-missiology in contrast with the FTL's church-driven missiology. The starting point for COMIBAM's missiology stemmed from an adaptation of Winter's writings. The significance of the book *Misión Mundial* [World Mission] (Lewis, 1990) is discussed in the latter part of this chapter. Eventually, COMIBAM developed a hybrid missiology that included aspects of both.

Although the FTL was not a catalytic agent for COMIBAM, it did contribute to the debate over how to achieve a contextualized missiology for Latin America. In their first official encounter, FTL and COMIBAM International leaders agreed that the nature of the organizations was interdisciplinary theological reflection and a cross-cultural missions movement, respectively. Additionally, FTL leaders played a significant role in the World Evangelical Fellowship (WEF) from 1975 to 1980 (Smith, 1983). The WEF would later contribute to COMIBAM. Thus, in spite of their distinct visions and even disagreements about missiology and strategy, the FTL and COMIBAM have related to one another and have both made contributions to the Latin American evangelical movements of the latter part of the twentieth century.

The desire to develop a more indigenous missiology resulted in the formation of the FTL (Escobar, 1987; Plou, 2004; Salinas, 2005). The advance of the integral mission in Latin America faced two challenges on opposite extremes. On the one side, liberation theology and liberalism had alienated the more conservative portion of evangelical leaders and participants (Avila, 1996, p. 25-26; Moreno, 2001, p. 2). On the other extreme, Latin American leaders shunned a wholesale adoption of North American fundamentalism, which seemed too individualistic and failed to give proper attention to the social concerns (Escobar, 1987; Lewis, 1990; Moreno, 2001; Padilla, n.d.; Plou, 2004). "In general, evangelicals maintained a fundamentalist theology and conservative political attitude towards social reality….Evangelical systems of biblical interpretation were dominated by dispensational, Pentecostal, and grammatical-historical hermeneutics, all of them unrelated and indifferent to the social reality of Latin America" (Avila, 1996, pp. 25-26). A holistic mission that took biblical authority seriously did not fit the existing Protestant North American categories of liberal and conservative (Bosch, 1991; Escobar, 1987; Moreno, 2001; Padilla, 2006). Padilla (n.d.) cited two representative extremes among Evangelicals in the face of the Latin American revolutionary context: the North American fundamentalist theologian C.I. Scofield who suggested the way for pastors to face social problems was to pray humbly and preach a pure gospel of tender love, and the Cuban theologian Sergio Martinez Arce who proposed that revolution is a means for the establishment of the Kingdom of God and that revolutionaries are servants of God. Either of these two extremes was inadequate. Moreno (2001) further wrote,

> The complaint most often heard in various seminaries during the decade of the 1970s was in regard to the scarcity of real theological reflection on the part of the Latin American evangelical theologians, the lack of abundance of translations, the trans-culturalization of evangelical models, and the theological inability of the leadership to reflect on the problems of the continent from a truly Latin American perspective. (p. 2)

Thus, a new missiology was needed, one that was relevant to the Latin American context and true to the biblical commitment of evangelicals. Padilla (2006) stated that the resulting missiology was in fact more biblical and closer to the practice of Jesus and the first century church. Bush (2002) considered it a recovery of classical evangelicalism.

Emergence of a New and Proactive Indigenous Leadership

The establishment of the FTL took place between momentous congresses on world evangelization. At CLADE I in Bogota, Colombia, "the key point that marked the beginning of the FTL" (Avila, 1996, p. 27), Samuel Escobar delivered a speech entitled The Social Responsibility of the Church listing the basic themes that were to become the focus of the FTL in the succeeding years (Avila, 1996; Padilla, n.d). Moreno (2001) pointed out the importance of this paper,

> This paper manifested a cutting edge of theological reflection that made a significant impact during the following decades. Escobar was able to synthesize the thinking of a significant group of evangelicals, namely: the conviction that one could be profoundly evangelical doctrinally as well as relevant and committed socially. (p. 5)

During the first CLADE consultation in 1970 at Cochamba, Bolivia, Latin American leaders drafted the guidelines that essentially constituted the formation of the FTL (Coy, 1999; Escobar, 1999). The FTL established itself shortly after CLADE I and ensured an indigenous agenda and indigenous leadership for CLADE II (Plou, 2004; Taylor, 2000). The leaders' discernment and ability to articulate their position in a timely manner proved to be critical. The FTL established itself timely after the Berlin Conference and before the Lausanne Congress on World Evangelization. By the Lausanne 1974 Congress, the FTL had formulated and articulated its theological and missiological positions. Latin

American leaders were prepared to contribute to the developments at Lausanne 1974 and they did.

The FTL, with the participation of leaders such as Samuel Escobar, René Padilla, Orlando Costas, Emilio Nuñez, Peter Savage, Andrew Kirk, Pedro Arana, Tito Paredes offered biblical, conservative, evangelistic and holistic theological and missiological reflection (Avila, 1996; Escobar, 1987; Moreno, 2001; Padilla, n.d.; Padilla, 2006; Smith, 1983). Three specific factors shaped the work of the FTL: the need of an indigenous reflection, a strong criticism of Marxism, and a clear commitment both to the Scriptures and to Latin American reality (Avila, 1996). Yet, the FTL was a product of missiological concern, namely the need to advance a holistic mission in Latin America (Taylor, 2000).

René Padilla Advocates *Misión Integral*

Since the concept of *Misión Integral* [Integral Mission] is so central to the missiology of the FTL, it merits a brief overview. René Padilla, using a hermeneutic that affirmed the authority of the Bible and also took the social context seriously, developed a series of articles (1975) that reflected on the relationship of the gospel and social responsibility (Moreno, 2001). Eventually Padilla, in the context of the FTL, developed the concept of *Misión Integral* [Integral Mission] (Moreno, 2001). Padilla (2006) contrasted the integral mission approach with the traditional approach inherited by evangelical churches from the modern missionary movement. The traditional approach, he argued, is primarily a geographical concept, and thus it is limited to cross-cultural mission: "The purpose of missions was to save souls and to plant churches, mainly in foreign countries, by means of the preaching of the gospel. The agents of mission were principally missionaries" who related to missionary agencies and felt a special call to missions (Padilla, 2006). Moreno (2001) indicated that this was the reality for the majority of Latin American evangelical churches in the 1960s. Furthermore, Padilla (2006) mentioned four dichotomies created by this traditional approach: (a) between churches that send and churches that receive, (b) between home and the mission field, (c) between missionaries and ordinary Christians, (d) between the life and the mission of the church. Integral mission, on the other hand, means primarily crossing the frontier between faith and no faith,

> according to the testimony to Jesus Christ as Lord of the whole of life and of the whole creation…(Acts 1:8)…every church, wherever it may be, is called to share in God's mission, a mission that is local, regional and world-wide in scope…Commitment to mission is the very essence of being the church; therefore, the church that is not committed to the mission of witnessing to Jesus Christ and thus to crossing the frontier between faith and no faith is no longer the church. (Padilla, 2006)

Based on this understanding of the nature of church and mission, integral mission has several implications. The church is less concerned with numerical growth and prosperity and more concerned with incarnating the values of the Kingdom of God, including love and justice. There is a focus not just on conversion of individuals but also on the transformation of human life in all dimensions, including that of the community.

Before Padilla Orlando Costas had criticized a number of missiological currents that lacked an integral concept of mission, including the church growth movement and the socio-political approach of the World Council of Churches (Moreno, 2001). Bush (2002) called Costas' commitment to radical word and radical deed a bridge between the two main streams. Padilla's treatment found acceptance of a holistic gospel concept among most conservative evangelicals as an option to liberation theology (Moreno, 2001). The FTL also took issue with the church growth movement that was related to the School of World Mission of Fuller Theological Seminary in Pasadena, California and its proponents such as Donald McGavran (Padilla, n.d.).

Thus, the theological method of the FTL was heavily missiological in nature. The mission of the church was the pragmatic reality along which theological reflection took place. Moreno (2001) stated,

> Rene Padilla and Samuel Escobar serve…the…evangelical community in Latin America as the pioneers in contextualized missiological reflection. Their theological reflections have continually been accompanied by their missiological concern, and they have dealt with themes stressing that an integral mission constitutes the inevitable apex of theological work in Latin America. (p. 7)

The FTL emerged in a *kairos* moment of history and the swift actions of its leaders demonstrated such a conviction. Avila (1996) affirmed the timeliness of this development:

> By rethinking the fundamental doctrine of Scripture, in the light of the evangelical reality of Latin America, and with a lesser emphasis on the relationship and applicability of the doctrine to the socio-economical-political reality, the FTL became a landmark in the history of Latin American evangelical theology….we may be able to conclude that Latin American evangelicals started to do their own theological thinking with greater freedom and maturity. (p. 33)

This moment in the history of reflection among theologians in Latin America was signaled by the work of others beyond the confines of the FTL. "Scholars such as Pablo Deíros, Oscar Pereira, Damian Vivas, Samuel Escobar, Jorge Díaz, Floreal Ureta, Hector Llanes, Pablo Moreno and Juan Carlos Cevallos are only a few of the specialists whose biblical studies evidence a commitment to a more contextualized biblical exegesis" (Moreno, 2001, p. 4). Although, *Misión Integral* [Integral Mission] was not equivalent to cross-cultural mission, Escobar believed that Latin America will be the launching pad for mission to the rest of the world (Moreno, 2001, p. 7). Indigenous theological reflection and a keen sense of the changing times would be characteristic of the FTL and later of COMIBAM. Furthermore, the resulting missiological theology produced by the FTL influenced and, more frequently, challenged the Latin American missions movement.

National Mission Movements

COMIBAM helped to create international cooperation among various national missionary mobilization movements. Before the first COMIBAM Congress, individual countries in Latin America were developing these national networks. Some of these national movements were catalytic in the eventual multi-national network. They came to be known as *Movimientos Misioneros Nacionales* [National Missionary Movements] (MMN). The designation MMN has been used in three different ways: (a) an actual national movement, (b) a more formal national missionary network, or (c) COMIBAM's representation in a particular country. Earlier cases of MMN include the national movements in Brazil, Argentina, Chile, El Salvador, Guatemala, Costa Rica and Mexico (D. Bianchi, personal communication, May 8, 2009; L. Bush, personal communication, February 4, 2011; B. Ekström, personal communication, February 9, 2011). Daniel

Bianchi, an Argentine pastor, has been a leader in Argentina's national missionary movement and in COMIBAM International. Bertil Ekström, a Brazilian missionary, was one of COMIBAM's early leaders.

The early MMN contributed to the international cooperation in at least three ways. They kindled the sparks of missionary fervor in various regions of Latin America. They provided some of the leaders for COMIBAM. Thirdly, the seminal concept of a missionary network rather than a missionary agency had been tested at a national level before its implementation at the international level. Although there were various countries whose movements were strong before the rise of COMIBAM, Brazil, Argentina and El Salvador will be discussed in this section as examples of what was taking place in several other places.

Three Important National Movements

Ekström (2006) identified Brazil as the first country in South America to have a national missionary association. The Cross Cultural Missionary Association of Brazil (AMTB) was established in 1975 and Jonathan dos Santos became its first president (Ekström, 2006). The second such national network became the *Red Misiones Mundiales* [World Missions Network] (RMM) in Argentina. Established in 1982, under the original name of *Misiones Mundiales* [World Missions] (MM), the Argentine national missionary movement displayed characteristics that would later be reflected in the COMIBAM International movement (Bertuzzi, 2007, p. 12; E. Surenian, personal communication, May 27, 2010). Bertuzzi (2006a), an Argentine pastor, one of the founders of the RMM, and a COMIBAM leader in the area of publications, marked the date of AMTB's organization as 1982, coinciding with the date of the Argentine network's inception, thus suggesting Argentina and Brazil were on par in the beginning time of their respective networks. This discrepancy in the establishment date of the AMTB reflects the competitive spirit between Brazilians and Argentines. A grassroots beginning sparked by God's Spirit, leaders who responded enthusiastically in a timely manner, a choice for a cooperative organism rather than a sending agency approach were elements of the Argentine national movement which also found expression in COMIBAM International. The use of the term Ibero American for the scope of this missionary enterprise was already in use in Argentina with the formation of the *Misión Evangélica Iberoamericana* [Ibero American Evangelical Mission] (MEI) before 1982 (Bertuzzi, 2007, p. 17).

Not much later, the national missionary movement began to develop in El Salvador. Luis Bush, who later became COMIBAM's first president, was a pastor in that country at that time. The fervor overflowed from his church throughout the rest of that Central American country and beyond.

El Salvador. During the mid-eighties, *Iglesia Nazaret* [Nazareth Church], under the leadership of her pastor Luis Bush, planted various churches and directly supported 35 missionaries (Bush, 2001). Luis Martí (personal communication, February 4, 2011), a Salvadorian pastor, who was involved in the national missionary movement of his country and also served as a leader in COMIBAM International testified about the effect of *Iglesia Nazaret* in El Salvador. Not only was the church mobilizing young men and women for the mission field but it was also leading national mission conferences. *Misión '84* (Mission '84) was a significant conference that provided great momentum for what eventually became COMIBAM '87 (L. Bush, personal communication, February 4, 2011). *Misión '84* had 1000 registered participants from 11 countries in Central America

(Bush, 2001). After this Central American missions conference Bush was asked to visit each Latin American country to promote the continent wide event called COMIBAM 87 (Bush, 2001). Bush led in the founding of an inter-denominational mission agency to send and support Salvadoran missionaries (Bush, 2001). Although the formal organization of a national movement did not take place until the 1990s, there was certainly missionary fervor at a national level previous to COMIBAM's Congress in 1987. By the time of the 1987 COMIBAM congress, individuals such as Luis Martí were already serving on the international mission field (L. Martí, personal communication, February 4, 2011).

Argentina. The national missionary movement in Argentina is a classic example of how God's timing and indigenous leadership combined to produce a movement. The *Red Misiones Munidales* [World Missions Network] (RMM) in Argentina was, in some ways, prototypical of COMIBAM International a few years later. According to Juan Pablo Bongarrá, an Argentine pastor and one of the founders of the RMM, the emergence of the Argentine RMM network was almost unintentional (J. Bongarrá, personal communication, May 26, 2010).

A national conference for pastors, sponsored by the *Misión Evangélica Iberoamericana* [Ibero American Evangelical Mission] (MEI), was in the planning stages. MEI sought cross-denominational cooperation in Argentina. Tasked with the responsibility of determining topics to be used in promotional materials for a national pastors conference, Bongarrá came up with four. The first three topics: unity, strengthening the pastoral work and evangelism, were his primary concerns and appropriate provisions were made in the conference to address those issues. The fourth selected topic: world missions, was almost an afterthought according to Bongarrá (J. Bongarrá, personal communication, May 26, 2010). One of the keynote speakers of the 1982 pastors' conference was the evangelist Luis Palau (Bertuzzi, 2007). Palau, in one of his messages, addressed the potential that Argentina possessed of sending missionaries to other countries (Palau, 1982). In the audio file of the message, which is in Spanish, Palau references the Lausanne theme of world evangelization. Prodded by this word and by the fourth announced topic of the conference, participants inquired about the possibility of a seminar on this topic (Bertuzzi, 2007). Reluctantly, Bongarrá conceded to tightly schedule a seminar between lunch and a plenary session with Palau as a presenter (D. Bianchi, personal communication, May 8, 2009; J. Bongarrá, personal communication, May 26, 2010).

The response to the previously unscheduled seminar was overwhelming and the enthusiasm was such that an ad hoc commission was named. Those initially named to the commission were Juan Pablo Bongarrá, Juan Herrera, Guillermo Cotton, Francisco Cid and Federico Bertuzzi (Bertuzzi, 2007). Edgardo Surenian (personal communication, May 27, 2010) argued that *Misión Mundial* did not initiate cross-cultural missions mobilization in Argentina, but it became the catalyst of what was already beginning to happen. The commission eventually became the RMM network.

Several of the RMM meetings prepared the way for national mission conferences in 1983, 1984 and 1985. In the 1985 RMM conference Luis Bush, who at that time led *Iglesia Nazaret* in San Salvador, a guest speaker, suggested connecting *Misión '86*, a national missions conference, and the upcoming COMIBAM Congress in Sao Paulo (Surenian, personal communication, May 27, 2010). *Misión '86* was a breakthrough conference for Argentine evangelicals. A great number of young people and families surrendered to God's call for the mission field (J. Bongarrá, personal communication, May 26, 2010). The church Bongarrá led called a full-time missions pastor in 1993. This young mission pastor's name was Carlos Scott, who later became a national leader of the RMM and subsequently the president of COMIBAM International: an example of the relationship of church-based ministry, national movements and COMIBAM International.

A key figure in the developments of the Argentine national movement was Federico Bertuzzi (D. Bianchi, personal communication, May 8, 2009; J. Bongarrá, personal communication, May 26, 2010; E. Surenian, personal communication, May 27, 2010). Bertuzzi attended the Berlin Congress in 1966 as a young man, travelled on OM's *Doulous* ship and had the seed planted in his heart about Latin America rising to the challenge of world evangelization by Greg Livingstone, founder and first president of Frontier Missions, as early as 1970 (Bertuzzi, 2006, pp. 45, 90-91). The vision of Luis Palau, the experience and passion of Federico Bertuzzi and the timely response of Juan Pablo Bongarrá represent the spontaneity of the movements that were emerging in Latin America in the decade of the 1980s.

In the search for the best approach to fueling a missionary movement, there were moments in which some leaders considered making RMM a missionary agency. The idea of its being a cooperative network prevailed and proved to render it more effective (Bertuzzi, 2007). This spirit of a movement that exists to encourage prayer, cast vision, share information and coordinate the missionary task was characteristic of the RMM network, and later of COMIBAM International (Bertuzzi, 2007).

National missionary movements were essential precursors to the rise of the international COMIBAM movement. There were pockets of missionary fervor in several countries. In Brazil, it took the form of sending missionaries, in Argentina, of uniting evangelicals for the cause of cross cultural missions and in El Salvador, the rise of a church and a leader that would be influential for the international cooperation that came to fruition later. Ekström (B. Ekström, personal communication, February 9, 2011) pointed out that for the most part the idea of an international congress and movement is what motivated leaders such as Luis Bush, David Ruiz and Rudy Girón to enlist the participation of individual countries. Thus, in a reversal of roles the concept of international cooperation fueled the fires of national missionary movements where they existed and kindled the flames in countries where they did not.

Evangelical Organizations that Contributed to COMIBAM

Although the conferences, organizations and leaders mentioned above provide a general background for the formation of COMIBAM, the pre-existing organizations which had a significant influence on its establishment were the World Evangelical Fellowship, Operation Mobilization, CLADE, and the *Confraternidad Evangélica Latinoamericana* [the Latin American Evangelical Fellowship] (CONELA). Additionally, the publication and distribution of *Misión Mundial* [World mission] by Jonathan P. Lewis (1990) provided COMIBAM its primary missiological textbook. A brief discussion of these entities and how they prepared the way for the rise of COMIBAM International will be given below.

World Evangelical Fellowship

The WEF, which eventually changed its name to WEA preferring the nomenclature alliance to fellowship, played a significant role in preparing the ground for the emergence of the COMIBAM movement. The WEF, for example, was instrumental in the CONELA convocation where the idea of a continental congress was formalized (Ruiz, 2007). Financial support for COMIBAM training and for COMIBAM office operations on behalf of WEF was a direct contribution (J. Lewis, personal communication, November 1, 2009). According to Jonathan Lewis, who worked for the mission commission of the WEF, the organization's objective was to develop a model of cooperation in Latin America similar to what already existed in Africa and Asia. Lewis (personal communication, November 1, 2009) contended that since the WEF's Missions Commission was made up of continental mission network leaders, it was in the position to mentor COMIBAM and to help it connect to the other networks.

Interestingly, Bill Taylor (2007) wrote the following about COMIBAM in a WEA publication,

> This network/alliance is the regional mission movement of Latin America and as such, provides a significant model for such movements in other regions of the world. Regretfully, we do not have anything of this caliber in Asia, Africa, the Caribbean, South Pacific or even Europe. (p. 4)

Taylor's declaration stood in contradiction to Lewis' assessment. It is likely that WEF identified incipient missionary cooperation networks in other parts of the world and attempted to encourage them. COMIBAM was the biggest success story.

Smith (1983) stated that WEF was committed to a "network model with autonomous fellowships in every country" (p. 335). Smith (1983) argued that "the FTL engaged in styles of operations that were very similar, since both worked according to a "network" or "movement" model" (p. 340). Thus, while COMIBAM and the FTL did not share a missiology they did share an organizational model: the network. COMIBAM leaders shared this organizational philosophy. In a historical treatment of a movement like COMIBAM there is often the temptation to determine who had the original idea and the tendency of those who were protagonists to take credit for it. However, in considering a movement that arose in a precisely appropriate time period and context, it is a valid approach to identify those whose hearts and minds were being prepared simultaneously and who had the ability to identify the people and opportunities for the implementation of their shared vision. The network organizational concept was present in national movements, in the strategy model of the WEF and in the mind of COMIBAM leaders.

Another significant development in the WEF had to do with its stance on the evangelical response to the social realities in the world. "In 1983 another significant step forward was taken at a WEF consultation in Wheaton devoted to 'The Church in Response to Human Need.' For the first time in an official statement emanating from an international evangelical conference the perennial dichotomy was overcome" (Bosch, 1991, p. 407). This willingness to engage the social situation from an evangelical perspective was also relevant for Latin American evangelical leaders.

Operation Mobilization

Operation Mobilization (OM) contributed to the vision of cross-cultural missions in Latin America. OM's ship, *Doulos,* stopped in Latin American ports inviting young evangelicals to travel internationally on short-term mission assignments between 1979 and 1983. "Many Latin Americans had their first opportunity to speak with fellow believers from Africa or Asia and to feel very close to the global mission field" (Bertuzzi, 2006, p. 46). Daniel Bianchi (personal communication, May 8, 2009) reported that in 1979, 25 Argentines traveled on board OM's ship to Spain, Brazil, Uruguay and Mexico. Federico Bertuzzi and Daniel Bianchi are examples of young men who travelled on OM's *Doulos* and who became leaders in the missions movement in Argentina and COMIBAM International (D. Bianchi, personal communication, May 8, 2009; J. Lewis, personal communication, November 1, 2009). OM's contribution is not sufficiently documented in COMIBAM's publications. Nevertheless, it is highly significant in that OM provided a cross-cultural missionary vision for young evangelicals.

Congreso Latinoamericano de Evangelización

As discussed at the beginning of this chapter, CLADE was one of the events in a series of Congresses that had a more direct influence in the eventual birth of the COMIBAM movement. CLADE's appeal to the more conservative segment of the Protestant community was significant. CLADE was formed as an alternative to CELA, which was related to the World Council of Churches. The WCC represented the mainline Protestant ecumenical movement (Escobar, 1987; Plou, 2004; Ruiz, 2007).

On a global scale, the 1966 Berlin Congress was the conservative evangelical alternative to the more liberal mainline Protestant WCC missionary conferences (Bosch, 1991). The first CLADE was convened in 1969 in Bogotá, soon after the Berlin Congress (Escobar). CLADE I merged the themes of Latin American evangelization and social action as part of the church's mission which had been discussed at the Berlin Conference (Escobar, 1987; Plou, 2004). The contribution made by CLADE I to mission, according to Saracco (2000), was its emphasis on church mobilization, the inclusion of social and political concerns in the evangelical missionary agenda, the need to have a serious dialogue with the Catholic Church and the recognition of an outpouring of the Spirit on the South American continent. Padilla (1986), however, stated that CLADE II, which met in Lima, Perú, provided greater commitment to addressing the reality of poverty, oppression, corruption and abuse of power. As stated previously, since some evangelical leaders in Latin America perceived CLADE I as having too much influence from North America and sought to develop a more indigenous theology and missiology, they ensured that CLADE II took a step in the direction of affirming a Latin American model of mission (Taylor, 2000). It is important to remember that the formation of the FTL took place shortly after CLADE I both as a response and as a reaction to it. COMIBAM would benefit from the emphasis on church mobilization and from CLADE's involvement in CONELA.

Confraternidad Evangélica Latinoamericana

The most direct precursor of COMIBAM was CONELA. Theological reflection, the continued concern for the evangelization of the world and cross-denominational collaboration led the participants of CLADE II, the Luis Palau Evangelistic Association and the WEF to convoke this event called CONELA to meet in Panama in 1982 (Ruiz, 2007). In an email to the researcher and a subsequent interview, Luis Bush mentioned that the CONELA meeting in Panama took place in 1983 (Luis Bush, personal communication, January 26, 2011 and February 4, 2011). The 1982 date will be used since it is in published documents. Participants in the CONELA meeting in Panama planned a 1984 meeting of leaders in Mexico City. The purpose of the convocation in Mexico City was to discuss the organization of an international congress that would promote the missionary vision in Latin America (L. Bush, personal communication February 4, 2011; Ruiz, 2007). Rudy Girón, one of COMIBAM's early leaders, considered this occasion the birth of COMIBAM, thus marking the organization's anniversary from that point (R. Girón, personal communication, October 31, 2009). The convocation by CONELA of various leaders and initiatives helped to focus the shift in the thinking and activity of Latin American evangelicals in regard to missions advance (Escobar, 1999; J. Londoño, personal communication, September 25, 2008). Though missionaries had been sent from Latin America to other parts of the world since the beginning of the twentieth century (Escobar, 2007), the focus on evangelizing the world as a cooperative effort from the Latin American evangelical church was relatively new. Jesús Londoño (personal communication, September 25, 2008), clarified that COMIBAM was not purely a product of CONELA by pointing out that before the CONELA convocation in Mexico City, leaders like Federico Bertuzzi in Argentina, Edison Quiroz in Brazil and Roberto Gager in Columbia were already leading movements in their own countries. CONELA was not the sole contributing organization that fanned the flames of COMIBAM, but it would facilitate the planning of its first congress in Sao Paulo in 1987.

Misión Mundial [World Mission] Books

The book *Misión Mundial* [World Mission] edited by Jonathan P. Lewis (1990) was a three-volume adaptation in Spanish for the Latin American context of Ralph Winter's *Perspectives on the World Christian Movement* (Bertuzzi, 2007). The first volume was required reading for the COMIBAM '87 congress and the other two volumes were distributed at the congress in Sao Paulo (J. Lewis, personal communication, November 2, 2009; Lewis, 1990). Thus, this set of books became very important in the missiological formation of COMIBAM. Interestingly, Luis Bush acknowledged the importance of these books but felt they were not completely adequate.

Ralph Winter's missiology characterized COMIBAM's initial approach and strategy in contrast with the FTL's missiology. In Latin America, Winter's views were characterized as agency and Unreached People Groups (UPG) missiology, and the FTL perspectives as church-driven and holistic missiology (J. Lewis, personal communication, October 31, 2009). Ralph Winter's influence on the missiology of COMIBAM was as early as Lausanne 1974 when Winter proposed that missions advance needed to shift from a geographical to a people group strategy (Bush, 2002; Eshleman, 2010; A. Fernandez, personal communication, February 9, 2011; Lewis, 1990; Parks & Scott, 2010). Winter (1981b) and some COMIBAM authors credited Donald McGavran and Cameron Townsend with pioneering the people group concept (DeCarvalho, 2003). The strategic emphasis upon UPGs was a part of COMIBAM's strategy and structure since its early days, but a commitment to this understanding was formalized in the San José, Costa Rica, Declaration in 1992 (Londoño, 2006, p. 60). Winter's contribution continued as he caught the vision about the emerging missionary movement from Latin America at a 1986 regional meeting in Guatemala and subsequently published the idea in the *Mission Frontiers* magazine (L. Bush, personal communication, February 4, 2011).

With the objective of awakening among North American college students a passion for world missions, Ralph Winter designed a missiology course that compiled what he considered to be the best of missiological writings and offered it for the first time in the summer of 1964 (Lewis, 1990). Winter's *Perspectives On The World Christian*

Movement (2009) was adapted by Lewis to become the first textbook for the COMIBAM movement.

Winter's publication first influenced the COMIBAM movement through Lewis' Spanish digest *Misión Mundial*. The first volume of *Misión Mundial* [World Mission], edited by Lewis, presented the biblical basis for the mission and a brief overview of the expansion of Christianity. It approached missions from the perspective of *missio dei* or God's global mission and the Bible as God's revelation of his plan (Lewis, 1990). The first four chapters of the book gave an overview of Old and New Testament passages highlighting God's mission and his desire to carry it out through his people (Lewis, 1990). The last chapter gave an interpretive summary by Ralph Winter of redemptive history beginning with the Abrahamic covenant and proposing ten epochs for it: five before Christ and five after (Winter, 1981). Winter also offered three epochs of missionary expansion identified with respective leaders: William Carey (1790), Hudson Taylor (1865) and Cameron Townsend and Donald McGavran (1934), crediting these last two with the emphasis on what came to be known as UPGs (Winter, 1981). Additionally, the author offers four stages related to the cross-cultural mission enterprise: pioneer, paternal, partnership and participative (Winter, 1981). Laying down a biblical basis for the mission of the church is an important place to begin for evangelicals. The first volume was designed to lay the foundation and cast the vision of missionary advance in a historical context.

The second volume offered a chapter on the history of strategies and structures. In the first chapter, Winter (1981) introduced two terms that represented the two types of structures for the advancement of the mission: modality and sodality. Modality, he argued, is the type of structure where membership is generally biological, namely the church. Sodality, on the other hand, is the kind of fellowship where membership is based on a shared objective, namely an agency. The concept of sodality is the basis for his view of an agency-structure for missionary sending. This view of the church and its relation to the mission is limited at best. It is guided more by a pragmatic observation of church life than by theological reflection on the nature of the church. The FTL's church-driven missiology had a stronger biblical foundation.

The second chapter described the remaining task of world mission by providing terminology for its consideration (Winter, 1981) and by presenting a Lausanne Occasional Paper on Christian Witness to the Chinese People (Lewis, 1990). It included a discussion on the meaning of nation as a people group and of the Hindu, Muslim, Buddhist and Tribal mega spheres. Chapter three focused on reaching the unreached and it included an article by Peter Wagner on the four strategies for mission. These strategies consisted of the right goals, the right place at the right time, the right methodology and the right people. Two other articles in this chapter were A Church for Each People Group: A Simple Message About a Difficult Topic, by Donald A. McGavran and Reaching the Unreached, by Edward Dayton separated by a discussion on people movements. These ideas advanced by Wagner and McGavran are what Escobar and others in the FTL criticized as managerial missiology based more on sociological principles than on theological reflection (R. Girón, personal communication, October 31, 2009; Moreno, 2001; Padilla, n.d.). Volume 2 also covered a treatment of holistic mission (Lewis, 1990). The authors treated evangelism separately from social action. This treatment is not to be confused with the views of Padilla and the FTL in *Misión*

Integral. Nevertheless it states that ministering to the physical needs of people is an undeniable part of the mission (Lewis, 1990). The holistic mission section included an article by Robert C. Pickett and Steve C. Hawthorne entitled Helping Others Help Themselves: Christian Community Development, which provided four strategies for development: economic growth, political liberation, help and community development. Another article in this chapter was The Spontaneous Multiplication of Churches, by George Patterson. Based on the author's experience in Honduras, he outlined the steps to follow in order to have spontaneous multiplication of churches. The last chapter of volume two outlined the need for developing and working with a global mission team (Lewis, 1990). The chapter's articles included topics about global mission, prayer, the role of the local church in world missions, missions in the two-thirds world, and cooperation. This volume of *Misión Mundial* stood in contrast with the FTL missiology more than the first one.

The third volume of *Misión Mundial* [World Mission] (Lewis, 1990) was a concentrated set of chapters dealing with cross-cultural missions. The articles dealt with the foundational understanding of culture, practical implications of cross cultural relationships and biblical models for cross cultural ministry. There was descriptive and prescriptive material for the cross-cultural missionary. In addition, there were chapters on cross-cultural communication and social structures and the gospel. The concluding chapter was a treatment of the Lausanne document Gospel and Culture. The document dealt with the biblical basis for culture, its formal definition, its role in biblical revelation, the normative nature of Scripture, the cultural condition of Scripture and the continuing work of the Holy Spirit. This volume had a very pragmatic approach but its treatment of the topics is brief.

Misión Mundial [World Mission] (Lewis, 1990) became the timely textbook for the COMIBAM Congress in 1987. Since then the book has been published in several editions and used for cross-cultural training in churches and training centers throughout Latin America (Lewis, 1990). In some cases it has been adapted and abbreviated further by national movements. As such, this three-volume set had a significant role in casting the vision for thousands of Latin American evangelicals and in shaping their missiology. In the decades of the 1990s and 2000s mission leaders and practitioners in the Latin American context published several books. How these newer publications promulgated the same missiology and to what extent they offered fresh reflection are treated in subsequent chapters of the current study.

The manner in which the decision was made to use *Misión Mundial* [World Mission] (Lewis, 1986) is another demonstration of the momentous nature of the movement. Jonathan Lewis had translated Ralph Winter's materials to Spanish in 1983, but was not sure how he was going to publish or distribute this book. While in Guadalajara, Mexico, in 1985, he encountered Federico Bertuzzi and mentioned his translation and editing work. Luis Bush, who was also in Guadalajara on that occasion, had been looking for a book to use as pre-event reading for the upcoming COMIBAM 87. Unforeseen circumstances caused Luis Bush and Jonathan Lewis to stay in the same hotel room. After some conversation between the two, the decision was made that *Misión Mundial* [World Mission] would be the book used for that historic occasion. The publication schedule was put in motion (J. Lewis, personal communication, October 31,

2009). Even if *Misión Mundial* [World Mission] had not sufficiently contextualized missiology for Latin America, it did contribute to the mobilization of thousands of Latin Americans in cross-cultural missions.

Summary and Conclusions

The Ibero American Missionary Cooperation known as COMIBAM, emerged in Latin America in a context of continental change, religious renewal and maturing indigenous leadership among evangelicals. Global events, continental leadership, regional socio-economic and political instability, national missionary movements and strategic actions by evangelical organizations provided an ideal context for the rise of a mission sending movement from Latin America.

A multitude of missionary conferences that advanced the ideal of accomplishing world evangelization by cross-denominational cooperation took place during the twentieth century. COMIBAM's vision was to fully participate in this ideal by mobilizing Iberian and Latin American evangelicals. The more significant world evangelization conferences in relation to COMIBAM were the Edinburgh Missionary Conference in 1910, the Panama Congress in 1916, the Berlin Congress in 1966, and the Lausanne Congress in 1974. Continental congresses such as CLADE would also contribute to the development of this vision in Latin America. These series of congresses throughout the twentieth century had a systemic impact on the advancement of the church's mission, and consequently, on the rise of mission mobilization movements such as COMIBAM.

The socio-economic, political and religious context of the 1960s, 1970s and 1980s helped to shape the development of the Latin American church and its theology. The various segments of the church were affected in different ways. Some Latin American evangelicals responded constructively to the challenges while others reacted in a less positive manner. The adversity and continuous change contributed to the forging of mature reflection and action by Latin American evangelical leaders. This context included the rise and decline of multiple revolutionary movements and radical political changes in Latin America, the maturing stages of liberation theologies, the growth of the evangelical church in Latin America and the migration of Latin Americans to other parts of the world. Those decades were a ripe time for idealism and the mobilization of masses for a common vision.

Liberation theologies affected mainly the Roman Catholic and some of the mainline Protestant segments of the Latin American church. COMIBAM is primarily a movement among the more conservative evangelical church. A most significant development in evangelical theological reflection in the years leading up to COMIBAM's first congress was the FTL. Although the FTL did not directly contribute to the formation of COMIBAM, it paralleled it in that the FTL provided theological and missiological reflection while COMIBAM mobilized the church for cross-cultural mission within the conservative evangelical segment the Latin American church. Both organizations are examples of the emergence of indigenous leadership among evangelicals in the continent.

Before the first COMIBAM Congress, individual countries in Latin America were developing national missionary networks. Some of these national movements were catalytic in the eventual multi-national network called COMIBAM. Some of the earlier cases were Brazil, Argentina, Chile, El Salvador, Guatemala, Costa Rica and Mexico.

These movements kindled the missionary fervor in various regions of Latin America, provided leadership for the movement, and experimented with the organizational network model. Several other evangelical organizations and publications contributed directly to the success of COMIBAM's first Congress. The organizations which contributed in more direct manner were the World Evangelical Fellowship, Operation Mobilization, CLADE, CONELA and *Misión Munidal* [World Mission].

Decades of missionary and evangelistic fervor, a spirit of international cooperation among evangelicals, an indigenous missiology for Latin America and visionary leadership provided fertile ground for the launching of a movement.

CHAPTER 3. COMIBAM '87: THE BIRTH OF A MISSION MOVEMENT

The planning process, the first COMIBAM congress, and the events that followed this initial Ibero American meeting laid the groundwork for a pivotal missional movement. David Ruíz (2007) stated that the first Ibero American Missionary Congress COMIBAM '87

> has a place in history as the date when the Ibero American Church began to turn from being a mission field to becoming a mission force. Missions from Latin America to the rest of the world were born. Two phrases were coined at that congress. The first is "from mission field to mission force"…(and) the second saying… "Neither with dollars nor computers, but with my Spirit said the Lord."
> (p. 9)

Although Luís Bush pronounced the phrase from mission field to mission force, at the congress and he became identified with it, Ekström made it clear that it was not originally coined by Bush but by Jonathan Dos Santos (B. Ekström, personal communication, September 13, 2001). The first congress holds historical significance in the development of a native missionary vision and action within the Latin American church. Luís Bush (1985, October 5-16. *Reporte de viaje a los Estados Unidos* [Report of trip to the United States]. COMIBAM/Bertuzzi Archive Box 17) quoted Ralph Winter saying to him in a personal conversation, "COMIBAM '87 should be the most important congress in the history of Latin America." It definitely marked the heightened awareness of the fact that Latin American evangelicals had a commitment to God and to their churches to advance the Great Commission (Ekström, 2006). The effects of this continental congress rippled through missionary efforts. COMIBAM '87 influenced future congresses and retreats, contributed ideologically to the formation of missionary agencies, and propelled the sending of Latin Americans on cross-cultural missions (Bertuzzi, 2006; Ekström, 2006; Escobar, 2002). When and how was this idea of a COMIBAM born? What were the movement's objectives and how did it advance them? What was the role of the national mission movements? Who were the key leaders and how did they lead? What were the missiological assumptions and developments related to this watershed event? These and other questions will guide the contents of this chapter.

The First Congress

From its inception, COMIBAM '87 proved to be a watershed event for the Latin American church and for global missions. Thirty-one hundred delegates representing all Latin American countries attended the first Ibero American Missions Congress in Sao Paulo, Brazil, November 23-29, 1987 (DeCarvalho, 2007, p. 20; Escobar, 2002, p. 159; Escobar, 2007, p. 25; Ruíz, 2007, p. 9). Curiously, a letter from a Fuller Theological Seminary recipient of a doctorate in missiology to Roberto Hatch in Ecuador challenged the assertion that COMIBAM was the first Ibero American Missions. The author of the letter stated that she organized the first such congress in the mid-seventies, along with the help of leaders such as Rene Padilla and Samuel Escobar, in Brazil. The 600 participants of this congress came from throughout Latin America and even from Africa (Itioka, N. 1986, September 9. [Letter to Roberto Hatch]. COMIBAM/Bertuzzi Archive Box 17). Nevertheless, it is evident that this was a national missions congress that happened to have continental participation and not strictly a continental congress. COMIBAM stands indeed as the first Ibero American Missions congress. COMIBAM '87 was the largest international Latin American evangelical event up to that time (Bertuzzi, 2006). The delegates represented 25 Ibero American countries and 59 other countries around the world (Girón, 2000). These attendance statistics reflect the deliberate Pan-American planning by the leaders in Mexico City in 1984, who conceived the idea of the congress (Bertuzzi, 2006; Escobar, 2002; Ruiz, 2007). The organizers intended to launch a process, not just an event, which would continue after the meeting (Bertuzzi, 2006). Thus, the leaders set an ambitious agenda to secure the support of national leaders, to survey the missionary history in Ibero America and to assess the future of its missionary movement. They pursued this agenda during the three years leading up to the congress.

The thesis statement of the current study posits that COMIBAM serves as a case study of how right leadership in the right context produces an effective missionary network. The Sao Paulo 1987 congress did indeed launch the platform for a new network and process. Thus, this chapter seeks to analyze the congress by identifying the process for its conceptualization, reviewing the proposed scope of the congress, and examining the content of the plenary sessions. Other components leading up to the congress will be discussed under the headings of National Mission Movements, Leaders and Leadership, and Missiological Reflection.

The Process for the Conceptualization of the Congress

The organization of the first congress, and subsequently, the birth of the COMIBAM movement depended on the leadership's ability to recognize and seize this *kairos* moment. As Burns (1978) so eloquently put it, "intellectual leadership at its best anticipates, mediates, and ultimately subdues Experience with the weapons of imagination and intelligence" (p. 168). The founding leaders of the COMIBAM movement demonstrated this kind of leadership. The range of leaders and organizations that contributed to the conceptualization and organization of the congress prove that the idea came from various sources at the same time. Additionally, through the planning stages, there is the recurring theme of the leaders' vision that the congress would have a life beyond the event itself.

Visionary leaders recognized an important shift occurring in the Latin America missional landscape of the early 1980's. Before the first Brazilian Evangelism Congress in 1983, Jonathan dos Santos, president of the *Associção de Missões Transculturais Brasileiras* [Brazilian Cross-cultural Missionary Association], shared his desire to expand the missionary vision throughout the entire continent with Luís Bush, pastor of the *Nazaret* Church in El Salvador. In that exchange, dos Santos suggested the idea of an Ibero American conference (Bush, 1987, March-April; Ekström, 2006). In 1984, Bush's church in El Salvador organized *Misión '84* probing the international interest in a continental missions congress. Theodore Williams, who at the time was the executive secretary of the WEA's Missions Committee, and Lawrence Keyes, a missiologist serving through SEPAL (Spanish acronym for "Evangelization Service for Latin America"), expressed to Bush on different occasions the same conviction that the time was right for a continental wide missions conference (Bush, 1987). During the 1984 meeting in Germany, the Lausanne committee challenged the Latin American representatives to move forward in the process of missions awareness. As a result, CONELA's meeting in December of that same year discussed the feasibility of a congress (Bush, 1987, March-April; Ekstrom, 2006). This meeting took place on December 12-14, 1984 in Mexico City (Bush, L., 1985, *Congreso Iberoamericano de*

Misiones, informe de abril 1985 [Ibero American Missions Congress, April 1985 report. COMIBAM/Bertuzzi Archive Box 17; Entre Nos, 1984). By June of 1985, the first meeting of the coordinating committee for COMIBAM in Brazil documented the commitment to move forward with such a congress (Bush, L. K., 1985, *Reporte COMIBAM 87 b* [COMIBAM 87 Report b. COMIBAM/Bertuzzi Archive Box 17). In 1986, the first Ibero American Theological Conference took place in Antigua, Guatemala, providing much of the base topics for the COMIBAM congress in 1987 (Bush, 1986, July; Ekström, 2006). Thus, Ekström (2006) made a case for the roles of Jonathan Dos Santos, Luís Bush, *Misión '84* (San Salvador), the WEA, the Lausanne Committee and CONELA in conceptualizing the COMIBAM '87 congress and what might follow. Although the influence of the Lausanne movement is listed as a contributing element to the formation of COMIBAM, an examination of how influential the ideals of Lausanne were outside the scope of the current study. Further research in this area is recommended. Ekström's view coincided with what Luís Bush (1987, March-April) reported via COMIBAM's newsletter in its March-April issue. This demonstrates how innovative leadership captured the emergence of like-minded ideas in the Latin American landscape of the 1980s and put them into action.

Born of visionary conversations, the 1984 Mexico meeting served to cement the foundational concept for an Ibero American missionary congress. Representatives of seven different organizations, namely Luís Bush representing CNEC, Marcelino Ortiz and Galo Vasquez representing CONELA, Dr. Samuel Wilson representing LCWE, Larry Pate representing SEPAL, Richard Griffin representing OM, H.O. Espinoza representing PROMESA, and Tom Chandler representing WEF, met in Mexico City on

December 12-14, 1984 to consider the possibility of a continental missions conference. Luís Bush was appointed president of the coordinating committee and continued to serve as pastor of *Nazaret* Church in El Salvador. CONELA sponsored the meeting and it resulted in an affirmative decision to organize a conference (Bush, L. 1985, April. *Congreso Iberoamericano de Misiones, informe* [Ibero American Missions Congress, report. COMIBAM/Bertuzzi Archive Box 17; Entre Nos, 1984). At this preliminary stage, leaders determined that the congress should emphasize world evangelism, the sending and going of missionaries, and that the approach should focus on launching a process rather than simply holding an event. At that point, the leadership intended for the congress to involve 2,500 to 3,000 delegates and to include denominational leaders with an interest in missions, youth leaders with the potential for becoming missionaries, pastors, evangelical organization leaders, representatives of para-church organizations, representatives of missionary agencies, missiology professors, key missionaries in Latin America and mission leaders from other continents.

Shortly after the Mexico City meeting, Luís Bush corrected an apparent misunderstanding that was being publicized throughout the continent. Bush (1985, April. *Congreso Iberoamericano de Misiones, informe* [Ibero American Missions Congress, report. COMIBAM/Bertuzzi Archive Box 17) made it clear that CONELA had sponsored the Mexico City meeting, but was not the sole sponsor of the COMIBAM '87 congress. All those who came to the table at the Mexico City meeting recognized the critical importance that COMIBAM '87's sponsorship not come from one sole organization but have broad support. This distinguished the event and process as the networking of multiple entities. This decision intentionally sowed the seeds for broader partner participation and for the creation of a network of those partners.

Taking initiative after the Mexico 1984 meeting, Luís Bush continued to develop concrete plans for the congress. In personal correspondence, Bush (1985, April 26. [Letter to Luis Perfetti] COMIBAM/Bertuzzi Archive Box 17) communicated to Luís Perfetti that they should select congress participants based on the percentage of evangelicals in each country, namely 43% from Brazil, 13% from Mexico, 8% from USA/Canada, 7% from Chile, 4% from Guatemala, Argentina and Colombia and 16% from the rest of Ibero America. The leadership also adopted a strategy of accessibility to attract and gather the top leadership across the various domains that related to missions in Ibero America. They selected Brazil as the congress location to reduce travel costs. COMIBAM '87 encouraged attendance by helping to cover the travel expenses of delegates, many of whom were from Brazil. This comprehensive leadership approach that sought to involve multiple domains of leaders from a cross-section of Latin America at a financially affordable venue proved a strategic one in order to mobilize the church in Ibero America.

The Proposed Scope of the Congress

Once leaders decided to hold the congress, the planning teams began to work shortly thereafter to cement and implement the strategic vision. The proposed scope of the congress was ambitious, but its success validated such boldness. Ralph Winter (1988) declared, "I am writing right in the midst of COMIBAM, here in Brazil—a meeting the like of which has never been held in all of human history. I believe we can see the future of missions more closely by looking at the meeting more closely" (p. 1).

The first coordinating committee meeting for COMIBAM '87 took place in Sao Paulo, Brazil June 26-28, 1985 with sixteen members representing eleven countries (Bush, 1985, October). The October newsletter reported the number of members in the coordinating committee and the countries from which they came, without listing their names. The newsletter provided the following photo, shown in figure 4, which included Luís Bush on the bottom left and Federico Bertuzzi at the top, the third one from the left:

Figure 1. Photo of the COMIBAM '87's first coordinating committee which met in Sao Paulo, Brazil June 26-28, 1985.

In COMIBAM '87's first newsletter, after the Sao Paulo coordinating committee meeting, Luís Bush (1985) stated his desire that this congress would ignite a change in Latin American missions:

> This congress, more than an event, seeks to generate a process of awakening and missionary participation among the churches, to emphasize world evangelization, to find, equip and support missionaries, and the participation of all the church for this purpose. (p. 3)

Furthermore, the coordinating committee documented a declaration that expressed their conviction that now was the right time, under God, for the Ibero American church to mobilize as a mission force. They recognized and articulated: (a) the need for churches and pastors to experience a missionary awakening, (b) the need for biblical and theological reflection, (c) the inclusion of missiology in theological training, (d) the need for research about current missionary methodology and about unreached people groups, and (e) the need for cross-cultural training for the missionary task. Such ambitious desires fueled the motivation and informed the strategic choices in the planning of the Ibero American Missionary Congress in 1987.

The leaders' emphasis on biblical, theological and missiological reflection demonstrates the emerging search for a contextualized missiology during this era. Based on the latest and best missiological assumptions from North America, the focus on unreached people groups and on cross-cultural training categorized the movement as cross-cultural missionary mobilization. The struggle between defining and implementing a contextualized native missiology and the pragmatic approach that took for granted the more developed North American missiology would continue throughout the first years of the movement. Nevertheless, the coordinating committee established the following goals as it launched the preparations for the first congress: (a) hold missionary conferences in each of the twenty-three Ibero American countries, (b) organize national committees at the conferences, (c) research and document missionary activity in the most needy mission fields, (d) publish the data discovered in a series of books in Spanish, Portuguese and English, and (e) publish a biblical manual of missiology and a manual of missionary practice for the cross-cultural work to be carried out by churches (COMIBAM, 1985, October 25. *Research proposal submitted to World Vision*. COMIBAM/Bertuzzi Archive Box 17).

Even if the movement came to be known more for its pragmatic mobilization than by its missiological reflection, there was a clear intent to build on informed research. Consequently, Luís Bush (COMIBAM, 1985, April. *Congreso Iberoamericano de Misiones, plan de investigación* [Ibero American Missions Congress research plan]. COMIBAM/Bertuzzi Archive Box 17) drafted an ambitious plan for published research. This plan included historical, contextual, missiological, geographical, and biblical research. National Christians, once selected and approved by the COMIBAM '87 national committee according to their own country, were to conduct the historical research. Marc Publications was to conduct the contextual research through the national World Vision office in Ibero America. The missiological research consisted of gathering data regarding missionary activity and needs. Overseas Crusades was to conduct the missiological research. The geographical research was to be the task of the Global Mapping Project. Emilio Antonio Nuñez was to write the biblical research. The proposal called for Latin Americans to conduct the research as much as possible and envisioned the involvement of missionary organizations. The resulting research was to be published before COMIBAM '87 as a 350-page book in Spanish, Portuguese and English. Those involved in editing this work and writing the introductory and concluding chapters were to be Emilio Antonio Nuñez, Synesio Lyra, Luís Bush, Luís Palau, Nilson Fannini and Galo Vasquez, respectively. Six months after the initial proposal, Bush (1985, October 25. *Research proposal submitted to World Vision*. COMIBAM/Bertuzzi Archive Box 17) presented a proposal to World Vision with a flow chart of information resulting in the editing and printing of the missions research in Spanish and Portuguese by the COMIBAM office and in English by World Vision. Marc Publications had final editorial control over the books (Bush, L., 1985, October 5-16. *Reporte de viaje a los Estados Unidos* [Report of trip to the United States]. COMIBAM/Bertuzzi Archive Box 17). This proposal also assigned research of specific countries to various organizations such as Overseas Crusades, Puente, VELA, IMDELA and DAWN, and provided a time-line and a budget for the project. The 350-page comprehensive book was never published as proposed. However, significant portions of it did come to fruition. The works that were published in relation to COMIBAM between 1985 and 1987 included the following:

Manual de intercession misionera [Missionary intercession manual].

Atlas de COMIBAM [COMIBAM Atlas].

Reto Iberoamericano [Ibero American Challenge].

Manual de misiones para la iglesia local [Missions manual for the local church].

Misión mundial: Un Análisis del movimiento cristiano mundial; Vols. 1, 2 y 3 [World mission: An analysis of the world Christian movement; Vols 1, 2 & 3].

Misión para el tercer milenio [Mission for the third millennium].

Introducción a la misiología Latinoamericana [Introduction to Latin American missiology].

Misionología: Nuestro cometido transcultural [Missiology: Our cross-cultural assignment].

Ayudas educativas en misiones para la iglesia local [Educational helps in missions for the local church].

Introducción a la misiología Latinoamericana was not published by COMIBAM, but it was published in the context of the current dialogue in 1986. The author of *Introducción a la misiología Latinoamericana,* McIntosh, participated in COMIBAM's first theological conference. *Misionología: Nuestro cometido transcultural* was not published by COMIBAM, but the author, Pate, was present at the Mexico 1984 meeting and he mentions COMIBAM '87 in the book's prologue. *Ayudas educativas en misiones para la iglesia local* is the third book on the list that was not published by COMIBAM, but it is included here because of the publisher's, SEPAL, connection with COMIBAM. In spite of the fact that the 350-page proposed project was not published as originally planned, this list of published volumes is impressive for such a brief period of time and for an organization still in its infancy. Clearly, the movement asserted itself through publications from its inception.

The delegate selection process for the congress proved essential to ensuring that COMIBAM '87 resulted in the mobilization of the Latin American church and not just an event. A continental movement required proportionate participation from each country and delegate-readiness to capture the vision and return home to share it. The organizers recognized the significance of getting the right leaders from each country. The leadership chose a process in which individuals from each country had the opportunity to apply and be selected based on previously announced criteria. Approximately six months after the leadership committed to move forward with the congress, the COMIBAM continental office in Guatemala announced, via its newsletter, the opportunity to apply for a delegate seat at the congress (COMIBAM, 1986, February).

Congress leaders sought 3,000 participants who were committed to a national or international missionary ministry. Congress organizers expected to have representation from all twenty-three Ibero American countries. Applicants for one of these 3,000 seats had to meet five criteria: (1) total consecration; (2) a proven track record of service in their local church; (3) development of spiritual gifts; (4) certification of local and national leadership; and (5) participation in an intercessory group with a missionary emphasis. Approved delegates were sent instructions to form a weekly intercessory group and received materials to use in the group after pre-registration (Calderón, 1986). The materials included the book *Misión Mundial, Part I* (1986) and a missions intercession manual (Calderón, 1986). Each approved congress participant was to involve eight to twelve others in missionary study and intercession, thereby exponentially increasing the strength of the movement beyond the 3,000 delegates (Calderón, 1986). These criteria demonstrated the leadership's value of participants' spirituality, praxis, and leadership ability. Furthermore, beyond the spiritual value of the study/prayer groups, this process provided the establishment of a network of approximately 30,000 people before the congress even took place, potentially providing a platform for vision dissemination almost simultaneous to the congress. This entire process for enlisting and preparing the 3,000 delegates proved an insightful organizational leadership decision.

The development of a budget presented significant opportunities to materialize the vision for an autonomous indigenous missions movement. For a first-time event on a continent that considered itself part of the so-called third world, participation depended on affordability. Notwithstanding, it would be important for the congress to avoid a paternalistic pattern in terms of its financing. From the onset, organizers envisioned a congress budget that covered a significant portion of the travel expense, meals and lodging for participants (Bush, L. K., 1986, May 5. [Letter to Federico Bertuzzi]. COMIBAM/Bertuzzi Archive Box 17). The proposed budget for the Ibero American Congress designated that the travel expenses for delegates be covered 40% by national committees; 20% by the delegates; and 40% by COMIBAM. All of the meals and lodging for delegates while in Sao Paulo would be the responsibility of COMIBAM (COMIBAM, 1985, August 1. *Budget summary.* COMIBAM/Bertuzzi Archive Box 17). This approach reflected unusual cultural context awareness on the part of the leaders and ensured equal access to all potential delegates. Lanier (2000) suggested that people from hot-climate cultures have contrasting concepts about hospitality from those of cold-climate cultures. Namely, "in most hot-climate cultures, hospitality automatically means taking in and caring for the travelor" (p. 74). Additionally, the budget approach demonstrated the maturity of the Latin American evangelical church, which was poised to take greater responsibility, indeed moving from mission field to mission force.

Financing this endeavor presented a challenge. Obtaining funding for an endeavor that had not been done before and for which no single organization could take the credit required high entrepreneurial intelligence. Furthermore, the manner of funding for the first congress, and subsequently the movement, would make a tremendous cultural difference. Would this movement truly be an autonomous Latin American enterprise or would it be another Northern-financed project? Corbett and Fikkert (2009) stated that the North American church often hurts itself and the materially poor by attempting to help with a distorted view and with an approach that contributes to the feelings of inferiority in the materially poor. Furthermore, Corbett and Fikkert (2009) defined material poverty alleviation as, "working to reconcile the four foundational relationships so that people can fulfill their callings of glorifying God by working and supporting themselves" (p. 78). According to Corbett and Fikkert (2009) these four foundational relationships are relationship with God, with self, with others and with the rest of creation. Although the COMIBAM '87 congress was not a poverty alleviation endeavor, the principle holds that the ultimate success of a movement in a materially disadvantaged part of the world depends on its eventual ability to support itself. Though self-support proved unrealistic at the beginning, good leadership articulated it as an ultimate goal. By this time, Bush estimated a $2 million budget for COMIBAM '87 and he hoped to raise about $700,000 from U.S. sources. The budget summary in Table 2 provides a general overview of the finances needed and their sources.

This approach demonstrates a genuine effort to give ownership of the process to Latin Americans. Bush set the expectation that Latin American sources would cover well over half of the cost. The unstated, but essential, assumption was that as local sources contributed more than half of the total budget, local ownership was demonstrated. The proportion expected from indigenous sources was a significant achievement considering these were the beginning stages of the COMIBAM movement. Nevertheless it should be noted that the effort received significant financial support from outside Latin America.

The budget format implemented the COMIBAM strategy that the majority of resources come from local funds to ensure local ownership. Of the total budget, 65% was expected to come from Latin American sources.

Table 2

COMIBAM operations budget summary from August 1985 to December 1987
(COMIBAM, 1985, August 1. COMIBAM/Bertuzzi Archive Box 17)

Line Item	To be raised in Latin America	To be raised in Western Countries	Total
Intercession—communication	$450	$1,050	$1,500
Information—monthly bulletin	$1,600	$8,200	$9,800
Investigation—(research)	0	$3,300	$3,300
Instruction—12 books	$25,500	$51,000	$76,500
Involvement—national conferences	$16,345	$6,020	$22,365
Inspiration—national congresses	$112,000	0	$112000
Infrastructure—missions agencies	0	0	0
Invitation to consecration—Ibero American Congress	$1,119,200	$568,000	$1,687,200
Coordination	$16,700	$28,900	$45,600
Administration—Guatemala and Sao Paulo offices	0	$28,060	$28,060
Total	$1,291,795	$694,530	$1,986,325

The proportion of funds coming from Latin America was not uniformly applied in each of the ten budget areas. More than half of the intercession, information, investigation or research, instruction and administration budgets were to come from outside Latin America. Sixty-three percent of the coordination budget was to come from outside sources also. The involvement, namely the national conferences, budget expected 73% to come from Latin Americans, the inspiration, namely the national congresses, budget called for 100% from Latin Americans, and the Ibero American Congress budget projected 66% to come from the same source. This distribution most likely reflected the leaders' ability to identify what the sources inside and outside Latin America were willing to fund. Allowing Latin Americans to absorb the greater share of the cost for the national conferences, national congresses and the Ibero American Congress represented a significant step away from paternalism.

Corbett and Fikkert (2009) defined paternalism as "doing for people what they can do for themselves" (p. 115) listing five types of paternalism: resource, spiritual, knowledge, labor and managerial. One of the significant dangers for the nascent COMIBAM movement would be the progression from resource paternalism to managerial paternalism. Managerial paternalism, according to Corbett and Fikkert (2009), is the tendency of North Americans to take over initiatives out of the innate desire for efficiency and tangible results. The need to demonstrate to donors efficiency and results as defined by North American standards carried with it the implicit danger that a Latin American missions movement could be managed by North Americans.

This initial budget, nevertheless, permitted participating countries to fund the more tangible experiences. The challenge of leading Latin American evangelicals to value funding research and literature in the area of missions was apparently left for future leadership. Acknowledging how much past financial support came from outside sources, Jonathan Lewis (2009) rejoiced that the 2009 COMIBAM IV General Assembly in Bogotá, Colombia marked the first COMIBAM meeting where travel and lodging of delegates was not subsidized (J. P. Lewis, personal communication, October 30, 2009). It would take almost twenty-five years for COMIBAM to end travel and lodging subsidies for its international meetings, but COMIBAM accomplished its initial intention.

From the inception of the idea among various leaders, the three years after the Mexico '84 meeting were filled with planning, casting the vision throughout Latin America, and investing in the preparation of the would-be delegates. Congress leadership demonstrated great ability as they provided research and publishing, and as they budgeted for the congress. God blessed the results of visionary leadership acting at the right moment for Latin America.

Plenary Sessions: Topics and Personalities

Beyond the participation and the scope of the congress, the program for the COMIBAM '87 reveals the intentional gathering of seminal ideas and innovative minds to catalyze a paradigm shift within the Ibero American evangelical church. What schedule format did the congress have? What topics were discussed at the congress? Who were the personalities that were invited to help cast the vision? The decisions related to these questions reveal the organizing committee's priorities.

The executive committee decided that the Congress program would consist of a Bible Hour each day with biblical/theological exposition toward an Ibero American missiology, small groups that would discuss and document conclusions, intercessory prayer groups, the availability of spiritual and vocational counseling, a combined international musical concert, missions exhibits, missionary testimonies and seminars (COMIBAM, 1986, October. *Acta de reunion del comité ejecutivo COMIBAM* Minutes of the COMIBAM executive committee meeting]. COMIBAM/Bertuzzi

Archive Box 17). The suggestions within the planning time reveal the struggle to balance academic reflection and practical application. A year before the congress, Roberto Hatch (1986, November 12. [Letter to Luís Bush]. COMIBAM/Bertuzzi Archive Box 17), a continental leader living in Ecuador, suggested that the biblical exposition at the congress should be exegetical, deep, and done by one single individual. He further alluded to building on the work of Russell Shedd, John Stott, and the Urbana conferences. The suggestions he gave for COMIBAM '87 presenters were Emilio Nuñez from Guatemala, Samuel Escobar from Philadelphia, Hector Piño from Peru, Pablo Pérez from Dallas, Jaime Ortíz from Colombia, Luciano Jaramillo from Miami and Pablo Deíros from Argentina, none of which were actually COMIBAM '87 plenary session speakers.

While Hatch may have desired presenters with a more academic approach, other COMIBAM '87 planners seemed to have had in mind a broader perspective for the selection of presenters. The names listed by the executive committee as possibilities were Daniel Reiz, Emilio Nuñez, Roberto Hatch, Pablo Deíros, Rudy Girón, Guillermo Milovan, Arnoldo Canolín, Teodoro Williams, Rusch Sludd, Guillermo Taylor, Luís Palau, Luís Bush, Calo Fabio, George Verwer, Frank Dietz, Edison Queiróz (COMIBAM, 1986, October. *Acta de reunion del comité ejecutivo COMIBAM* [Minutes of the COMIBAM executive committee meeting]. COMIBAM/Bertuzzi Archive Box 17). Although several of these possessed significant academic recognition, many were better known as practitioners. Beyond the theological and biblical exposition ability of speakers, the committee also sought presenters with missiological training, cross-cultural vision, demonstrated praxis, and Spanish-speaking ability. The committee overtly decided to minimize English and Portuguese language participation during the program

(COMIBAM, 1986, October. *Acta de reunion del comité ejectuivo COMIBAM* [Minutes of the COMIBAM executive committee meeting]. COMIBAM/Bertuzzi Archive Box 17). The minimization of Portuguese language participants potentially endangered the higher involvement of Brazilians in the movement. From its very beginning the movement was known to prioritize praxis over theological/missiological reflection (B. Ekström, personal communication, February 9, 2011). The plenary sessions approach further confirmed this preference.

The plenary session topics intentionally set the stage for a total paradigm shift that seized upon the current landscape of ideas, yet emphasized practical application over mere academic reflection. The topics covered in these plenary sessions included assessment of the current situation as well as biblical, theological, and missiological considerations. Alberto Barrientos dealt with the Ibero American situation and missions. He presented the challenges facing the Ibero American evangelical church in order to become a mission force, mostly in terms of set mental models, and suggested new possibilities by presenting new mental models (Barrientos, 1987, November). Calo Fabio presented a brief exposition of Revelation 5:1-14 and its implications, primarily painting an eschatological vision as inspiration for the mission (Fabio, 1987, November). Edison Queiróz treated the topic of the church and missions (Queiróz, 1987, November). The subject of prayer and missions was covered by Francisco Anabalón (Anabalón, 1987, November). Luís Bush interpreted the congress' theme, "Light to the Nations," providing a clear, compelling and graphic vision for the task of mobilizing Ibero America for cross-cultural missions (Bush, 1987, November). Luís Palau encouraged participants to "dream big dreams" using John 14:12 as a text (Palau, 1987, November, pp. 24-27).

Roberto Hatch provided an insightful treatment of missionary lessons and models, delivered with a tone of realism (Hatch, 1987, November). The role of the Holy Spirit in the mission of God's People was treated by Rudy Girón, offering the memorable and enigmatic paraphrase of Zechariah 4:6: "Not with computers, not with dollars, but with my Spirit, said the Lord of Hosts" (Girón, 1987, November, pp. 37-40). Theodore Williams offered a pragmatic treatment of finances and missions (Williams, 1987, November). Bill Taylor presented the session on the cross-cultural challenge, by offering a biblical, missiological, and practical perspective on the topic (Taylor, 1987, November). These presentations exceeded mere inspirational encouragement to mobilize the Ibero American church for missions. The quality of their original approach provided seeds for reflection and further development.

The Congress Becomes a *Cooperación*: COMIBAM International

Congress leaders continually announced their intention of catalyzing a process that would continue beyond the event itself. Eventually COMIBAM became a network of networks. This, however, did not develop overnight. COMIBAM first evolved from a vision to a congress and then to a *cooperación*. Since in standard English usage the word "cooperation" does not name a kind of organization, the Spanish word, which also suggests an organizational structure similar to a network, will be used in the current study. Visionary leaders played an instrumental role in carrying out the congress. The new leaders who followed the founders carried the visionary torch and developed the implementation of the cooperation stage.

Planners for the first conference laid the foundation for establishment a mobilization process. Subsequent leadership faced the task of building the organizational structure for this continuing network. Bertil Ekström stated, "There was no structure for it. It was an event with the desire to mobilize people" (B. Ekström, personal communication, February 9, 2011). Furthermore, Ekström, who became COMIBAM's third president, considered that the consolidation of the international movement really took place under the leadership of Rudy Girón, along with the work of others like Federico Bertuzzi, Carlos Calderón and Edison Queiróz. Girón (2000) acknowledged his role in that development but suggested a wider time frame. According to Girón, the first phase of turning the event into an ongoing process of cooperation took place between 1983 and 1990. The first congress, thus, served to cast the vision, to create enthusiasm among evangelical leadership throughout the continent, and to provide connecting points for the future. After the congress, the leadership had to figure out how to continue the movement and to design the vehicle that would carry these goals forward. The success of the movement depended upon the interaction of continental leadership with each country. The emerging leadership in each country began organizing and linking with the continental leadership. The word *cooperación* replaced *congreso* in the COMIBAM acronym. As such, the identity of COMIBAM as a loose network transitioned to the development of a more formal network structure.

Leadership Theory and COMIBAM Leaders

The successful development of COMIBAM as an organization can be contributed to the creativity and discipline of its leadership. Collins (2001) and Bolman and Deal (2003) provided theoretical criteria to analyze COMIBAM's leadership during this period of its history. As an event inspires a movement, one must consider the role of vision and how that vision is implemented into an organization. Collins (2001) developed a matrix of creative discipline that categorized organizations into one of four quadrants: hierarchical, bureaucratic, start-up and great. Figure 2 displays this matrix. These quadrants are formed by the intersection of what Collins (2001) labels "ethic of entrepreneurship" and "culture of discipline." COMIBAM soon moved from Collins (2001) "start-up organization" quadrant, which consists of high ethic of entrepreneurship and low culture of discipline, to the "great organization" quadrant, which consists of high ethic of entrepreneurship and high culture of discipline.

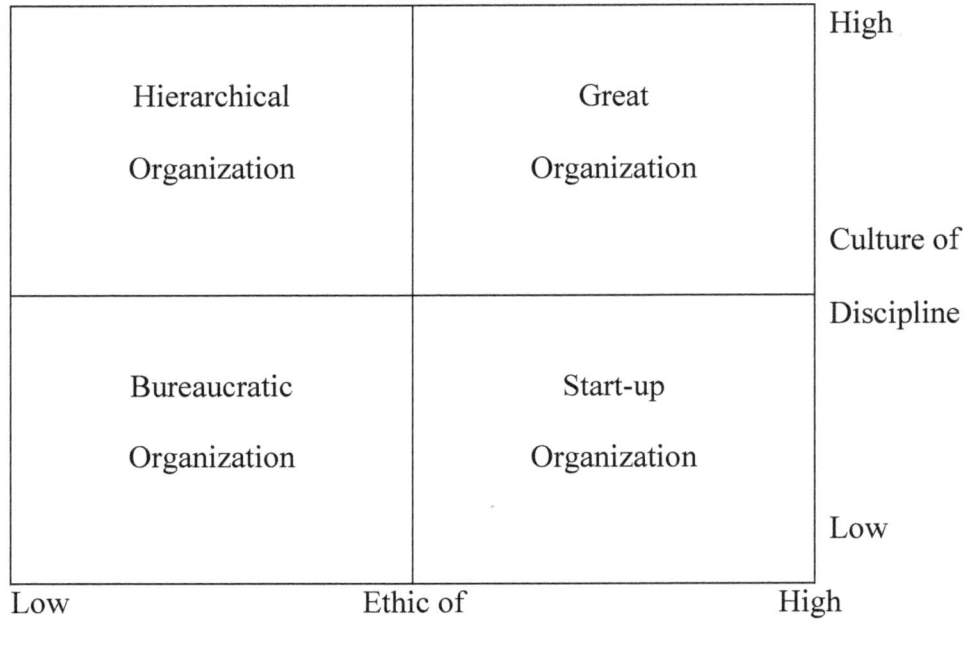

Figure 2. Collins' (2001) "Good-to-Great matrix of creative discipline" which uses the "culture of disciple" and the "ethic of entrepreneurship."

Beyond the roles of vision and organizational discipline, another aspect that requires leadership discernment has to do with organizational frames. Bolman and Deal (2003) introduced four organizational frames: structural, human resource, political, and symbolic each with respective characteristics. The authors presented the concept of "reframing organizations" as follows, "Reframing requires an ability to understand and use multiple perspectives, to think about the same thing in more than one way…The effective leader changes lenses when things don't make sense or aren't working" (pp. 5, 331).

As COMIBAM moved from an event to an organization, the ability of its leadership to reframe proved critical. Although some desired to establish a more formal organizational structure to ensure that the objectives of the first Congress would be carried out, the majority of the leadership insisted in maintaining a looser network-like structure that would allow national leadership to form grassroots organizations (Bertuzzi, 2006). David Ruíz (2002) championed the network model early in the process. He proposed a network organization with characteristics such as, "unity based on the objective not on the organization, voluntary association, permanence in the service function, shared leadership, and a flat organization." This concept did not develop instantly, nor did the leadership share a unified concept about it in the beginning. Luís Bush, for example, suggested to the coordinating committee in October of 1985 that they consider forming three associations at the first COMIBAM congress: (a) an association for mobilization of churches; (b) an association of missions professors; and (c) an association of missionary agencies in Latin America (Bush, L. K., 1985, October. *Reporte COMIBAM '87 b* [COMIBAM '87 Report b]. COMIBAM/Bertuzzi Archive Box 17). To use Bolman and Deal's (2003) terminology, Bush envisioned using primarily a structural organizational frame to start COMIBAM. The six assumptions of the structural organizational frame are:

1. Organizations exist to achieve established goals and objectives

2. Organizations increase efficiency and enhance performance through specialization and a clear division of labor

3. Appropriate forms of coordination and control ensure that diverse efforts of individuals and units mesh

4. Organizations work best when rationality prevails over personal preferences and extraneous pressures

5. Structures must be designed to fit an organization's circumstance (including its goals, technology, workforce, and environment)

6. Problems and performance gaps arise from structural deficiencies and can be remedied through analysis and restructuring (p. 45)

The structural organizational frame may have been appropriate for organizing a continental congress. Nevertheless, for COMIBAM to become a movement, reframing was necessary. If the kind of continental level of associations that Bush suggested had actually formed, they may have provided a simpler organization but COMIBAM would have lost the opportunity to function as a network. COMIBAM would have become a hierarchical organization at best or a bureaucratic one at worst. If COMIBAM had become a hierarchical or bureaucratic organization it might have become an expensive agency that relied on sources outside Latin America, or struggled to survive financially. Furthermore, without depending on the grass-roots national networks, it might have become detached from the diverse needs as understood by the churches and, consequently, lost credibility and relevancy.

The idea of COMIBAM becoming more than an event had been communicated and accepted from the beginning. The plan for transition took time to emerge. This evolution of COMIBAM from a congress to a *cooperación* required the disciplined work of leaders. Additionally, it called for discernment as to the most appropriate organizational model and the willingness to experiment with a new and untested organizational structure. Grassroots groups could find channels of expression through this infrastructure. This organizational structure was innovative. It is remarkable that COMIBAM was not fashioned after existing missionary organizations in Ibero America. The longevity of the movement, including two additional international congresses, gives evidence of highly disciplined leadership and the durability of the *cooperación* structure.

National Mission Movements: The Network's First Level

The dream of coordinated but autonomous movements arising in every nation of Ibero America to mobilize evangelical churches into global missions materialized in the MMN. The desire to mobilize the Ibero American church for world evangelization implies the connection of evangelicals in each of the geo-political states that comprise Ibero America. The success or failure of a continent-wide movement depended on the degree to which MMN organized throughout Ibero America. The vision of autonomous but interconnected national movements in each country had implications for the organizational model that prevailed. In this section we will examine the MMN. This portion will identify the conferences and congresses that took place in each country leading up to COMIBAM '87 along with the leaders that emerged and the committees that formed. The identification of these leaders and the establishment of these committees helped to determine COMIBAM's destiny after its Sao Paulo congress.

MMN are national mission movements. This nomenclature refers to the mission sending fervor, activity and networking taking place at the national levels in the various

Latin American and Iberian countries. Some of the earlier cases of the nascent MMN fervor were the national movements in Brazil, Argentina, Chile, El Salvador, Guatemala, Costa Rica and Mexico (L. K. Bush, personal communication, February 4, 2011; B. Ekström, personal communication, February 9, 2011). Daniel Bianchi, an Argentine pastor, a leader in Argentina's national missionary movement and in COMIBAM International, also attested to this (D. Bianchi, personal communication, May 8, 2009).

These movements continued to develop after the first congress and became the essence of the movement. What had been taking place in the various countries before the first congress underpinned the success of the congress. Two types of events became normative for most of the countries: national missions conferences and congresses. The conferences were gatherings of representative leadership to cast the vision. Often at these conferences, committees formed and organized to promote the missionary cause at a national level and to link to COMIBAM '87.

Luís Bush (1985, April. *Consultas misioneras nacionales* [National missions consultations]. COMIBAM/Bertuzzi Archive Box 17) drafted the blueprint for the missions conferences, which included the objectives, the target audience, the topics to be covered, and even a recommended schedule. The objectives included: (a) encouragement of the national Christians, (b) review of the national church's participation in the mission task, (c) identification of the unfinished task in relation to the unreached in each country, (d) promotion of the plans for COMIBAM '87, (e) introduction of continental leadership, (f) selection of a national committee that would relate to COMIBAM '87, and (g) selection of the person who would conduct the historical research for that particular country. The conferences generally targeted a select group of approximately 30 leaders who represented missionary agencies, mission-minded pastors, missions professors, missionaries interested in helping the church send missionaries, and youth leaders. The topics for the national conferences included: (a) the missionary challenge for the Latin American church, (b) presentation of the plans for the COMIBAM '87 congress, (c) introduction of a common terminology for missionary cooperation, (d) the role of the church in cross-cultural missions, (e) report of the advance of cross-cultural missions within the country, (f) the progress of denominational missions, (g) report of the unreached within the country, (h) missionary training, (i) evaluation of missionary conferences, (j) women and missions, and (k) youth and missions. Congresses, by contrast, appealed to a wider segment of the evangelical church in each country. Usually conferences preceded congresses.

Appendix G lists thirty missions conferences and congresses throughout Ibero America. Calderón (1986, September) reported that conferences also took place in Uruguay and Paraguay. These meetings reflect the missionary fervor brewing throughout the continent and demonstrate the strategic preparation for COMIBAM '87 by its leaders. The COMIBAM leadership seized the missionary zeal which was present throughout the continent already and provided the vehicle for an organized movement.

The conferences offered discussions on the biblical basis for missions, missiology, the need for evangelicals to rise to the missionary challenge, and the urgency of prayer. The vision of the upcoming COMIBAM '87 congress was also presented at these national meetings. A common thread to all of the conferences was emphasis on prayer and the communication of a sense of God's *kairos* moment. These national missions conferences laid the strategic foundation for missiological discussion across denominations, they identified key national leadership, and they secured commitment for the continental congress. The presence of leaders such as Luís Bush, Rudy Girón, Roberto Hatch and Moisés Mejía in multiple national conferences provided the opportunity for national leaders to relate closely to continental leaders, thus keeping the pulse of the national movements and the heartbeat of the continental congress synchronized. The missions conferences and congresses targeted the leaders of various denominations. Some of the congresses targeted the participation of young people and of women. This approach secured representation of significant segments of the evangelical church throughout the continent. The early participation of indigenous people group leaders from various tribes in Latin America demonstrated COMIBAM's commitment to being inclusive and to the people-group approach to missions.

While there was certainly widespread excitement taking place, not all national missionary movements experienced a uniform level of readiness. Implementing the COMIBAM strategy in all twenty-three countries did not happen automatically. COMIBAM acknowledged that evangelical leaders in Peru were not initially receptive to the work of COMIBAM (COMIBAM, 1986, November). Bush also shared a prayer request for Honduras to avoid a potential division over which group would carry forward the COMIBAM vision (Bush,L. K., 1986, August 8. [Letter to the COMIBAM coordinating committee]. COMIBAM/Bertuzzi Archive Box 17). By October of 1986, at the meeting of the continental executive committee, the regional leaders reported the following in regard to the national situations: (a) Chile, Ecuador, Honduras and Panama had demonstrated nominal interest and some difficulties, ; (b) Peru, USA, Canada, Puerto Rico and the Dominican Republic had a good level of participation but evidenced a more regional focus; (c) Uruguay, Paraguay, Colombia, Venezuela, Bolivia, and Mexico had a higher level of readiness evidenced by the establishing of organizational channels to promote the process; (d) Argentina, Brazil, Guatemala, El Salvador and Costa Rica displayed a high level of readiness for the COMIBAM process, and also showed the ability to be pacesetters. Of all the countries, Panama had participated least in the process. The Costa Rica NMM, on the other extreme, functioned efficiently through their indigenous interdenominational missionary agency FEDEMEC and had the commitment of 22 organizations at the national level (COMIBAM, 1986, October. *Acta de reunión del comité ejecutivo COMIBAM* [Minutes of the COMIBAM executive committee meeting]. COMIBAM/Bertuzzi Archive Box 17).

Luís Bush's (1985, October. *Reporte COMIBAM '87 a* [COMIBAM '87 Report a]. COMIBAM/Bertuzzi Archive Box 17) report of the first missionary congress in Venezuela illustrates the momentous beginnings of national missionary movements across denominations. The congress in Venezuela took place much earlier than some of the other national conferences and yet it secured the participation of 325 pastors and youth from various areas of the country—and, it seemed important enough that the Caracas seminary canceled classes in order for students to attend. The congress sought to define the mission of the church, to awaken a missionary awareness for Venezuelan evangelicals to accept their role in the task, to provide information about mission agencies, methodology and practice, and to establish criteria for the formation of a Venezuelan missionary-sending agency. This ambitious agenda for the first congress of this kind demonstrates the enthusiasm and fervor of both continental and national leaders.

In addition to the Spanish and Portuguese speaking countries, the organizers intentionally reached out to involve Hispanics in the United States early in the process. Luís Bush reported about a visit to the Rio Grande Bible Institute, near McAllen, Texas on October 28 through November 1, 1985 (Bush, L. K., 1985, October. *Reporte COMIBAM 87 a* [COMIBAM 87 Report a]. COMIBAM/Bertuzzi Archive Box 17). During that visit Bush spoke to students, faculty and pastors from Hispanic churches in the area. Having shared the COMIBAM vision, the students expressed their desire to attend the continental congress. Potential leaders for an Ad Hoc committee to organize a regional missions conference were identified, namely, Rafael Contreras, Noé Mendoza, Isaías Uc and Teófilo Aguillón. Ernesto Johnson, rector of the RGBI school offered to broadcast the COMIBAM sessions from the site's radio station. The possibility of other regional missions conferences for Hispanics in the United States was discussed with H.O. Espinoza, Alberto Motessi, Galo Vásquez and Juan Carlos Miranda. They decided to present such concepts for further development, along with the COMIBAM vision, at the National Radio Broadcasters convention in Washington. The list of prayer petitions in Bush's letters to the leadership continued to include this Hispanic population in the U.S. (Bush, L. K., 1986, August 8. [Letter to the COMIBAM coordinating committee]. COMIBAM/Bertuzzi ARchive Box 17). These visits demonstrated the continental leadership's awareness of the presence of Hispanic evangelicals in the U.S. and an intentional effort to include them in the continent-wide movement.

Two national missionary movements demonstrated their commitment to the COMIBAM cause by organizing formally very early in the process: Bolivia and Costa Rica. José Moreno reported to Luís Bush in a letter that after a conference with

COMIBAM leadership and representatives of eight denominations in Bolivia, the COMIBAM vision was shared in the National Assembly of Evangelicals. This meeting resulted in a commitment to the process and the formation of a national committee (Moreno, J., 1985, December 2. [Letter to Luís Bush]. COMIBAM/Bertuzzi Archive Box 17). The national committee for Bolivia consisted of José Moreno, Julián Coronel, Ulíses Sánchez, Tito Montero, Filemón Soto, Demetrio Castro and David Morales. Most of the national conferences elected national committees. However, Bolivia formed a national committee one year before its first national conference. This organizational step secured a great level of support for COMIBAM in Bolivia.

In Central America, Rafael Baltodano reported in a letter to Luís Bush that at the first Costa Rican missions conference, leaders from the 44 denominations and entities present organized a committee in order to establish the ground work for the formation of a missionary agency, adopt the constitution and bylaws for the same, and conduct a second missions conference (Baltodano, R., 1985, November 8. [Letter to Luís Bush]. COMIBAM/Bertuzzi Archive Box 17). Rafael Baltodano, Enrique Várgas, Alejandro Castro, Luís Leandro, Sixto Pórras, Eduardo Mena and Rubén Shedden, each representing a different denomination or evangelical organization, formed this committee. The committee completed the first objective of their assignment within the same calendar year. This level of proactive commitment characterized Costa Rica as one of the leading national missionary movements within the COMIBAM process. Ekström pointed out that this exemplified the kind of national networking that COMIBAM attempted to catalyze (B. Ekström, personal communication, February 9, 2011).

Not only were there important national conferences before COMIBAM '87 but these kinds of meetings continued fueling national movements after the Sao Paulo congress. In Argentina, various follow-up congresses to COMIBAM '87 took place: Buenos Aires, Santa Fe & Córdoba in 1988 and *Misión '89* [Mission '89] in Mar de Plata (Ekström, 2006, p. 12). In 1993, the first Brazilian Missionary Congress and the first North American Hispanics Congress, COMHINA '93, were held in Minas Gerais, Brazil and Orlando, Florida, respectively (Ekström, 2006; Girón, 2000). Rudy Girón (2000) described this period vividly:

> All over the continent national and regional missionary conferences were celebrated. The missionary spirit started to flourish in the continent. By the end of 1989 the Spirit of God clearly had raised up in the continent a missionary movement. Many new leaders were identified and discipled, a new generation of mobilizers started to spread out the new vision among the churches in the continent. Though, without a recognizable structure, the movement was alive.

National mission conferences fueled the national mission movements and connected them to the continental movement. Argentina, Brazil and Hispanics in North America were early examples of what was taking place throughout the continent. The networks in Argentina and Brazil formed before COMIBAM '87. Eventually, each national mission movement came to have its own designation that identified it with COMIBAM. Even the Central American region organized itself as COMCA, which stands for COMIBAM in Central America (C. Cordero, personal communication, October 30, 2009). Table 3 contains the list of each MMN by country and designation.

Table 3

Ibero American National Mission Movements by Country

Country	Acronym	Full Name
Argentina	RMM	*Red de Misiones Munidales* [World Missions Network]
Bolivia	COMIBAM Bolivia	
Brazil	AMTB	*Associação de Missões Transculturais Braisileiras* [Cross-cultural Brazilian Missionary Association]
Chile	COMIBAM Chile	
Colombia	COMIBAM Colombia	
Costa Rica	COMIBAM Costa Rica	
Dominican Republic	COMIDOM	*Cooperación Misionera Dominicana* [Dominican Missionary Cooperation]
Ecuador	COMEC	*Cooperación Misionera Ecuatoriana* [Ecuatorian Missionary Cooperation]
El Salvador	COMISAL	*Cooperación Misionera Salvadoreña* [Salvadorian Missionary Cooperation]
Guatemala	CONEM	*Cooperación Nacional Evangélica de Misiones* [National Evangelical Missionary Cooperation]

Country	Acronym	Full Name
Honduras	FEMEH	*Federación Evangélica Misonera de Honduras* [Honduran Evangelical Missionary Federation]
Mexico	COMIMEX	*Cooperación Misionera Mexicana* [Mexican Missionary Cooperation]
Nicaragua	MMTN	*Movimiento Misionero Transcultural de Nicaragua* [Nicaraguan Cross-cultural Missionary Movement]
Panama	CMP	*Cooperación Misionera Panameña* [Panamanian Missionary Cooperation]
Paraguay	CONAMI	*Cooperación Nacional Misionera* [National Missionary Cooperation]
Peru	CONAMI	*Cooperación Nacional Misionera* [National Missionary Cooperation]
Portugal	COMIBAM Portugal	
Puerto Rico	RECOMI	*Red de Cooperación Misionera* [Missionary Cooperation Network]
USA/Canada	COMHINA	*Cooperación Misionera Hispana Norte Americana* [North American Hispanic Missionary Cooperation]
Spain	COMIES	*Cooperación Misionera Española* [Spanish Missionary Cooperation]

Country	Acronym	Full Name
Uruguay	COMIBAM Uruguay	
Venezuela	COMIBAM Venezuela	

Not all of these national missionary movements had organized themselves or taken on these names before the second COMIBAM congress. Nevertheless, these eventually became their designations.

In addition to the national conferences taking place between COMIBAM '87 and COMIBAM '97, some continental level meetings also took place. Ekström (2006) listed the four most important of these:

- Two missionary training conferences held in 1990, one in Córdoba, Argentina, and the other in Guatemala resulting in the development of the profile for the ideal missionary and a teaching strategy for the missionary training centers

- The first Ibero American Adopt-a-People Conference in San José, Costa Rica in 1992 which brought this emphasis to the forefront of the COMIBAM movement

- The first meeting of churches and missionary agencies related to COMIBAM in 1994 in Panama City resulting in the commitment of all those present to establish churches, sending agencies and training centers networks.

This last one marked an important step toward the establishment of networks within national networks, which would in turn relate to COMIBAM. The birth and development of national missionary movements provided solid elements for the formation of a strong continental missionary network.

Leaders and Leadership at the Continental Level

The establishment of COMIBAM as a network of networks signified an important development for the effectiveness of the organization. The leaders of this developing network and their leadership styles played a critical role in its success. James MacGregor Burns (1978) wrote, "Leadership over human beings is exercised when persons with certain motives and purposes mobilize, in competition or conflict with others, institutional, political, psychological, and other resources so as to arouse, engage, and satisfy the motives of followers" (p. 18). This understanding of leadership is especially relevant to an evangelical context where participation in a shared vision is completely voluntary. How was this leadership exercised during the beginning of the COMIBAM movement? Who were the key players in this leadership? In this section we will identify the primary continental leaders and the manner in which they mobilized resources for the first congress and beyond.

Leadership through Communicating the Vision

Leading organizational change requires vision development (Yukl, 2002). This is especially true of leading a new movement. Research has shown that the desirable characteristics for vision:

1. Are simple and idealistic, a picture of a desirable future, not a complex plan with quantitative objectives and detailed action steps;
2. Should appeal to the values, hopes, and ideals of organization members and other stakeholders whose support is needed;

3. Emphasize distant ideological objectives rather than immediate tangible benefits;
4. Should be challenging but realistic;
5. Should not be a wishful fantasy, but rather an attainable future grounded in the present reality;
6. Address basic assumptions about what is important for the organization, how it should relate to the environment, and how people should be treated;
7. Focused enough to guide decisions and actions but general enough to allow initiative and creativity in the strategies for attaining it;
8. Simple enough to be communicated clearly in five minutes or less (Yukl, 2002, p. 303).

The manner in which the congress leaders organized and communicated the vision demonstrate an intentional vision-casting strategy. The organization and communication plan included a plan to secure the participation of evangelicals from throughout Latin America. One of the earliest COMIBAM publications from its Guatemala office described COMIBAM as an Ibero American congress to be celebrated in November 23-29, 1987 in Sao Paulo, Brazil, "with the primary purpose of glorifying God by encouraging Ibero American churches to have a greater participation in the world missions task" (Bush, 1985, October, p. 3).

Communicating the vision effectively meant describing thoroughly what constituted this new thing called COMIBAM. COMIBAM leadership described the who of COMIBAM, including all of the following: (a) a coordinating council representing the twenty-three Ibero American countries, (b) a sponsoring committee which was formed in

Mexico in December 1984 and is made up of Christian organization and denominational entities, (c) an advisory committee made up of a person from each country and some from without the continent, (d) national coordinating committees by country, and (e) all those who desire to be a part of the process that seeks to mobilize the Ibero American church to fulfill the missionary task (COMIBAM, 1985, December). This description of who is COMIBAM demonstrated the leaders' attempt to communicate the scope of this missionary movement. Continental leaders and leaders in the participating countries could own the vision as they participated in what was described.

COMIBAM leadership was also intentional about communicating that COMIBAM was part of a process and how COMIBAM '87 fit into the process. The Guatemala COMIBAM office presented eight elements to the process, each with a corresponding action: (a) Intercession: intercessory groups in all of the countries, (b) Information: a monthly newsletter, (c) Investigation (Research): about the reached and unreached, (d) Instruction: promoting and publishing books, (e) Involvement: national conferences, (f) Inspiration: national congresses, (g) Infrastructure: missionary agencies, and (h) Invitation to consecration: COMIBAM '87 (COMIBAM, 1986, February). The inclusion of missionary agencies as part of the infrastructure demonstrated the movement gave prominence to missionary agencies betraying the influence of the missiology from North America in contrast with a purely local church-driven missiology. This work-plan for the congress communicated to would-be participants the role of the first congress and the leadership's intention to hold more than just an event (Calderón, 1986b). The alliteration of eight words that begin with the letter I in Spanish made these steps easier to remember and to communicate in a brief manner.

Blackaby and Blackaby (2001) wrote that the crux of spiritual leadership is when "Leaders seek to move people on to God's agenda, all the while being aware that only the Holy Spirit can ultimately accomplish the task" (p. 21). COMIBAM leadership expressed the importance of laying a spiritual and organizational infrastructure in preparation for the first congress through three objectives during the formative 1985 year: (a) organize at least one men's intercessory prayer group, one women's intercessory prayer group, and one youth intercessory prayer group in each country; (b) establish at least one mission-sending agency in each country by December 1987; and (c) secure the commitment of 10,000 Ibero Americans to mission work by December 1987 (COMIBAM 87, 1985. *Grupos de intercesión* [Intercessory groups]. COMIBAM/Bertuzzi Archive Box 17). The *Manual de intercesión misionera* [Manual for missionary intercession] (Bush, 1986), one of the first publications by COMIBAM, demonstrated the commitment to intercessory prayer. This 90-page manual introduced intercessory prayer as foundational for world evangelization, gave guidance as to the organization of intercessory groups and as to how to conduct an missionary intercessory prayer meeting, shared a strategy for prayer and gave information on various people groups around the world for whom to pray. It was clear that the leadership placed a high priority on spiritual preparation through prayer. The three objectives above also demonstrate a vision that encompassed more than a successful event and that provided the groundwork for the continuation of the COMIBAM movement in a quantifiable manner.

In the book *Good to Great*, Collins (2001) contrasted great and good companies by identifying great companies with a Level 5 Management Team and good companies with a Genius with a Thousand Helpers. The primary difference, according to Collins, is that great companies decide the who, in other words, getting the right people, and then the what, namely the vision path, while good companies inverse this process. In the case of COMIBAM's leadership development, the vision came first and then people were asked to join the team. Nevertheless, as people joined the movement they helped shape the vision and the vision path. This hybrid of deciding the what before the who and allowing the who to shape the what proved to be effective for COMIBAM as an organization. It should be noted that a network of voluntary participants does not share all the characteristics of a corporation with paid employees like those Collins (2001) researched. Notwithstanding, the COMIBAM leadership sought to enlist the right people throughout the continent.

Coordinating Committee and Administrative Staff

The group of continental leaders increased in number according to the need. The coordinating committee that met in Sao Paulo in June of 1985 under the leadership of Luís Bush had been the primary official group for several months. By the beginning of 1986 it became evident that for greater logistical efficiency, a team of regional coordinators was needed (Bush, L., K., 1986, May 5. [Letter to Federico Bertuzzi]. COMIBAM/Bertuzzi Archive Box 17; COMIBAM, 1986, April, p. 8). The new executive committee and its members were Luís Bush, General Coordinator and President; Jonathan Dos Santos, Vice-President; Carlos Calderón, Spanish-Language Regional Office Administrator; Alexandre Areaujo, Portuguese-Language Regional Office Administrator; Federico Bertuzzi, South Cone Coordinator; Roberto Hatch, Andes Zone Coordinator; Francisco Fiorenza, North America and Mexico Coordinator; Moisés

Mejia, Central America Coordinator; Rodolfo, known as Rudy, Girón, Caribbean Coordinator; Juan Gili, Spain and Portugal Coordinator; and Wade, known as Tomás, Cogging, Honorary Treasurer (COMIBAM, 1986, July, p. 8). Leaders like Bush, Dos Santos, Calderón, Bertuzzi, Hatch and Girón maintained a strong leadership presence in the continental organizational structure, the regional leadership and the national conferences.

While the coordinating committee provided general leadership, staff teams oversaw day-to-day operations in preparation for the congress. These administrative hubs operated in two different locations and were led by two members of the coordinating committee. Alex Areaujo, one of the members of the coordinating committee, moved from San Jose, California to Sao Paulo, Brazil to give logistical leadership for the congress (Bush, L. K., 1986, May 5. [Letter to Federico Bertuzzi]. COMIBAM/Bertuzzi Archive Box 17). The Brazilian coordinating committee consisted of Jonathan Dos Santos, Elben César, Luís Carlos Pinto, Paulo Mello Cintra Damiao, Sergio Schwantes, Norival Trindade, Lidia Almedia de Menezes, Rinaldo de Mattos, Roberto George Harvey, Ken Kudo, Jesse Teixeira, Alan Bachman, Edison Queiróz de Oliveira, Manoel Ferreira and Manfred Grellert (COMIBAM, 1985, December). Carlos Calderón, who had been an elder in Luís Bush's church in El Salvador and the coordinator for Bush's *Misión '84*, moved to Guatemala to lead the continental office (Bush, L. K., 1986, January 4. *Asuntos varios de COMIBAM 87* [Various matters about COMIBAM 87]. COMIBAM/Bertuzzi Archive Box 17). The Guatemala office staff consisted of Carlos Calderón as administrator, Fernando Mazariegos in charge of communications, Silvia Cordón Paz in charge of literature, Sonia Marroquín coordinating pre-registration, Luís Rodas heading research, Lissethe Eguizabal in charge of information systems, Marga Calderón in charge of finances, Moisés Mejía leading the area of youth ministries, Abel Morales leading ministry to professionals, and Beatríz de Zapata leading women's ministry (COMIBAM, 1986, July). Luís Bush and his family moved to San Jose, California in June of 1986 as he assumed the vice-presidency of Christian Nationals. From there he maintained contact with Alex Areaujo, Carlos Calderón and the regional coordinators while he also channeled all North American and European contributions for COMIBAM through his office (Bush, L. K., 1986, May 5. [Letter to Federico Bertuzzi]. COMIBAM/Bertuzzi Archive Box 17). These leaders and locations ensured a connection of the congress with the Portuguese-speaking and Spanish-speaking segments of Ibero America and divided the task of local arrangements and continental promotion and participation.

Connecting with the Rest of the World and Theological Conference

Luís Bush, as the primary leader of the congress, connected those who demonstrated interest in the development of Ibero American missionary mobilization with what was taking place in other parts of the world. He also provided a common terminology for the missions dialogue. Bush communicated the importance of sharing a common missions vocabulary in order to have a unified movement.

The unanimous thinking about these words will determine, in great part, the direction and reach of the ministerial activity that will bring into reality the participation of our continent in the historic task of effectively evangelizing "all the nations." (Bush, L. K., 1986, February 21. *Terminología: Significado de palabras importantes* [Terminology: Meaning of important words].

COMIBAM/Bertuzzi Archive Box 17, p. 1)

Bush traced the process of developing this glossary from its first mention at the Mexico 1984 meeting through the Ibero American Theological Conference, which would take place in June of 1986.

Bush became an instrumental communicator to the world about COMIBAM and to COMIBAM about the world. During this time, Bush travelled extensively within Latin America and throughout other parts of the world. While these trips allowed him to promote COMIBAM '87, he also remained in contact with missionary developments outside of Ibero America and communicated these developments through the COMIBAM information channels. In June 1985, he attended a meeting of Bible Societies' leadership in Miami and promoted COMIBAM '87 among them (Bush, L. K., 1985, September. [Letter to Federico Bertuzzi]. COMIBAM/Bertuzzi Archive Box 17). In the same letter, Bush reported about a trip he made to Nigeria where he shared the plans for COMIBAM '87 and where he discussed plans of exchanging missionaries with the Nigerian leadership. A report about a trip to the United States demonstrates Bush's ability to network and communicate efficiently in one trip. The reported stated that Bush (a) promoted COMIBAM '87 in churches in Detroit, Wisconsin; (b) visited with Bill Taylor about COMIBAM '87; (c) enlisted Carlos and Lorena Calderón in Texas for COMIBAM '87's staff; (d) met with Global Mapping leadership; (e) met with Ralph Winter, and (f) met with Hispanic leaders (Bush, L. K., 1985, October 5-16. *Reporte de viaje a los Estados Unidos* [Report of trip to the United States]. COMIBAM/Bertuzzi Archive Box 17). Much of Bush's travels in the United States had to do with fundraising. The

Proposed scope of the Congress section earlier in this chapter treated the financing of the mission. Bush was definitely the *paladín* [champion] of the COMIBAM movement.

Leadership Transition after the First Congress

Luís Bush exercised his leadership through extensive communication, travel, and vision casting. This kind of leadership contributed to the success of the first congress and to the visibility of COMIBAM. Much of the success of the congress and much of the survival of the movement depended on Bush. Some, including Jonathan Lewis (personal communication, October 30, 2009), and even Girón himself (2000), have acknowledged that Bush and Girón were seen as charismatic leaders. Yukl (200) indicated that charisma occurs when there is a social crisis, a leader emerges with a radical vision, they experience some successes that make the vision appear attainable, and the followers come to perceive the leader as extraordinary. Girón (2000) indicated that some thought the movement would die without the leadership of Bush. How did this charismatic type of leadership affect COMIBAM's sustainability? Yukl (2002) warned about the dangers of charismatic leadership in organizations. He wrote,

> Charisma is a transitory phenomenon when it is dependent on personal identification with an individual leader who is perceived to be extraordinary. When the leader departs or dies, a succession crisis is likely. Many organizations founded by an autocratic charismatic leader fail to survive this succession crisis. (p. 269)

Succession, thus, becomes the greatest challenge for the kind of charismatic leadership that launches a movement such as COMIBAM. COMIBAM transitioned successfully after Luis Bush stepped down from his primary leadership role.

The COMIBAM leaders that followed Bush successfully shepherded the transition from congress to a sustainable movement by shifting from a personality-driven leadership model to a shared leadership approach. From 1987 to 1989, as the movement advanced with great momentum, Luís Bush from Argentina, who had been the Congress' coordinator, served as the first president of the newly formed COMIBAM. Initially the concept of president combined the role of chairman of the board and executive director but eventually, the presidency came to refer more precisely to the function of a chairman (J. P. Lewis, personal communication, October 30, 2009). Alexandre Araéujo from Brazil, who served as the Congress' executive secretary, passed the baton to Edison Queiróz from Brazil. The international office of COMIBAM was established in Quito, Ecuador and Roberto Hatch served as the administrator (Ekström, 2006). In 1990, Rudy Girón, an architect from Guatemala, who felt called by God at an intercessory group led by Luís Bush in Guatemala and who became very involved in the initial COMIBAM process, became its second president (Ekstrom, 2006; Girón, 2000).

Leaders like Bush, Hatch, and Girón maintained close contact with national movements, as seen in the list of conferences in Appendix G, while they also provided continental leadership. Bush's contact with national movements took place mainly around the time of the first continental congress, while Girón's arduous travels and relationship-building followed the congress and sustained the movement for many years (A. Amigo, personal communication, February 2, 2011; B. Ekström, personal communication, February 9, 2011). David Ruíz, from Guatemala, became COMIBAM's first executive director in 1995, while Girón continued as president (Ekström, 2006, p. 14). This new role shared the power and responsibilities of the COMIBAM president.

A new style of leadership emerged in the movement when Rudy Girón invited Bertil Ekström from Brazil to serve on the executive team in 1995. In 1997, when Girón was ready to step down from the presidency, Girón worked closely with Ekström to pass the mantle to him (B. Ekström, personal communication, February 9, 2011). Girón left the presidency of COMIBAM to go serve as a missionary in Russia (Girón, 2000). Immediately before the second COMIBAM congress in Acapulco, Mexico, Bertil Ekström was named its third president (Ekström, 2006). Ekström ushered in a style of shared leadership and advocated separating the roles of president as an international representative and of executive director as a full-time leader. Jonathan Lewis, who had served as training coordinator under Girón's leadership and who became Vice-President of COMIBAM, worked closely with Ekström to prepare the bylaws that would ensure this (J. P. Lewis, personal communication, October 31, 2009). David Ruíz filled the role of executive director when Ekström became president (B. Ekström, personal communication, February 9, 2011). This transitioned the movement from the personality-driven leadership of Bush and Girón to a more shared-leadership approach.

Yukl (2002) suggested that there are three approaches to perpetuate an organization whose leadership has been personality-driven: transfer charisma to a designated successor through rites and ceremonies, create an administrative structure that will continue to implement the leader's vision with rational-legal authority, and embed it in the culture of the organization by influencing followers to internalize it and empowering them to implement it. While certainly steps had been taken along the lines of the third approach, Lewis and Ekström made effective use of the second one. Other important leaders at the international level during this time were Federico Bertuzzi from

Argentina, Carlos Calderón from Guatemala, Edison Queiróz from Brazil, Moisés López from Mexico, and Jonathan Lewis from the USA, among others (B. Ekström, personal communication, February 9, 2011). These leaders championed the COMIBAM cause in their countries, spoke at international conferences, published articles and books, and helped to launch various missions programs. While Bush cast the vision and mobilized enthusiasm for the first congress, Girón sustained the momentum between the first and the second congresses, and Ekström, Lewis and Ruíz provided the organizational structure that allowed COMIBAM to continue as a network. Each of these men exemplified what Collins (2001) termed Level 5 leaders; namely, leaders who built "enduring greatness through a paradoxical blend of personal humility and professional will" (p. 20). He further clarified,

> Level 5 leaders channel their ego needs away from themselves and into the larger goal of building a great company. It's not that Level 5 leaders have no ego or self-interest. Indeed, they are incredibly ambitious—but their ambition is first and foremost for the institution, not themselves. (p. 21)

The COMIBAM leaders that birthed and secured the sustainability and vitality of the movement displayed an ambition for the greater missionary cause.

The highly visible leadership of Luís Bush was very important in the years immediately before, during and after the congress. Bush stands out as the *paladin*, the champion warrior, of COMIBAM. His tireless work, charisma and visionary leadership were extraordinary. The movement continued beyond its infancy to maturing because of successful and timely leadership transitions. Bush succeeded in passing the torch in a timely manner to capable leaders. Many shared and further developed Bush's vision.

The network structure invited new participants and made them stakeholders almost immediately. Others who provided leadership at the continental level before and during the first congress were Jonathan Dos Santos, Carlos Calderón, Alex Araéujo, Federico Bertuzzi, Roberto Hatch, Francisco Fiorenza, Roberto Hatch, Moisés Mejía, Rudy Girón, Juan Gili, Tomás (Wade) Cogging. During the congress and shortly thereafter Bertil Ekström, David Ruíz, Moisés Lopez, Edison Queiróz and Jonathan Lewis shared the continental leadership. These leaders representing different countries and denominations led the COMIBAM process by communicating the vision, encouraging spiritual preparation, organized planning through a coordinating committee, execution of the plans by administrative staff in Spanish and Portuguese regions, constant communication with the national mission movements, two-way communication between COMIBAM and the rest of the world, and organizational developments that allowed the movement to continue. Combined, these initial and subsequent leaders provided a model for the initiation of a movement that had sustainability.

Missiological Reflection at the Onset of the Movement

The COMIBAM '87 initiative was a world missions endeavor. Missiological reflection arises as a relevant issue on two levels: informing the process and developing a contextualized missiology. From its inception the leadership desired missiological reflection to inform the process. Most importantly the development of a contextualized missiology contributed to the autonomy of a missionary movement. There were primarily three possible outcomes. COMIBAM could be an Ibero American movement with North American missiology. As a second alternative, COMIBAM could be thoroughly Ibero American movement in missiology and practice. The third possible outcome was for COMIBAM to become an Ibero American movement with a hybrid missiology. Eventually the COMIBAM movement advanced while it undergirded a hybrid missiology.

The primary objective of the COMIBAM movement dictated the missiological outcome. COMIBAM leadership focused its attention on missionary mobilization more than on missiological reflection. While leaders acknowledged the tension between North American and indigenous missiological ideas, their pragmatic objective prevented them from a more systematic reflection. Samuel Escobar (2002) noted that the first COMIBAM congress and endeavors were strongly influenced by what he terms "managerial missiology" from the United States. He noted terms such as unreached peoples, 10-40 window, and adopt-a-people as evidence of this. Interestingly, Luís Bush (1990) developed the concept of the 10/40 window. Rudy Girón also acknowledged this tension and indicated that the primary reason for this is that COMIBAM was a mobilizing network not a reflection organization (R. Girón, personal communication, November 1, 2009). Furthermore, Escobar regretted that the first congress neglected to deal with the more important theological issues that Latin American missiologists had been exploring since the 1960s. Ekström indicated that COMIBAM's strength did not come from its missiological reflection but its pragmatism (B. Ekström, personal communication, February 9, 2011). Alvaro Fernández in Mexico also maintained the assessment that COMIBAM displayed a pragmatic emphasis (A. Fernández, personal communication, February 18, 2011). In the beginning, COMIBAM adopted many aspects of the agency/UPG missiology characteristic of Ralph Winter, but it also integrated some of the aspects characteristic of a more holistic, church-driven missiology. This hybrid of missiological perspectives can be observed in the content of COMIBAM '87's plenary sessions. However, missiological developments were taking place in the movement for months before the first congress. Some of the themes of discussion are identified below.

Missiological Dialogue Before COMIBAM '87

The missiological dialogue within the COMIBAM movement had begun during the thirty months of preparation for the congress, corresponding with the national conferences that convened during that time. The conversation took place in both directions: continental-to-national and national-to-continental. The COMIBAM leadership and staff at the Guatemala office published brief columns in their newsletters offering information about what was taking place in missions around the world. Additionally, COMIBAM held a conference at the continental level to address some foundational missiological concepts (COMIBAM, 1985, December; COMIBAM, 1986, February; COMIBAM, 1986, July; COMIBAM, 1987, March-April). From the national-to-continental direction, as conferences were taking place in each country, conference leaders also documented their conclusions and convictions. Although, many of the conferences had the influence from the continental leadership and from foreign conference speakers, there was a healthy measure of grassroots missiological development.

COMIBAM's newsletter columns. The columns in COMIBAM's newsletter reported what was taking place in missions in other parts of the world beyond Latin America. COMIBAM leadership used this medium to cast the vision and to stimulate missiological reflection throughout the continent. The October, 1985 issue of *COMIBAM Informa* reported a missionary conference attended by Luís Bush which took place in

Nigeria. The brief report included a summary of the topics presented at this conference and the potential for partnership between the African continent and Latin America. The topics were, Emerging Missions; Past, Present and Future of Missions in Nigeria; The Church-Mission relation in Nigeria; and The Challenge of the Unreached People Groups in Nigeria.

In a subsequent issue of the newsletter, Luís Bush (1986, July) reported on a trip he made to the Philippines sharing a personal perspective on the missionary need in Asia and the relevance of Hispanic history for both the Philippines and Latin America. In the same issue, the writer presented Europe as one of the greatest mission fields and suggested the priority of Latin America sending missionaries to South Europe, namely, Spain, Italy, Portugal and Belgium. Antonio Peralta (1986, September) wrote about his experience serving among Muslims in Egypt and presented the challenge of Latin Americans going to the Muslim world, giving some practical advice on the subject. Similarly, Nahomy Finley (1986, September) reported on the condition and missionary need of Australia. In an article titled, Discipleship with Missionary Vision, Sonia Marroquín (1986, November) briefly treated the Great Commission from the perspective of discipling the nations. Luís Bush (1986, November) made a case for the timeliness of the mobilization of the Latin American church by pointing out how crises in Latin America, namely, natural disasters, national debt, drug wars, violence, unemployment and political instability, had given rise to revival in various sectors of the church and to new opportunities to share the gospel. Furthermore, he traces the historical beginning of missions from Latin America to 1916, when a Brazilian church sent a missionary to Portugal. Other columns were more generic, offering reminders of the urgency of the missionary task, the need to be filled with the Spirit for the mission, the necessity of being informed about the mission field, the willingness to go, and the conviction that the Great Commission is God's heart for the nations (Morales, 1987). Additionally, Jonathan Dos Santos (1987, May-June) wrote on the changing perception about missionaries and the church's role in sending out missionaries from Brazil, the leading mission-sending country in Latin America. In the same issue, the newsletter identified the majority-world countries that were sending the most missionaries at that time, namely, India, South Africa, Burma, Brazil, Nigeria, the Philippines, Indonesia, Kenya, Peru and Chile. In summary, these brief articles presented readers across the continent with the possibility and the urgency of Latin Americans going on mission to every part of the world. The articles were not formal treatises on missiology, but they offered biblical basis, historical background, and the rationale for going on cross-cultural missions. Basically, the COMIBAM newsletters created legitimacy for Latin Americans engaging in cross-cultural missions.

Reflection at National Missions Conferences. The national missions conferences also produced some documented, albeit brief, missiological reflection. The conference in Ecuador, which took place on May 27, 1985, included discussion of the understanding of God's mission for the church, mission as part of the Trinity, traditional mission models, and the Christological model based on the ministry of Jesus (COMIBAM, 1985). In response to the call for developing missionary models that did not merely copy the North American models, the conference participants agreed on ten principles among which are the following three: Understanding that the mission demands serious biblical-theological reflection; the church needs to move from the static state of maintaining to the dynamic state of the mission; and a missionary is a sent one not a professional, and should respect the existing culture and work on the field. While these three are not necessarily antithetical to North American missiology, they demonstrate the desire of Latin Americans to do missiological reflection from the base.

In Chile's conference, which met on June 19-20, 1985, the primary topics discussed were (a) the Unreached, (b) the Church Involved in Missions, (c) Denominational Missions, and (d) Women and Missions (COMIBAM, 1986, February). The dialogue emphasized the need for humility in cross-cultural missions, the need for training and strategic development in reaching the unreached, and the numerical prominence of women in missions. The Honduras conference, which occurred on January 9-11, 1986, emphasized the responsibility of making disciples among all ethnic groups (COMIBAM, 1986). At the conference in Spain, which took place on March 14-15, 1986, Luís Bush presented the need for Spain to partner with Latin America and the urgency of the missionary task (COMIBAM, 1986, April). It was at this conference that the participants identified the key role of Spain as a link and preparation base for missionaries to the Arab world. The Nicaragua conference, which convened on September 23-24, 1986, affirmed that the biblical and theological basis for the church's mission consists of who God is, His Word and His Plan (COMIBAM, 1986).

Although the terminology varied from country to country, the recognition of the mission as God's mission, the identification of the biblical basis for the mission, the realization that there were unreached people groups that needed to be reached, and the need for Latin Americans to go on cross-cultural mission emerged as unifying themes. The influence of Ralph Winter, as a U.S. missiologist, and Luís Bush, as an Argentine compatible with U.S. missiology, on these reflections is evident by their focus on unreached people groups and cross-cultural missions. These incipient reflections laid the foundation for more formal discussions at national mission congresses and provided context to the missiological discussions at COMIBAM '87.

COMIBAM's Theological Conference. The continental leadership of COMIBAM convened a theological conference, called the First Ibero American Conference on the Church's Mission and World Missions, which took place June 2-4, 1986 (Bush, L. K., 1986, February 5. [Letter to Federico Bertuzzi]. COMIBAM/Bertuzzi Arhcive Box 17; COMIBAM, 1986, February, p. 4). Having identified the need for a common glossary of missiological terminology at the Mexico 1984 meeting, an international group of missiologists gathered to compile a rough draft for it during the first months of 1985 (Bush, 1986). Leaders sent this rough draft to 200 missiologists, pastors and Christian leaders in four continents in order to seek their feedback. Subsequently, these leaders made modifications to the glossary from correspondence with the experts and as part of the national conferences process (Bush, L. K., 1986, February 21. *Terminología: Significado de palabras importantes* [Terminology: Meaning of important words]. COMIBAM/Bertuzzi Archive Box 17). The resulting list of terms and definitions is found in the Appendix H.

This initial document reflected particular missiological positions, as seen in Appendix H of the current study. It understood missions as the cross-cultural or cross-geographical activity of the church. Thus, it distinguished between evangelism and missions on the basis of cultural and geographical context. Furthermore, it distinguished the mission of the church from missions in that it saw missions as one aspect of the church's mission. Bosch (2006) made a distinction between mission and missions to refer *missio Dei* and *missiones ecclesiae* respectively. Nevertheless, this initial definition by COMIBAM leadership referred to both mission and missions as *missiones ecclesiae*; in other words, as belonging to the church. Initially in the COMIBAM dialogue there was no explicit emphasis upon the *missio dei* and of the church's mission in relation to it.

Eventually, COMIBAM invited theologians and missiologists from Central America, South America, Spain and the United States to define the most important terms in relation to the church's mission and world missions at the June, 1986 conference in Guatemala (Bush, L. K., 1986, February 21. *Terminología: Signficado de palabras importantes* [Terminology: Meaning of important words]. COMIBAM/Bertuzzi Archives Box 17, p. 5). The purpose for developing this list of working definitions was to publish it and distribute it before the continental congress to all those interested in the missions task (Bush, 1986d). The conference published and distributed a document to those interested in mission sending throughout Latin America and to those who attended COMIBAM '87 (COMIBAM, 1986). The conference organizing committee and conference moderators included Emilio Antonio Nuñez, a member of the FTL, Mardoqueo Muñoz and Luís Bush. The conference participants were Alexandre Costa Araéujo of Brazil, Carlos Calderón of Guatemala, David Harms of Honduras, David Suazo Jiménez of Guatemala, David E. Kornfield of the USA, Emilio Antonio Nuñez of Guatemala, Federico Bertuzzi of Argentina, Guillermo W. Méndez of Guatemala, Hector Ladislao Leíva of El Salvador, Ismael Morales of Guatemala, Jonathan Dos Santos of Brazil, Lorenzo D. Pate of the USA, Mardoqueo Muñoz of Guatemala, Moisés Mejía of Guatemala, Robert Allen Hatch of Ecuador, Rudy J. Girón of Guatemala, Synesio Lyra of the USA, and Luís Bush of Argentina (Bush, 1986). Thus, the representation included one delegate from Ecuador, one from Honduras, one from El Salvador, two from Brazil, two from Argentina, three from the USA, and eight from Guatemala. Central America was over-represented. South America was underrepresented. Mexico and the Caribbean were not represented. The location of the conference, including its proximity to the Central American Theological Seminary in Guatemala, most probably influenced this pattern of representation.

Prior to the conference, each presenter submitted a paper to the rest in order to be read in advance and to be discussed at the Antigua meeting (Bush, 1986). Conclusions were drawn and submitted to an editing committee which prepared a document for the approval of the group by the end of the event. The topics for this conference are shown in Table 4.

Table 4

Antigua Theological Conference Topics and Presenters

Presenter	Topic
Emilio A. Nuñez	The mission of the church
Guillermo W. Méndez	The kingdom of God and the world mission of the church
David Harms	The holistic ministry of the church
Estuardo McIntosh	Mission for the third millennium
Mardoqueo Muñoz	A macro-missiological focus
Larry Pate	Ethics and doing missions
David Suazo	Urban evangelization
Federico A. Bertuzzi	Universalism and world missions
Synesio Lyra, Jr.	The missionary and world missions
David Kornfield	The nature of the church and world missions
Roberto Hatch	Missionary Associations and the mission of the church

At the conclusion of the conference the group approved a document which they called the Affirmation of Antigua, named after the city where the meeting took place.

This serious effort at missiological reflection was a good beginning and it provided some commonly agreed concepts for the new movement. In this Affirmation of Antigua, the group defined mission as follows:

> The mission of the church is the expression and the expansion of the Kingdom of God in word and deed, through the power of the Holy Spirit, for the glory of God, for the holistic growth of believers in Christ and the evangelization of those who have not surrendered to Him. (Bush, 1986)

Furthermore the document stated that the essence of this mission included church planting, church-driven disciple-making and church-driven holistic ministry. The emphasis on holistic mission points to the missiological influence of the FTL. The declaration acknowledged the centrality of the local church in the mission (Bush, 1986). Additionally, the conference participants stated that, after considering the various missiological models in church history, they recognized that the mission-sending task from Latin America would demand great sacrifice on the part of the sending churches and of the missionaries (Bush, 1986). Furthermore, the document identified urban centers as areas of focus for the missionary task and established the centrality of Scripture for the mission (Bush, 1986). The affirmation defined a missionary and the church in the following manner:

> A missionary is a disciple called and sent by God through the local church, who crosses geographical and/or cultural barriers in order to communicate all of the gospel for either the establishment or the holistic growth of the church. (Bush, 1986, p. 32)

> The church is the assembly of believers in Christ called to worship God in a community that, in submission to Him and to each other, penetrates the world in the power of the Holy Spirit. (Bush, 1986, p. 32)

These definitions retain the concepts of the integral mission and the centrality of the church's role in the mission. The missionary definition departs from the integral mission missiology. It defines missionary exclusively as one who crosses geographical and/or cultural barriers. The last paragraph of the declaration highlights the centrality of the church with the support of mission sending institutions:

> We affirm that the process of sending missionaries is a divine initiative. God carries this process forward through the local church, which is the instrument that He has established for the fulfillment of the mission. Thus, the missionary responsibility belongs mainly to the local church. This responsibility includes recognition, motivation, preparation, support and pastoral care of those who are called. Mission entities in their specialization help the church in fulfilling its mission. (Bush, 1986, p. 32)

Interestingly, this portion of the Antigua declaration foreshadows the *missio Dei* concept that would later be treated by some missiologists. In fact, participants acknowledged that the participation of the third world in the third millennium required the recognition of new challenges, concepts, methodologies and mentality (Bush, 1986). As Bosch (2006) so wisely noted in referring to the global missionary task:

> We require a new vision to break out of the present stalemate toward a different kind of missionary involvement—which need not mean jettisoning everything

> generations of Christians have done before us or haughty condemnations of all their blunders. (p. 7)

It is a difficult thing to develop a new vision without first looking at the past critically. The understanding of a distinction between the mission owned by the church or by God, according to Bosch (2006), can be traced back to 1952 as a contribution from Barth at the Willingen Conference of the IMC. Bosch stated,

> It was here that the idea (not the exact term) *missio Dei* first surfaced clearly. Mission was understood as being derived from the very nature of God. It was thus put in the context of the doctrine of the Trinity, not of ecclesiology or soteriology…In the new image mission is not primarily an activity of the church, but an attribute of God…There is a church because there is mission, not vice versa. (p. 390)

Nevertheless this concept did not receive wide treatment in either North America or Latin America until much later. Guder (1998) put it this way,

> it has taken us decades to realize that mission is not just a program of the church. It defines the church as God's sent people. Either we are defined by mission, or we reduce the scope of the gospel and the mandate of the church. Thus our challenge today is to move from church with mission to missional church. (p. 6)

Similarly, Minatrea (2004), in defining the missional church as the community of disciples sent by God to live and proclaim His Kingdom in the world, stated that this community does not own the mission but is invited to share in it (p. 12). This development of *missio Dei*, which took decades for North American missiologists to adopt, was also absent, for the most part, in the missiological development of

COMIBAM's beginnings. Additionally, the Antigua affirmation also demonstrated a moderate position that included aspects of the FTL missiology and that of Ralph Winter. One of the primary points in this tension between the two missiological outlooks had to do with the role of the church and the place of missionary agencies. Girón (2000) acknowledged the struggle between these two and affirmed that COMIBAM's leadership came to the conclusion that missionary agencies were to be servants, partners and instruments to the local church. In essence, the position of the Antigua statement was church-centered in relation to the missionary task but not church-driven.

This first theological conference demonstrated a serious intention to do missiological reflection from the Latin American perspective. The movement's missiology at times and in specific contexts approximated Ralph Winter's model but it definitely was not a thoroughly North American missiology. Furthermore, although some criticized COMIBAM for lack of missiological reflection, it must be noted that COMIBAM occasionally served as the catalyst for missiological reflection in Latin America.

Plenary Sessions: Missiological Observations

By the time the first Ibero American missionary congress took place, much conversation about missions strategy and missiology had already taken place. The plenary session topics of the first congress represented the important themes in casting the vision for the movement and in continuing to lead its participants in a paradigm shift toward mission sending. After all, this was the climactic gathering of over 3,000 delegates from throughout the continent who could go back to their countries and share the vision. The topics and the content of the plenary sessions revealed the basis, rationale and methodology for this missions advance. The hybrid of the church-driven, holistic missiology and the agency-driven missiology appears. The themes fell into three broad categories which were labeled using presenters' language as follows in this treatment: developing an Ibero American perspective versus Anglo-Saxon, developing a holistic mission versus a merely spiritual kingdom, and committing to cross the frontier between faith and no-faith versus defining missions by cross-cultural crossover.

From an Anglo-Saxon perspective toward an Ibero American perspective. The awareness of the tension between the Anglo-Saxon and the Ibero American missions paradigms emerged clearly in three of the plenary sessions. Alberto Barrientos (1987) argued that the reality of the Anglo-Saxon missionary presence in Latin America created the perception that missionary sending is done from the economic, political and cultural basis of developed countries to under-developed countries. Furthermore, he acknowledged the perception promoted by Marxist ideologies that Protestantism is nothing other than the promulgation of capitalism. Roberto Hatch (1987), in developing a model for missionary strategy, questioned the managerial schools of thought within missiology that focus on setting fixed objectives and plans without leaving room for the Divine. Bill Taylor (1987), in referring to the Anglo-Saxon missionary advance, acknowledged the numerous cases of lack of cultural adaptation, lack of absolute contextualization, and poor cross-cultural communication. Taylor additionally recognized missionaries' cultural insensitivity, the presence of colonial paternalism, and the importing of evangelism methods, dress codes, church architecture, life-style, promotion of capitalism and democracy as the divine politics, educational models, leadership hierarchies, Robert's Rules of Order, problem-solving methods, and a foreign ethos that belittles the local ethos. The recognition, however amiable, of these realities by COMIBAM '87 presenters proved that the movement would not accept all Anglo-Saxon models for missions and evangelism without some critical reflection.

From a merely spiritual kingdom outlook toward a holistic missions posture. The plenary sessions did not advance a well-developed holistic missiology. Bosch (2006) traced the evolution in evangelicalism from a one-mandate strategy, evangelism only, to a two-mandate strategy, evangelism and social responsibility, from the 1966 Wheaton Declaration to the 1966 Berlin Congress and on to Lausanne '74. He further indicated that most evangelical movements operated with an evangelism-is-primary approach rather than with Stott's eventual position that both were absolutely necessary. The evangelism-is-primary tendency clearly emerged in the plenary session messages. The focus on a primarily spiritual kingdom was clear. Nevertheless, an awakening to the need to confront the social and economic realities that existed in Ibero America also began to appear. Calo Fabio (1987) presented an eschatological understanding of the Kingdom using Revelation 5:1-14 as his text. In this exposition he posited this vision of the future and coming kingdom as the inspiration and the force that advances the mission of the people of God. Fabio (1987) concluded that this eschatological Kingdom should lead God's people to pray with the confidence of the world's destiny, to evangelize all peoples as future citizens of the cosmos, to give everything in the present for the cause of the future, and to rejoice in the vision of the future Kingdom of God. When God's people hear about the injustices in the world, Fabio argued, they should accept the need to confront them, but should trust in prayer that God holds history in his hands. There was the recognition that the Kingdom is here and now as well as there and then. So while

Fabio (1987) acknowledged the social realities in the mission's context, he did not fully represent the two-mandate strategy.

Luís Bush (1987), who interpreted the congress' theme, Light for the Nations, alluded to aspects of a holistic mission in his presentation. The second of six questions he used to guide his conference was, "What does it mean to be light for the nations?" (p. 18). He answers his own question by stating that it means that God's people should be holy, should proclaim the gospel, and should influence their communities with their presence. Using Matthew 5:16 as his basis, Bush (1987) stated,

> "To be light," means to influence for good the community where we are, to influence society in a positive way and to influence the very course of secular history by our very presence. It has to do with good works…It is so that you and I work together for good in the economic, political and social life of the nations. Let us contribute with hospitals, clinics, etc., and let us care about our neighborhoods, the marginalized, the poor, the widows, the orphans, and others. (p. 19)

Although not the focus in Bush's presentation, this emphasis does demonstrate an interest in carrying out a more holistic mission.

From an exclusive cross-cultural missions view toward an understanding of mission as crossing the frontier between no-faith and faith. The previous chapter presented the contrast between Padilla's (1986) *Misión Integral* and what he considered the traditional approach inherited from the modern missionary movement. The traditional approach is primarily a geographical and cross-cultural concept. The *Misión Integral* approach is primarily a concept that focuses on crossing the frontier between faith and no faith, and attempts to eliminate the dichotomies that the exclusively cross-cultural approach creates. The tone and content of much of the COMIBAM '87 plenary sessions assumed a primarily cross-cultural approach. Luís Bush's (1987) rallying cry included the words, "In 1918 foreign missionaries met to talk about how to send missionaries to Latin America. In 1987 national missionaries meet to talk about how to send missionaries from Latin America" (p. 16). Bill Taylor's (1987) entire session addressed the subject of the cross-cultural challenge. Taylor discussed the concepts of culture, contextualization, cross-cultural communication, culture in the Scriptures, and the Ibero American cross-cultural challenge. Bush and Taylor clearly saw the nature of COMIBAM as a call to cross-cultural missions. Even so, Latin Americans engaging in cross-cultural mission was a fresh and inspiring paradigm shift for evangelicals throughout the continent. The movement ignited the flame among the Ibero American people who awakened to the challenge and opportunity to change the world with the message of the gospel.

As significant as the cross-cultural paradigm shift was, a broader understanding of mission also surfaced in some of the presentations. Barrientos (1987) acknowledged the mental model that sees missionary work as a cultural transplant rather than a sowing of Kingdom principles. While he refuted this notion primarily to argue that missionary sending is not limited to superior cultures or economically-developed countries, he advanced the view that the mission is directed not on the basis of geography, economy, politics or culture but on the basis of man's spiritual condition. Furthermore, Barrientos (1987) recognized Ibero America as a large mission field, without denying that Ibero American evangelicals are a mission-sending force. He stated, "The missionary motivation can begin for many churches in their own nation, in geographical or ethnic zones that need the testimony of the Gospel" (p. 8). Thus, while he did not completely abandon the cross-geographical/cultural notion, he addressed the frontier between faith and no faith. Barrientos also presented a model for the missionary task that consisted of proclamation, disciple-making, missionary-sending and church-planting. This model failed to include aspects of a more holistic mission. The prevailing mental model in Barrientos presentation remained more akin to what Padilla called the traditional approach.

In his keynote speech, Luís Bush (1987) presented missions history as the passing of the torch from Israel to Jesus, to his disciples, to the early church in the Middle East, to the church in Europe, to the church in North America and finally to the church in the third world. For Bush, COMIBAM '87 presented the timely occasion for calling the church in Ibero America to take up the torch that brings "light for the nations" (p. 18). This implied a cross-cultural and cross-geographical view of the mission. After redefining the word "nations" as people groups, Bush clearly stated the focus of COMIBAM as follows,

> COMIBAM's emphasis is…cross-cultural, that of going to another culture and penetrating a group that is different in the anthropological or sociological sense, whether a social group or an ethnic group. And in particular, going to an unreached people group, a group among whom there is no community of believers or resources for the evangelization of the group without external support. COMIBAM's emphasis is on the unreached people groups of the world,

both in the great urban centers as in the rural areas, within and without the Latin

American continent. (p. 20)

While this is broad and inclusive in scope, it is very much along the lines of the Ralph Winter missiology in the *Misión Mundial* publication treated in the previous chapter.

Roberto Hatch (1987) offered a more balanced approach in his presentation of missionary lessons and models. While, he took for granted the need for cross-cultural mission, he provided two warnings in this endeavor. In regard to what has been termed managerial missiology, a label used as a critique of the efforts of North American missions agencies to quantify results, Hatch stated,

Today there are certain management schools that have penetrated the church and the missionary movement with a strong push for establishing objectives and plans. Such an approach can be very helpful in regard to our tendency of improvising, but to the measure that our plans cease to be tentative, provisional and humble, we lose the possibility of listening to the voice of the Spirit or receiving his visions and dreams because of our pride. (pp. 30-31)

Hatch, thus, emphasized a more flexible and fluid approach to the mission that gives room to the divine in contrast with a human-driven management approach. His second warning in regard to the cross-cultural mission was against the cultural superiority tendencies of both Spanish Catholic missionaries and North American evangelical missionaries (pp. 32-33). Hatch exhorted missionaries to hand over the mission to indigenous leadership as soon as possible even when that required great courage, trust and humility. Lastly, Hatch presented the model of the historical Moravian missions as support for the bi-vocational and business-as-mission models for the present. The exhortation to hand over the mission to indigenous leadership expediently and the bi-vocational model for missions presented a softening of the dichotomies created by the traditional approach that Padilla (1986) criticized.

The plenary sessions, designed to cast the vision for Ibero America becoming a mission force, retained many North American missiological assumptions, but included contextualized reflection from the Latin American experience. These plenary sessions did not coincide in every point with the content of the First Ibero American Theological Conference in Antigua, Guatemala, which took place in June of 1986. Nevertheless, the plenary sessions represented significant steps toward a more contextualized Latin American missiology. There was evidence of deliberate blending of missiological ideas, creating a new hybrid that accepted the best practices from missiologists while distancing themselves from North American idiosyncrasies, and framing the process within a developing Latin American perspective.

The amount of missiological communication and discussion that took place in the COMIBAM process from 1985 to 1987 is vast. The topics were numerous and the perspectives were varied. The participants included strategists, theologians, practitioners and others. The information flowed from the top-down most often, but on occasion a bottom-up flow of ideas welled upward. The fact that these principles found a home in the grass roots of Latin American evangelicals is of singular significance. In spite of the criticism that COMIBAM lacked much in indigenous missiological development, COMIBAM leadership maintained open dialogue, listened to the various perspectives and incorporated ideas from both North American missiologists and from Latin American theologians such as René Padilla and Samuel Escobar. For a movement whose primary objective was missionary mobilization, its missiological development demonstrated a significant maturing for Latin American evangelicals.

Summary and Conclusions

The first COMIBAM congress and the events that surrounded it laid the foundation for what would become a movement. Ralph Winter (1988), reporting from COMIBAM '87 said,

> This meeting represents the first time that the final geographic limits of the earth's surface have provided both representatives and the very initiators of a global level congress focused exclusively on the missionary dimensions of world evangelization. You would have to actually be here to sense the pulse, the presence, the power, the phenomenal potential of these key, third-world leaders, running this immense meeting.

The first Ibero American Missions Congress took place in Sao Paulo, Brazil on November 23-29, 1987, with the participation of 3,100 delegates from 25 Ibero American countries. From the beginning, organizers intended to launch a process that would continue after the event itself. To ensure this, during the three years preceding the congress, COMIBAM leaders advanced and set in motion an ambitious agenda to secure the support of national leaders, to survey the missionary history and current situation, and to assess the future of the missionary movement.

The idea of an Ibero American missions congress came simultaneously from individuals and organizations such as Jonathan Dos Santos, Luís Bush, *Misión '84*, serving in San Salvador at that time, the WEA, the Lausanne Committee and CONELA. The key meeting to consider this took place in Mexico City on December 12-14, 1984.

The first coordinating committee meeting for COMIBAM '87 took place in Sao Paulo, Brazil on June 26-28, 1985, with 16 members representing 11 countries. The committee established goals to hold conferences in 23 Ibero American countries, organize national committees, research and document missionary activity; publish a series of books including a manual of missiology and one of praxis. Ten books were actually published. Bush developed an innovative budget of $2 million with the idea that $700,000 would come from U.S. sources but the majority would emanate from Latin American sources so they would own their movement. The missions movement from Ibero America relied on the ground swell of missionary interest taking place simultaneously in certain parts of Latin America and on the timely leadership of COMIBAM leaders who propelled this interest forward and ensured that the same interest penetrated areas of Ibero America where it had been absent.

The program for the congress included Bible exposition toward an Ibero American missiology, discussion groups, intercessory prayer groups, missionary testimonies and seminars, and missions exhibits. The plenary sessions topics addressed the current situation in missions, as well as biblical, theological, and missiological considerations.

COMIBAM evolved from the 1987 Congress to a *cooperación*. In other words, it went from an event to a loose network partnership. Although a clear plan for it had not been developed before the congress, the consolidation of the movement took place under the leadership of Rudy Girón and others. While it took time to determine which organizational model to implement post-congress, eventually the components for a network organization came into place. The organizational model that ensured the continuation of COMIBAM's work after the congress eventually evolved into a network of networks.

Before the 1987 Congress, COMIBAM leadership engaged the national mission movements in the countries where they already existed and catalyzed movements in countries where they did not exist formally. Over 30 national conferences and congresses were held throughout Ibero America in preparation for COMIBAM '87. These conferences offered missiological discussions, vision casting for the movement, and promotion for COMIBAM '87. This phase marks a period of creativity and innovation essential for the later influence of COMIBAM International. National congresses and conferences were also held after COMIBAM '87. Additionally, continental level meetings took place after the first congress: missionary training conferences; the adopt-a-people conference; and the first meeting of churches and missionary agencies related to COMIBAM.

Luís Bush emerged as the primary leader, in fact, the *paladin* [champion], of the congress and the process that launched it. He cast a vision for the movement, the congress and the process. The eight elements of the process were intercession, information, investigation, instruction, involvement, inspiration, infrastructure and invitation to consecration. Each element had a single strategy corresponding to it. Bush shared his leadership with a coordinating committee at the continental level and with executive staff in two offices that related to Spanish- and Portuguese-speaking countries. While Bush cast the vision and mobilized enthusiasm for the first congress, Rudy Girón sustained the momentum between the first and the second congress. Bertil Ekström,

Jonathan Lewis and David Ruíz later provided the organizational structure that allowed COMIBAM to continue as a network.

Missiological reflection clearly interested the COMIBAM leadership. This was relevant to the movement's desire to build on an Ibero American missiology. Although the movement received initial criticism for lack of indigenous missiological reflection and for being influenced by missiology from North America, the COMIBAM process catalyzed missiological discussion through its newsletter, national conferences, the first congress' plenary sessions and a very important Ibero American theological conference in Antigua, Guatemala. The missiological developments that resulted from these formed a hybrid of North American and Latin American ideas.

COMIBAM leadership displayed extraordinary vision, perception and execution in launching a missionary movement from the COMIBAM '87 platform. The ability to mobilize leaders from approximately 23 countries and from multiple denominations around the cause of world evangelization is admirable. COMIBAM leadership demonstrated the ability to perceive God's timing for Latin American missions mobilization, to cast the vision, and to produce a comprehensive process to see it through. The process of preparation for the congress, the amount of data gathering and publications, the stated intention for the congress to become a cooperation, the ability to gather leaders and organize them for national mission movements and the promotion of missiological dialogue all contributed to the success of the first congress and that laid the foundation for the future of the movement. Charismatic leadership, effective vision casting with a network organization, transition of power, and innovative funding process ensured the perpetuation of the movement.

CHAPTER 4. COMIBAM II: A MISSIONS NETWORK CONSOLIDATES

At the arrival of the twenty-first century the mission from Latin America showed great promise for advancement. Churches throughout the continent developed a missionary outlook and they sent thousands of cross-cultural missionaries from Latin America. They established new missionary organizations for training, sending, and networking. Escobar (2002) declared during that time period: "Latin America is now the base for a growing Christian missionary movement to other parts of the world…(T)here is a vigorous willingness to assume responsibilities in Christian mission on a global level" (p. 153). As COMIBAM International entered its second decade of work, Ted Limpic (2002) reported that there were almost 6,000 missionaries sent cross-culturally from Ibero America. COMIBAM International ("¿Qué Es COMIBAM?", n.d.) estimated that there were 1,600 cross-cultural missionaries sent by 70 agencies in 1987. This number had quadrupled in a decade! This represents remarkable numerical growth in the mission sending force from Latin America. The COMIBAM movement contributed to the new mission reality in Latin America during this period.

Is it possible to know if COMIBAM was the driving force behind the new mission fervor or if COMIBAM was catching the wave of a new spirit in the continent? How did the movement mature since its first decade of work? What were the characteristics of the second decade of the COMIBAM movement? Who were its leaders? In what areas did their missiology continue to develop after the first decade, and how did it affect their mission praxis? These are the questions that this chapter explores. The chapter focuses on the developments around the COMIBAM '97 congress in Acapulco, giving special attention to the missiological developments.

The COMIBAM '97 congress recognized the importance of describing clearly the immediate past and current state of the Ibero American missionary movement. Federico Bertuzzi (2006a) addressed these questions at COMIBAM '97 and identified the following key elements: (a) the recent recognition that missiological reflection should include the work of Spanish and Portuguese Catholics since the 16th century and not only that of English-speaking Protestants since the 19th century, (b) the start of mission sending from Latin America since the beginning of the 20th century, (c) the necessity for Latin American evangelicals to discover and advance a missionary vision by their own initiative since the Anglo-Saxon missionary advancement in the same context failed to instill it, and (d) the recent emergence of national movements, which include the formation of missionary agencies and missionary networks across denominational lines. Thus, the Ibero American missionary movement, at this time, reflected critically on its past while it also maintained an appreciation for the contributions that connected the movement with history. Each of these four observations progressively ties the missionary zeal more closely to Ibero America while stepping away from depending on North America. Through COMIBAM Ibero American missions gave evidence of coming of age. The congress received the encouraging report of multiple national movements that were already engaged in the missionary task. Ultimately, COMIBAM was concerned with the advancement of mission and with helping Latin Americans to own their missionary efforts.

This chapter will explore missiological currents in Latin America around the time of the Acapulco congress, examine the congress itself and the significant developments related to it, analyze the status of the national mission movements during this era, identify the significance of continental meetings that followed the second congress, evaluate the continental leadership of COMIBAM International, and assess the contribution that the Ibero American missionary enterprise made to the cause of world missions. The study will reveal that the COMIBAM movement reached a new level of maturity during its second decade and marched boldly forward.

Missiological Currents in Latin America

Previous chapters have discussed dominant missiological currents present at the inception of the COMIBAM movement. It remains to examine three aspects of COMIBAM to determine the degree to which it is an indigenous missionary movement: leadership, financing, and missiology. Who controls it? Who supports it financially? Whose ideas are implemented? This idea relates closely to Venn's three-self formula for indigenous churches. Henry Venn (1796-1873), Secretary of the Church Missionary Society for thirty-one years from 1841-1873, was one of the key figures of the nineteenth century missionary and evangelical movement. Venn is known as the father of the indigenous church principle, namely self-supporting, self-governing and self-propagating (Papers of Henry Venn, 2013). Venn proposed that a truly indigenous church was self-sustaining, namely in terms of finances; self-governing, which is an issue of leadership; and self-propagating, in other words, evangelism and missions (Shenk, 2000). Similarly, an indigenous missionary movement requires indigenous leadership and indigenous financing. A missionary movement, by nature, exists for the purpose of propagating. Indigenous missiological reflection also contributes to the autonomy of a missionary movement.

COMIBAM took giant steps in the area of indigenous leadership and financing. On the other hand, COMIBAM developed a hybrid of foreign and domestic missiological tendencies from the beginning. This pattern continued through the second decade of the movement. COMIBAM's missiology was indigenous to the extent that it operated between the tension of U.S. and Latin American missiological models. Reciprocally, at least one Latin American missions leader, Luis Bush, influenced U.S. missiology.

For the purposes of this chapter the two primary currents will be identified as U.S. and Latin American missiological paradigms. However, these very generic designations require description. Escobar (2002) proposes three missiological currents in evangelical Latin America: post-imperial missiology, managerial missiology, and holistic missiology. These more specific descriptions are helpful in the present analysis.

Post-Imperial Missiology

According to Escobar (2002), the post-imperial missiology current came primarily from Europe and, more particularly from Great Britain. In these circles there was much missionary activity, biblical scholarship and theological reflection. Its designation derives from the assumption that colonialism is no longer a valid paradigm, if it ever was, for advancing the mission. While British scholars recognized the shift of the center of Christianity from the West to the South as early as the 1970s (Jenkins, 2002), this assumption was the basis for the Missional Church movement in North America at the turn of the 21st century (Guder, 1998). In other words, post-imperial missiology eventually had its proponents in North America also. This missiology current maintained spiritual zeal and serious biblical scholarship, and it resulted in new forms of non-colonialist cooperation with national churches. Representative individuals of post-imperial missiology are Michael Green, Stephen Neill, Max Warren and Andrew Walls (Escobar, 2002). This was a welcomed missiology for many of the Latin American evangelical leaders within the COMIBAM movement, especially as it related to the development of partnership models.

Managerial Missiology

Escobar (2002) gave the designation managerial missiology to the school of missiology developed in the United States that utilizes information technology, marketing techniques and management-by-objectives leadership for mission practice. It is pragmatic in focus; thus concerned with quantifiable data and with precision. The concepts it produced include unreached people groups, homogeneous units, and the 10-40 window. Specific programmatic expressions of this type of missiology are Disciple a Whole Nation (DAWN), AD 2000 and Beyond, *Iglecrecimiento* [Church Growth], Spiritual Warfare, and Adopt-a-People. One of the strengths of this approach, according to Escobar (2002), was the zeal and sense of urgency for the mission and the desire to evaluate missionary action realistically. One of the weaknesses of this missiology was that "The managerial focus gives rise to the suspicion that its proponents see mission as an activity that makes it possible to grow and crown its missionary centers in the United States with success" (p. 19). Those that are directly related to this kind of missiology are Ralph D. Winter, Donald A. McGavran, and the U.S. Center for World Mission. Since Ralph Winter gained much prominence as a missiologist and since he was a primary proponent of this school, this missiological current occasionally bears his name. The influence of managerial missiology did not disappear from COMIBAM after its first decade of existence. For example, Londoño (2006b) incorporated many U.S. concepts into his missiological glossary as the movement celebrated its third congress. In this missiological glossary the author lists the terms that relate to the adopt-a-people-group strategy, namely, the 10/40 window; E0, E1, E2 and E3 evangelism; various people group designations, mega blocks, mission agencies, etc. (Londoño, 2006b). These are the concepts presented in *Misión Mundial* (Lewis, 1990).

Holistic Missiology

Holistic missiology came primarily from the Majority World and was concerned not only about how much missionary activity was needed, but also what kind of "activity reflects biblical teaching and responds to the context" (Escobar, 2002, 19). In addition to seeking a biblical foundation, it reflects on the ethnic, social, political, and ecclesiastical realities of the Majority World. Escobar (2002) argued for the relevance of such an approach based on the nominal Christianity environment that resulted from the 16th century Iberian missionary action on a continent where dire poverty and injustice have remained through the 21st century. While this was the missiology of the FTL, Escobar admitted that it failed to systematize the approach in a way that would make it more accessible at the practical level of the missionary enterprise. Hints of this type of missiology were more visibly present in some areas of the COMIBAM missiological dialogue during its second decade of existence.

Missiological Currents of the FTL and COMIBAM

Chapter 2 of the current study included a thorough discussion from the contrasting missiological perspectives of the FTL and COMIBAM. The FTL missiological paradigm focused on indigenous Latin American reflection and emphasized *misión integral* [holistic mission], the centrality of the local church, and understanding the Kingdom of

God as a present reality, not only as a future eschatological fulfillment. Interestingly, Bertil Ekström (2006), as a COMIBAM leader, recognized the Latin American missiological contribution made by Samuel Escobar and René Padilla to the world evangelical community as early as Lausanne 1974. A different voice at the 1974 Lausanne congress also greatly influenced COMIBAM. Ralph Winter's missiology, as expressed in his *Perspectives on the World Christian Movement* (2009), influenced both Lausanne 1974 and COMIBAM's missiological paradigms. The primary instrument for this influence was the adaptation and translation of Winter's work into *Misión Mundial* [World Mission] (Lewis, 1990), which was required reading for the delegates of COMIBAM 87 in Sao Paulo. This missiological current is connected to the U.S. Center for World Mission founded by Ralph Winter and the School of World Mission and Church Growth at Fuller Theological Seminary. It emphasizes unreached people groups, agency-driven missionary sending and Church Growth theories that emphasize numerical growth. This current is in essence what Escobar terms managerial missiology.

While some of the FTL members participated in COMIBAM events, the FTL had initially been critical of COMIBAM's missiology until both organizations held a meeting to discuss their differences in Miami, Florida on April 24-26, 1995 (*Comunicado de Prensa* [Press Release] April 26, 1995. COMIBAM/Bertuzzi Archive file 201). Leaders of both organizations did not arrive at complete agreement on missiological paradigms, but it should be noted that participants of the encounter between the FTL and COMIBAM wished to minimize the dichotomy between the two organizations. In fact, many of the leaders had been involved in both organizations (Bertuzzi et al., 1995). They did agree significantly that the FTL focused on theological reflection, while COMIBAM focused on the mobilization of Latin Americans to cross-cultural mission.

The missionary experience in Latin America shaped the thinking about missions as well as the sentiments about who the key players were. Latin Americans conducted missiological dialogue against a backdrop where many U.S. missionaries continued to work in Latin America, and more than a few still practiced a paternalistic paradigm. Consequently, many of the leaders campaigned against any trace of U.S. ownership of the mission from Ibero America, and thus of COMIBAM.

The Second Congress

The second COMIBAM continental congress (*II Congreso Misionero Iberoamericano COMIBAM '97)* was held in Acapulco, Mexico in 1997 (Bertuzzi, 2006a, p. 165; Ekström, 2006). A hurricane and the difficulty of obtaining visas from Mexican officials preceded the Acapulco congress (Bertuzzi, 2006a). In spite of these challenges, the congress maintained an ambitious agenda and accomplished remarkable objectives. Ekström (2006) reports that 2,711 delegates attended the congress. David Ruíz (2001), who served as the Executive Director of COMIBAM International, stated that the four primary concerns of the congress were (a) an evaluation of the current Ibero American missionary movement, (b) an projection of the movement for the future, (c) the training of those who would go to the mission field, those who were already on the field, and those who would prepare and pastor them, and (d) inspiration from the Bible for congress participants, their respective churches, the seminaries and the missionary agencies. This second congress did not demonstrate numerical growth when compared to the attendance at 1987 congress. However, the congress demonstrated COMIBAM's growth in regard to content of the meeting's agenda. COMIBAM '97 addressed the issues of missionary sending from Ibero America based on experience in the first decade of the movement's existence.

This section on the second congress consists of a review of the numerical status of the Ibero American missionary sending at the turn of the 21st century; the congress presenters, topics, testimonies and reports; missiological publications in Latin America at the time of the second congress and COMIBAM publications after the second congress. A great number of missionaries from Ibero America were serving and demonstrating by their sacrificial service a truly continental movement in vision and engagement. The selection of program personalities and topics revealed an intentional effort to provide diversity in missiological perspective, academic and practitioner focus, location in the globe, denominational affiliation and ethnicity. The publications around the time of the second congress included U.S. and Latin American missiological currents. Clearly, by the time of this second congress, the Ibero American missionary movement had matured significantly.

Numerical Status of Ibero American Missionary Sending

Where statistics about how many foreign missionaries were sent out from Latin America were difficult to obtain for the 1987 COMIBAM congress, by the 1997 COMIBAM congress, Ted Limpic (1997) addressed this problem by providing extensive numerical data. This report was updated in 2002 and it revealed that approximately 5,900 Ibero American missionaries were on the field. The data suggested that the Ibero American mission-sending movement had a significant level of direct church involvement in sending missionaries, but it was primarily an agency-driven endeavor, consistent with the model inherited from U.S. missionaries and promoted by the Ralph Winter publications; that the mission-sending force was overwhelmingly an Ibero American enterprise but enjoyed significant support of Western partners; and that, although there was diversity in the denominational affiliation of those being sent, the proportion of Pentecostal missionaries was much greater in relation to the number of sending organizations (Limpic, 2002).

The statistics reported tell their own story. In terms of the organizations that were sending Ibero American missionaries, denominational boards sent 31% of those missionaries, Ibero American agencies sent 30%, international agencies with Ibero American leadership sent 18%, local churches sent 10%, international agencies 8%, and Ibero American agencies with Western leadership 1% (Limpic, 2002). Thus, agencies were involved in the sending of 90% of missionaries from Latin America. Of these at least 27% utilized resources from the church in the North. The missionary sending movement from Latin America was primarily agency-driven and strongly indigenous.

The affiliation of sending agencies and the number of missionaries they sent revealed some interesting facts. Of the mission-sending organizations, 46% were interdenominational, 31% were traditional, or non-Pentecostal Evangelical, denominations, 19% were Pentecostal, and 4% were independent (Limpic, 2002). Interestingly the denominational affiliation proportion of sending organizations did not exactly mirror that of the missionaries being sent. Of the Ibero American missionaries sent, 36% were interdenominational, 36% were Pentecostal, 26% were traditional (non-Pentecostal Evangelical), and 1% was independent (Limpic, 2006). The proportion of Pentecostal missionaries almost doubled that of Pentecostal sending organizations. The number of Pentecostal missionaries was in keeping with the growth of Pentecostalism and Charismatic movements in Latin America (Bertuzzi, 2006a, p. 179; Escobar, 2002). Anderson (2005) stated, "As Christian history enters a new millennium, Pentecostals have become the predominant face of Latin American Evangelicals" (p. 595). The denominational and theological tradition proportion of Ibero American missionaries has implications for the shape of the global church in the future.

The list of countries that sent missionaries provided another piece of the Ibero American picture. These figures demonstrated that by the turn of the 21st century, missionary sending from Ibero America was truly a continental enterprise. Of the countries that sent Ibero American missionaries cross-culturally, the top five in descending in order, were (a) Brazil, (b) United States, (c) Spain, (d) Mexico, and (e) Peru (Limpic, 2002). The United States is considered part of the Ibero American movement because it sends Latin Americans on cross-cultural mission. This classification included both domestic and foreign missionaries including those that served as cross-cultural missionaries within their own country along with those that cross geographical borders. COMIBAM was interested in cross-cultural missions from the perspective of people groups not of geo-political nations. Thus, it should be noted that the overwhelming majority of cross-cultural missionaries from Brazil stayed within its own geographical boundaries (Limpic, 2002). When considering only the number of missionaries sent out of their own country, the United States, Spain, Mexico, Peru, Bolivia, Paraguay, and Argentina each sent more missionaries than Brazil (Limpic, 2002). Ibero American missionaries represented North America, South America and the Iberian Peninsula in a significant way. The movement was indeed continentally Ibero

American not only in vision, but also in actual engagement reflected in the country of origin for missionaries.

Congress Presenters

The selection of program personalities for COMIBAM '97 demonstrated an intentional effort to provide balance in missiological perspective, between academia and praxis, and representation from various key segments of the globe. The speakers also represented denominational and ethnic diversity. These presenters included Valdir R. Steuernagel, Federico A. Bertuzzi, David D. Ruíz, Met Castillo, William D. Taylor, Jonathan P. Lewis, Maher Rizk, Luís Bush, Oswaldo Prado, Dieter L. Knospe, Patrick Joshua, David Tai Woong Lee, Fernando Quicaña and Rudy Girón (Bertuzzi, 2001).

In terms of missiological perspective the speakers represented both currents: the U.S. and the Latin American models. In general leaders who related to COMIBAM, the WEF and the AD2000-and-Beyond movement supported the agency-driven model characteristic of U.S. missions. Such leaders included Federico Bertuzzi, David Ruíz, Jonathan Lewis, Luís Bush and Rudy Girón, who were COMIBAM's current leaders; William Taylor, (WEF representative); Met Castillo, doctor in missiology from Fuller Theological Seminary (Bertuzzi, 2001, p. 55); Oswaldo Prado, a Brazilian Presbyterian, coordinator of the AD2000 movement in Brazil, and member of the WEF missions committee (Bertuzzi, 2001); and David Tai Woong Lee, Korean leader and president of the WEF Missions Commission (Bertuzzi, 2001). Steuernagel, a Brazilian Lutheran who held a doctoral degree in theology, with a concentration in missiology from the Lutheran College in Chicago (Bertuzzi, 2001), and who was at the time the president of the FTL (Bertuzzi, 2001) and Fernando Quicaña, a Peruvian Presbyterian pastor and also a member of the FTL represented the Latin American missiological current. It must be noted, that while the proportion of speakers concerned with the practical aspects characteristic of agency-driven missiology was greater, the FTL missiology was never absent from the COMIBAM dialogue.

In addition to the speakers mentioned above, Maher Rizk, an Egyptian, director of Arab Evangelical Ministers, an organization representing over twenty countries in the Middle East and North Africa (Bertuzzi, 2001); Dieter L. Knospe, a German leader of the Church of God denomination in his own country and church planter in Eastern Europe (Bertuzzi, 2001); and Patrick Joshua, a Indian national and general secretary of the Missionary Prayer League of Friends, one of the largest Majority World missionary agencies (Bertuzzi, 2001) represented significant areas of the globe where Ibero Americans were serving. COMIBAM leaders diligently offered a comprehensive picture of the global missionary situation at that time.

Topics of Discussion at the Second Congress

COMIBAM '97 provided help for the selection, training, sending and caring for Latin American missionaries (Ekström, 2006). The program addressed this objective by considering theological, practical and contextual aspects of each step of the process. David Ruíz (2001), in the prologue to the COMIBAM '97 Handbook, declares,

> We will travel here and there, according to the geographical point where the presenters live. It will be a true specialization to see the perspective of the diverse nationalities on the selection, training values, the seriousness of the sending aspect, and the challenge of pastoral care, or to evaluate from their viewpoint the missionary task of those who came to them from Ibero America. (p. 7)

Thus, the ambitious agenda sought to provide a broad and global perspective of the state of the mission across Ibero America.

At least two of the presentations dealt with theological subjects such as the nature of the mission (Steuernagel, 2001) and the missiological implications of eschatology (Taylor, 2001). Several of the topics covered the past and present realities of the Ibero American missionary movement (Bertuzzi, 2001), the sending of missionaries from Latin America (Prado, 2001), and the future of the movement (Girón, 2001). Three of the presentations covered practical matters of the mission including the selection of missionaries (Ruíz, 2001), missionary training (Lewis, 2001), pastoral care and supervision of missionaries (Lee, 2001), and spiritual warfare (Joshua, 2001). The majority of the presentations described segments of the global reality for Latin American missionaries. Bush (2001a) spoke on the globalization of the missionary movement and new paradigms while other speakers looked at the fields where missionaries served. Castillo (2001) spoke of the Asia reality, Risk (2001) of the Arabic Middle East, Knospe (2001) of Eastern Europe, and Quicaña (2001) of Indigenous communities in the Americas. Congress participants were exposed to missiological reflection and received essential information and inspiration that allowed them to participate in missions around the world.

Missionary Testimonies and National Consultation Reports

The COMIBAM '97 congress heard testimonies from missionaries who were serving in various parts of the world, and received statements from the national consultations that were held in the Ibero American countries. Missionaries shared testimonies about their respective missions fields. Rodrigo Arce in North Africa,

Reynaldo Torres in Muslim World, Andrés Duncan in the Middle East, Lucimara Rocha in Senegal, David de la Rosa in Spain, Ninette Jiménez in Guatemala, and Paulo Moreira in Eastern Europe brought inspiration to the congress (Bertuzzi, 2001). While these spheres did not reflect proportionately the areas where Ibero American missionaries were serving during that time, however, it did represent new fields where the COMIBAM leadership wanted to focus, especially in North Africa, the Muslim World, and the Middle East. As early as 1990, Rudy Girón led the first Latin consultation for the evangelization of the Islamic world, called CLAME '90, which was co-sponsored by COMIBAM (Ekström 2006). Citing historical, linguistic, sociopolitical, physical appearance and cultural reasons, Bertuzzi (2006a) declared at a mid-90s missions conference, "If there is a people who can ideally communicate with relative ease with the one hundred and sixty million Arabs, it is our people: the Latin people!" (p. 51). The selection of testimonies for the Acapulco congress was in keeping with the expanding vision for sending missionaries of the COMIBAM leadership. Clearly, as many Latin Americans continued to answer the call to engage in cross-cultural missions, COMIBAM pointed with intentionality to the places they should go.

COMIBAM organizers had requested that each country in Ibero America conduct an evaluation consultation and to report at Acapulco, in order to help the congress participants have a better idea of the status of the missionary task across Ibero America (Ekström, 2006). Reports from these consultations were submitted in writing by Argentina, Brazil, Canada, Chile, Colombia, Costa Rica, the Dominican Republic, Ecuador, Guatemala, Honduras, Mexico, Nicaragua, Paraguay, Peru, Portugal, Puerto Rico, and Venezuela (Bertuzzi, 2001). The diligence required for each of these seventeen countries to meet and subsequently to prepare a report for the continental congress demonstrated the cooperative spirit that existed at that time. Whereas the preparation for COMIBAM 87 in Sao Paulo, Brazil consisted of delegates who had led a group to study and pray about missions, as stated in chapter 3 of the current study, the preparation for COMIBAM '97 in Acapulco, Mexico consisted of an evaluation of each country's missionary activity to date. COMIBAM had moved from vision sharing to mobilization mode. COMIBAM had encouraged the nascent cross-cultural mission engagement in Ibero America for over a decade. The movement's leaders had developed a more global and strategic perspective on international missions. Furthermore, COMIBAM maintained a healthy appetite for useful information. The organization consciously based its mobilization efforts on theological reflection, evaluation of the progress of mission in each of its sectors, and the study of the context where mission was being carried out.

Publications Surrounding the Second COMIBAM Congress

At the beginning of the 21st century COMIBAM publications displayed the missiological currents in the movement at that time. The various publications incorporated the best elements from the missiology from the North, specifically that of the U.S. Center for World missions, and a missiology developed in Latin America. In result the COMIBAM movement created its own hybrid of these two currents. COMIBAM leaders did not develop a systematic missiology at the theoretical level. Rather, these missionary mobilizers and practitioners strived for a missiological reflection that was practical.

COMIBAM sponsored writing of textbooks on missions. Shortly after the COMIBAM 87 congress, COMIBAM International commissioned Emilio Antonio

Nuñez, a member of the FTL, with the development of a Latin American Evangelical missiology (Nuñez, 1997). This afforded the opportunity for the indigenous missionary movement to possess its own indigenous missiology. The resulting publication was *Hacia una misionología evangélica Latinoamericana: Bases bíblicas de la misión (Antiguo Testamento)* [Toward a Latin American Evangelical missiology: Biblical bases for the mission (Old Testament)]. The 359-page volume was written with the objective of training students of the Latin American missionary training centers in order to provide them a biblical basis for the mission and the content of the message to be communicated in cross-cultural mission (Nuñez, 1997). Shortly after COMIBAM '87 Larry D. Pate (1987) published *Misionología: Nuestro cometido transcultural* [Missiology: Our cross-cultural commitment]. This practical work had many parallels to the earlier book *Misión Mundial* (1990) written for the first COMIBAM congress. Peter Wagner (1987), professor at Fuller Theological Seminary in Pasadena, California, stated in the prologue that Pate's work was the most complete Spanish-language work in missiology and declared that it was the main textbook for the training of missionaries who had been mobilized by COMIBAM 87. Curiously, even though COMIBAM's officially commissioned Nuñez' (1997) work rather than Pate's (1987), it is evident that Pate's book represented a missiological agenda for the developing COMIBAM movement.

While Nuñez promised a missiology that spoke from Latin America, Pate's work was an agenda for Latin America. Regrettably, Nuñez' work was not published until ten years after the first congress. Pate's text and Lewis' *Misión Mundial* [World Mission] (1990) are both adaptations of the mindset that is represented in Winter's *Perspectives on the world Christian movement* (2009). These works represent the U.S. missiology that influenced the COMIBAM movement the most. Almost every COMIBAM publication betrays traces of this U.S. missiology combined with some indigenous reflection and adaptation by Latin Americans.

Because Pate's textbook *Misionología* (1987) was so important an influence upon the outlook of the missionary zeal in Ibero America, it will be examined to identify the primary themes that appeared in COMIBAM publications and discussions. Many of Pate's ideas did not originate with him, but his work advanced and popularized them in Ibero America. Pate's (1987) missiology textbook was a pragmatic handbook for cross-cultural mission. One of its ten chapters discussed the biblical basis for mission. The book omitted the history of mission. The greatest portion of its contents covered the social science aspect of missiology, especially as it related to missionaries adapting to the cross-cultural task. Thus, it was a work of applied missiology. The other topics covered in *Misionología* mirrored content already published in the second and third volumes of *Misión mundial* [World mission] (1990). *Misionología* (1987) emphasizes the biblical bases for the mission, the unreached-people-groups strategy, the establishing of indigenous churches and the strategies for cross-cultural evangelism.

Biblical basis. The U.S. missiology legacy sought to have a solid biblical base. In that endeavor it labored to find the common thread of God's plan for cross-cultural mission throughout the entire biblical record rather than in specific "missionary" portions of the Bible.

Pate (1987) provided biblical bases for validating cross-cultural ministry as coming from the very nature of God and His mission. Taking God's love as the foundation for His redemptive purpose, the *Missio Dei* or God's mission is to bring people to repentance through the work of Christ. The author maintained that a cross-cultural mission had always been God's plan. The cross-cultural plan of God was revealed first in the Abrahamic promise (Genesis 12:3). All nations of the earth would be blessed through Abraham's line (Pate, 1987). This cross-cultural mission continues to unfold throughout the entire biblical record (Pate, 1987). The true meaning of the day of Pentecost (Acts 2) was to declare that the church, no longer Israel, would be God's instrument for His mission and that the message would be delivered in the mother tongue or heart language of every people (Pate, 1987). Londoño (2006) shared this view of the Acts 2 event. Pate stated, "God was declaring the Holy Spirit's plan of action in the Church of Jesus Christ to establish churches among every people group on the earth" (p. 28).

Other COMIBAM publications shared this approach to the biblical basis for the mission. COMIBAM authors included other Old and New Testament passages. Bertuzzi (2006a) included Genesis 11; Jeremiah 1:5; Matthew 4:15, 24:13, 28:18-20; Mark 13:10, 16:15; Luke 24:47; John 17:18, 20:21; Acts 1:8, 11:19-21, 13:1-3, 15; and Revelation 5:9 in his treatment (pp. 58-65, 98-102). Londoño (2006) dealt briefly with Genesis 1-11,12; John 4:32-35; Acts 1:8, 2:1-21, 37-47; and 1 Peter 1:20. In summary, a shared understanding of this biblical foundation provided divine sanction for the movement's focus on cross-cultural ministry, people groups, and an evangelism-only approach.

Unreached people groups and the unfinished task. The focus on unreached people groups as a strategy for finishing the Great Commission remained a growing theme in the COMIBAM movement. Pate (1987) provided clear theological bases for the focus on people groups by stating that (a) God is the Creator of human diversity, (b) the church's unity consists of spiritual unity not cultural uniformity, (c) God sees the world from a people group perspective not from a geo-political nation perspective, (d) The Great Commission is an ethnocentric mandate, (d) Cross-cultural evangelism is a foundational part of the nature of the church, and (e) Jesus' model for reaching the world was to focus ethnocentrically on a mono-cultural group before sending them to do the same across other cultures.

The key text. The Great Commission (Matthew 28:19-20) provided a key text for the focus on people groups. The Greek words transliterated *panta ta ethne* which are translated *all the nations*, should also be translated, "Go, therefore, make disciples of all the peoples, " since the word nations has changed meaning within the last century of nationalism (Pate, 1987). Jesus commanded his followers to go as cross-cultural missionaries to every people group on the earth rather than to every geo-political nation. Bertuzzi (2006a) and Londoño (2006b) treated the meaning of *ethne* in the same manner.

The basic principle. Pate (1987) argued that reaching one ethnic group at a time was the best strategy to accomplish the world evangelization task based on the fundamental principle of the homogenous unit, "People like to convert to Christianity without having to cross racial, linguistic or class barriers" (pp. 51-52). In addition he listed efficiency, namely, more conversions, more churches, in less time, clearer missionary objectives, and the ability to tangibly keep track of people groups, as another reason for the unreached people group strategy.

Ibero American adaptation. However, at COMIBAM's first General Assembly in Lima Peru (2000), Jesús Londoño tempered a sociological and managerial emphasis with a call to return to biblical and spiritual starting points in the Ibero American implementation of this strategy. Londoño (2006a), as a COMIBAM leader, explicitly rejected the notion that the unreached people group strategy belonged to a managerial paradigm. After the Reach an Ethnic Group committee strategy meeting in Guatemala (2000), he proposed biblical-theological justification for this emphasis from Genesis 3:15; 12, Exodus 19:1-6; Malachi 3:1-3; Matthew 4:15-16; 28:18-29; Mark 16:14-18; Luke 24:44-49; John 4:32-35; John 20:21-23; Acts 1:8; 1 Peter 1:20; 2:9; and 2 Peter 3:9; Revelation 5:9 (Londoño, 2006a, pp. 36-38; 2006b). Londoño (2006a) argued that the unreached people group strategy, "is not a goal in itself, nor an end. The motor that propels us is not the accomplishment of objectives or the enlargement of statistics, but the fulfillment of God's expressed will" (p. 38). In fact, Londoño (2006b) rejected as unworthy the following motivations for the adopt-a-people-group strategy: goal accomplishment, denominational growth, institutional growth and the need of the unreached people. He advanced the view that the only valid basis for reaching the people groups of the world was so that these peoples would ultimately worship God. Londoño's correction was in agreement with Steve Hawthorne's prolific article, "The Story of His Glory" (Hawthorne, 2009) which was originally published in *Perspectives on the World Christian Movement*'s second edition (1992). Londoño demonstrated the willingness and ability to engage in critical dialogue on the theology of mission. Ibero Americans were free to think for themselves, but also to recognize the validity of missiological thinking from other places.

An attractive strategy. Bertuzzi (2006a) recognized that there was not consensus on the number of unreached people groups, estimating that the number was somewhere between 8,000 and 16,500 such groups. Londoño (2006b) lamented the variance of reports that ranged from 11,000 unreached people groups in the 1980s to 2,700 by the first decade of the twenty first century. Looking at the world from a people-group-perspective instead of a geo-political-nations-perspective highlighted the difference between assessing the world as 75% unreached or 55% unreached, respectively (Pate, 1987). This view leads to the central conclusion of the UPG missiology: since 91% of the missionaries, that is 81,500, are in reached fields, which constitute 25% of the world, and 9% of the missionaries are serving in the unreached fields, which constitute 75% of the world, the strategic focus of missions, in order to finish the world evangelization task, needs to be on unreached people groups (Pate, 1987). Bertuzzi (2006a) listed the existence of unreached people groups as the first reason for the urgency of the missionary enterprise. The concept of unreached people groups relied heavily on the social sciences and on demographics. Nevertheless, the concept of a tangible strategy for accomplishing the Great Commission remained attractive for mission mobilizers and practitioners in Latin America. In fact, in a reciprocal manner, one Latin American contributed largely to Anglo-Saxon missiology.

Bush's influence on the UPG missiology. Luis Bush, the Argentine who helped conceptualize, and who initially led the COMIBAM movement, subsequently made significant contributions to the strategies identified with the U.S. Center for World Missions. Shortly after Bush passed the baton of the COMIBAM leadership, he developed the AD2000 Strategy, the 10/40 Window concept, and contributed to the Joshua 2000 Strategy (Bush, 2001b; Coote, 2000). All of these brilliant concepts provided manageable strategies for the UPG missiology.

The AD2000 movement evolved as a worldwide expression of the same principles Bush developed for COMIBAM. At COMIBAM 87, Thomas Wang, a Chinese who served then as the international director of the Lausanne Movement for World Evangelization asked Bush to write an article to be circulated among 20,000 world Christian leaders (Bush, 2001b). The article elaborated on principles for world evangelization by the year 2000, a year Wang thought significant for the missionary task (Bush, 2002; Coote, 2000). These principles, namely, "spiritual movement, indigenization, consultation, involvement of every population segment, research of the harvest field and the harvest force, the principle of order and cooperation, encouragement, and major event-focal point," became the seed bed for the AD2000 & Beyond Movement (Bush, 2001b, p. 16). The objective of this network was to "encourage existing and new movements to work together across prevailing barriers, in order to advance the cause of Jesus Christ and his Great Commission" (Bush, 2002, p. 129).

The rallying cry for this worldwide network was "a church for every people and the gospel for every person by the year 2000" (Bush, 2001b, p. 16). The Ralph Winter-led Edinburgh 1980 missions consultation had coined the phrase "A church for every people by A.D. 2000" (Coote, 2000, p. 161). Bush took his COMIBAM principles and the seminal ideas of Winter and Wang to catalyze a new world wide movement focused on reaching UPGs by the year 2000. He led the AD2000 & Beyond Movement for a decade (Bush, 2001b). Bush acknowledged that his strategy had been criticized as gospel reductionism and as managerial missiology but he defended it as a historically legitimate method (Bush, 2002).

U.S. and U.K. Baptist, Presbyterian, Reformed, Anglican and other evangelical denominations endorsed the AD2000 objective demonstrating the wide influence of this strategy (Coote, 2000). John Stott (1995) believed the AD2000 & Beyond Movement could conceivable attain its bold goals because of "the proliferation of indigenous missions in Africa, Latin America, and the Pacific rim of East Asia" (p. 56). Coote (2000) credited the AD2000 Movement as having an incalculable impact on the education of the world Christian community. By the early 1990s, Bush had begun the journey of influencing the thinking about missions in the North.

Almost simultaneous to Bush's involvement with the AD2000 network, he conceived the idea of the 10/40 Window. The AD2000 movement sought to plant a church among every major unreached people group. A natural follow-up question to such an endeavor is to ask where these UPGs are concentrated, if at all, in the world. While attending Lausanne 89 in Manila, Bush remarked, "most of the unreached people groups live in a belt that extends from West Africa across Asia, between ten degrees to forty degrees north of the equator…(including) the Muslim block, the Hindu block, and the Buddhist block" (Bush, 2001b, p. 16). Additionally Bush (2002) affirmed that approximately 97 percent of the population in the 55 least evangelized countries and 85 percent of the poorest of the poor lived in this "window" (p. 139). In December of that same year at the Urbana conference Bush presented this 10/40 Window concept in one of the plenary sessions. By July of 1990 Bush and Pete Holzmann, a specialist in computerized mapping, developed the 10/40 window map that would be widely used around the world for prayer and missions mobilization (Coote, 2000). The AD2000 international board, at their first meeting that same month and year, decided to concentrate their efforts on this 10/40 Window (Bush, 2002). Thus, the 10/40 Window focus became the primary strategy of the AD2000 & Beyond Movement. Bush published this concept in 1991, in a booklet titled *The 10/40 Window: Getting to the Core of the Core*. The 21st century edition of Johnstone & Mandryk's (2001) *Operation World,* the missionary education and prayer Bible of world evangelicals, featured the 10/40 Window as a prominent concept in the completing of the missionary task. Undoubtedly, the 10/40 Window concept was Bush's best-known contribution to world missions thinking.

Bush helped to develop yet another refinement of the AD2000 strategy. The Joshua Project 2000 was a global cooperative strategy with the goal of establishing a pioneer church planting movement within every ethno-linguistic people group of over 10,000 individuals within every country of the world by December 31, 2000 (Bush, 2002). The project combined the focus on UPGs with national movements and kept the AD2000 completion deadline. With this emphasis on national initiatives, in 1995 Bush convened a conference of leaders from 77 countries in Colorado Springs in order to set in motion the final thrust of AD2000 (Bush, 2002). The Joshua Project 2000 became the focus of the AD2000 movement. The 4,000 participants from 130 countries affirmed the Joshua Project at the 1997 Global Consultation on World Evangelization (GCOWE '97) in Pretoria South Africa. Bush again became a major contributor of a strategy for world evangelization with wide reception by evangelicals around the world.

Luis Bush possessed a multi-cultural heritage that facilitated his receiving influence from Anglo-Saxon thinking while also contributing to it. Bush was born in Argentina, grew up in Uruguay and Brazil, pastored a church in El Salvador and led the launching of COMIBAM 87 from Guatemala (Bush, 2001b; Bush 2002). The son of

British parents, Bush attended British boarding school in Argentina and received the religious heritage of the Church of England (Bush, 2001b). The spiritual and educational influences on Bush's life included Dr. Howard Henricks, Pastor Warren Wiersbe, Pastor George Thies of Word of Life in Sao Paulo, Professor Ron Blue, Pastor Bob Hoekstra of Dallas Bible Church, Watchman Nee, the University of North Carolina, Moody Church, and the Dallas Theological Seminary, (Bush, 2001b; Bush, 2002). Surely the influence of these individuals and institutions afforded Bush the ability to function within an Anglo-Saxon frame of thinking. By the time Bush enrolled in the doctoral program in the School of World Mission at Fuller Theological Seminary he had already been a missions practitioner and thinker. Not coincidentally, in 2002, the same school and the Lausanne Committee for World Evangelization sponsored Bush's Evangelizing Our World Inquiry (Bush, 2002). A Latin American missions mobilization leader had significantly shaped U.S. mobilization thinking.

The UPG missiology had its origins in the U.S. missiology. However, Latin America contributed to the further development of this focus on UPG. Some Latin American leaders found theological justification for adopting a UPG missiology. Those that adopted this strategy believing it to be an efficient way to carry out the mission task made it their battle cry. Londoño (2006b) assessed that the UPG strategy had resulted in only prayer and talk in Latin America. COMIBAM published Londoño's (2006b) *Alcance una etnia: Programa viable* [Reach a people group: A viable program] in order to urge and equip local churches to engage in this strategy. The UPG focus was an attractive tangible strategy for mission mobilization. COMIBAM helped to promote it.

Bush refined its development. This explains the deep and wide acceptance of the unreached people group strategy within the COMIBAM ranks.

Establishing indigenous churches. Perhaps the greatest contribution that U.S. missiology offered the Ibero American missionary movement was the concept of establishing indigenous churches in the mission field. This was, in fact, the primary purpose of *Misionología*: to present the principles for establishing indigenous churches as the key factor for success in cross-cultural mission (Pate, 1987).

The concept of indigenous churches can be traced back to two Anglican churchmen. Henry Venn (1796-1873), who was the Secretary of the Church Missionary Society from 1846 to 1873, is considered the father of the indigenous church principle: self-supporting, self-governing, and self-propagating (Shenk, 2000). An indigenous church is one that supports itself without foreign aid, is led by its own people rather than by a foreign missionary, and has the ability to multiply itself into other churches. Roland Allen (1868-1947), an English missionary to China, in 1912 published the book *Missionary Methods: St. Paul's or Ours?* The most recent edition of this work was published in 1962. Allen (1962) argued that St. Paul planted churches and equipped them to continue to function with permanence. Allen published a second work titled *The Spontaneous Expansion of the Church: And the Causes that Hinder it*. In a groundbreaking manner, Allen (1997) declared, "If the Church is to be indigenous it must spring up in the soil from the very first seeds planted," (p. 2) and "If we want to see spontaneous expansion we must establish native Churches free from our control" (p. 5). All contemporary work on indigenous churches, church planting and church growth stems from the original thinking of these missionary practitioners.

Smalley (1978), whose article was included in *Perspectives on the World Christian Movement,* affirmed Roland Allen's works but was critical of the three-self criteria. Smalley (1978) argued that it is possible for a church to be self-governing, self-supporting and self-propagating without being a truly indigenous church if it has not been contextualized culturally. Lewis (1990c) credits Smalley with the following definition of an indigenous church, "A group of believers who live their lives, including their social Christian activity, following the model provided by the local society, and for whom any social transformation derives from their perceived needs, under the direction of the Holy Spirit and the Bible" (p. 166). Pate (1987) essentially presented Smalley's definition and offered the same criticism of the three-self criteria. The indigenous church concept for church planting was a positive missiological contribution to the Ibero American missionary movement. Londoño (2006b) stated that planting indigenous and autonomous churches was the goal of the missionary enterprise, defining such churches as self-supported, self-governed and self-propagating. The extent to which Ibero American missionaries have been successful in planting indigenous churches as a result of their own cross-cultural efforts requires further research.

Strategies for cross-cultural evangelism. Strategies and organization for cross-cultural evangelism represent the fourth dominant theme of the U.S. missiology that influenced the COMIBAM movement. This theme occupied almost half of Pate's (1987) contents. The detailed treatment of planning, setting measurable goals, strategizing and organizing for cross-cultural mission demonstrated the pragmatic nature of this missiological paradigm. The local church base in Latin America required a practical missiology. Interestingly, Matamoros (2006) noted at COMIBAM's first general assembly in 2000, that one of the greatest areas of need in the current Latin American missions movement was the lack of planning and goal setting on the field.

According to Pate (1987), developing strategies for cross-cultural evangelism is based on the focus on people groups, the ability to measure the receptivity to the gospel in a particular people group and the relationship between faith and goal-setting. The respect for the cultural context was a strong aspect of this paradigm. Escobar (2002) offered a Christological basis for this, "That's why at different stages and in different contexts mission has been affected by the social process surrounding it…Jesus did not understand his own mission and work apart from the divine initiative that is at work in the world" (p. 45).

Pate (1987) offered a model for cross-cultural evangelism strategy planning that followed a sequential order: (a) selection and study of a people group, (b) selection and training of a team, (c) determination of methods, (d) development of strategy, (e) execution of the plan, and (f) evaluation of results. The agency-driven emphasis is evident in Pate's treatment of organization for cross-cultural mission. The author defined four types of organizations: the missionary church, the missionary agency, the receiving church, and the daughter missionary agency and provided instructions on how these organizations should work and relate to one another. In contrast, Escobar (2002) argued that the creation of para-church agencies for evangelism and missions was a deficiency of the Protestant model of missions, which, having its roots in the Pietist revival, is a result of extreme individualism.

The pragmatism that characterized this U.S. missiological current provided a helpful paradigm for Latin American leaders whose concern was missionary mobilization and whose base consisted of the local churches rather than theological institutions. The COMIBAM movement received the biblical basis, the emphasis on unreached people groups, the concept of planting indigenous churches and the practical strategies for cross-cultural evangelism from its partners in the North. Nevertheless, COMIBAM leaders did so with careful reflection. They adapted and developed their own hybrid brand of missiology.

COMIBAM Publications from the Acapulco Congress Forward

During the years surrounding the second congress in Acapulco, Mexico, COMIBAM published several books. These publications were both prescriptive and descriptive of the Ibero American missionary movement. Several of these books were a compilation of papers presented at conferences. Others were adaptations of portions of *Perspectives on the World Christian Movement*. A couple of paperbacks were expositions of COMIBAM's vision and strategy. As such these represent the official missiological position of COMIBAM. The list of books with respective information for each is shown in Table 5.

Table 5

COMIBAM Publications from the Acapulco Congress Forward

Publication	Author/Editor	Year	Description
El despertar de las misiones [The awakening of missions]	Bertuzzi	1997	A collection of papers the author presented at various mission conferences
Misión transcultural [Cross-cultural mission]	Bertuzzi	2000	The collection of papers presented at the Fourth Latin American Congress of Evangelization (CLADE IV) in Quito, Ecuador, September 2 through 8, 2000

Publication	Author/Editor	Year	Description
Manual de estructuras de envío: Conclusiones de la consulta continental de estructuras de envío, Ciudad de Panamá, febrero 11, 12 y 13 de 2003 [Sending mechanisms: Conclusions reached at the continental consultation on sending mechanisms, Panama City, February 11, 12 & 13, 2003]	Londoño	2003	Self-explanatory
Visión por las naciones [Vision for the nations]	DeCarvalho	2003	A manual prepared with the permission of the U.S. Center for World Mission in Pasadena, California, which essentially condenses the three *Misión Mundial* [World Mission] volumes into one very thin booklet.
El espíritu de COMIBAM [The COMIBAM spirit]	Ekström	2002	The collection of presentations made at the First COMIBAM General Assembly in Lima, Peru, November 13 through 18, 2000
Alcance una etnia [Reach a people group]	Londoño	2002	A description of COMIBAM's adopted strategy for unreached people groups and a report of the current goals and progress of the movement
Hacia una misionología evangélica Latinoamericana: Bases bíblicas de la misión (Antiguo Testamento) [Toward a Latin American Evangelical missiology: Biblical bases for the mission (Old Testament)]	Nuñez	1997	Although Nuñez was a member of the FTL, this project was commissioned by COMIBAM

Publication	Author/Editor	Year	Description
Guía para los movimientos misioneros nacionales: Una orientación para su formación y fortalecimiento [Guide for the national mission movements: An orientation for their formation and strengthening]	Ruiz	1997	Self-descriptive

Most of these books reflect insights from U.S. missiology similar to the indebtedness found in Pate's (1987) *Misionología* and in Lewis' (1990) *Misión Mundial.* Nevertheless the expositors reflected critically on U.S. missionary ideology and practice. Nuñez' (1997) wrote entirely from a Latin American perspective. *Misión Transcultural* represented one of the best efforts at missiological dialogue that included both U.S. and Latin American models. In general the authors of these publications clearly owned their missiological positions, whether they gave origin to the ideas or whether they adapted them from U.S. models.

The Ibero American missionary movement had matured since the days of its first congress in Sao Paulo. The number of missionaries, the denominations they represented, the countries they came from and the places where they served demonstrated a truly continental movement. The presenters and topics at the second congress and the publications at this time revealed a movement that was living in the tension of missiological reflection and missionary mobilization and of U.S. and Latin American missiological models. The strength of the continental movement related directly to the strength of the national movements.

National Mission Movements

COMIBAM International sought to be the network of national mission mobilization networks in Ibero America. Ibero American leaders labeled these national networks *movimientos misioneros nacionales* [national missionary movements] and often referred to them by their Spanish language initials: MMN. Around the time of the first congress, COMIBAM inspired at least thirty national missionary consultations and congresses to convene throughout Ibero America. These are listed in Appendix G. These consultations and congresses cast the vision and fueled the missionary sparks in the various countries. Before the second congress, Argentina, Bolivia, Brazil, Chile, Colombia, Costa Rica, the Dominican Republic, Ecuador, El Salvador, Guatemala, Honduras, Mexico, Nicaragua, Panama, Paraguay, Peru, Portugal, Puerto Rico, the U.S. and Canada, Spain, Uruguay and Venezuela had formally organized their networks. Chapter 3 includes additional information on this subject. In this important next phase, how did the vision and fervor shared in the individual countries after the Sao Paulo congress result in missionary mobilization? How many of these national mission movements successfully sustained the mobilization vision until the time of the Acapulco congress and to what extent?

The reports of the national mission movements to the second COMIBAM congress reveal the status of the vision and the mobilization progress in each country. The organizers invited national mission movements to conduct evaluation meetings prior to the congress and to report their findings at the Acapulco meeting (Ekström, 2006). Seventeen countries submitted their findings: Argentina, Brazil, Canada, Chile, Colombia, Costa Rica, Dominican Republic, Ecuador, Guatemala, Honduras, Mexico,

Nicaragua, Paraguay, Peru, Portugal, Puerto Rico and Venezuela. Most of these national mission networks shared similar experiences and concerns. They identified a growing awareness of the missionary task. Some of them reported significant progress in the training and sending of missionaries. All the reports lamented that the progress was minimal in comparison to the potential and the resources available. The lack of pastoral care for missionaries and the lack of cooperation between churches and missionary agencies constituted the greatest concern for the national missionary networks. National leaders demonstrated humility and a desire to reach their full potential. All of these networks committed themselves to greater cooperation and to higher involvement in encouraging and training churches.

The reports submitted by the national networks at the Acapulco congress counted on the broad participation of national leaders from various denominations, local churches, missionary agencies and para-church organizations (Bertuzzi, 2001). They provide a valid assessment of the status for the national mission movements. The strength of each national mission movement may be estimated in part by the numerical participation at the evaluation meetings. Argentina counted with approximately 500 individuals, Mexico with 723 and Puerto Rico with 180, placing these three countries in a high-participation level (Bertuzzi, 2001). Ninety-two people attended the Nicaragua evaluation meeting, 90 attended the one in Costa Rica and 35 attended the meeting in Peru (Bertuzzi, 2001).

Cooperation between Churches and Missionary Agencies

The Argentina, Brazil, Chile, Ecuador, Mexico and Venezuela networks reported the need and the desire for more effective communication and cooperation between church and missionary organizations (Bertuzzi, 2001). The Ecuador group included the foreign agencies in their concern for improved communication. National leadership for Brazil, Canada, Costa Rica, Guatemala, Mexico, Puerto Rico lamented the lack of pastoral care for missionaries and noted the premature return of missionaries from the field. The recognition of the need for improved cooperation between churches and missionary agencies evidenced maturity in each of these countries since they were far enough along the process to identify the need and perceptive enough to acknowledge it.

Comprehensive Missionary Training

Several of the national networks perceived the need for a more comprehensive missionary training process and for missionary training centers to work in coordination with the churches. Brazil, Costa Rica, Mexico, Puerto Rico related this concern (Bertuzzi, 2001). Chile celebrated the existence of 12 institutes and 29 denominational and interdenominational entities for missionary training but also regretted the limited access of missionary training due to geography. Costa Rica similarly recommended expanding the location of its training centers from urban areas to open branches in the rural areas as well. Guatemala indicated that its training centers existed only in the capital city and recommended that churches provide the practical training for missionaries in cooperation with the training centers. Venezuela simply rejoiced that theological institutions and training centers were doing the necessary theological reflection and missiological training. Clearly the national movements were concerned with improving the training process for missionaries but the establishing of training centers marked significant progress.

Enlistment and Screening of Missionary Candidates

National leaders in some of the networks acknowledged that, in addition to missionary training, missionary enlistment and screening were critical for either the permanence of the missionaries on the field or for their premature return. The Costa Rican leaders expressed the need for greater cooperation in the screening process. The Mexican network called for the wider use by missionary agencies and local churches of a screening instrument called the *Profile of the Mexican Missionary*. Puerto Rican national leaders expressed the same desire in regard to the *Profile for the Ideal Puerto Rican Missionary* and for a comprehensive screening process that would result in better match of missionaries to the respective mission fields. National leaders grew in their concern for the well being of both missionaries and the mission field in which they served.

The More Advanced National Mission Movements

Several national mission movements reported positive strides in missionary mobilization. The missionary networks in Chile, Costa Rica, Mexico, Puerto Rico and Venezuela displayed great maturity. Chile gladly announced that 88 cross-cultural missionaries were serving on the field, even while it recognized that this did not reflect the full potential of the country (Bertuzzi, 2001).

Costa Rica credited their success in part to the ten-year-old FEDEMEC, the interdenominational missionary agency created alongside the first COMIBAM congress (Bertuzzi, 2001). This Costa Rican agency gave continuity to the process of mobilization promotion, missionary training, missionary sending, and missionary support. FEDEMEC contributed to the sending of thirty-two missionaries during its first decade. This success was very significant for an agency completely indigenous to Costa Rica and which is not supported by any particular denomination. Costa Rica provided an exceptional opportunity to measure the success of the COMIBAM movement. Beyond the role of

FEDEMEC, the national movement in Costa Rica counted on the involvement of local churches and several para-church and missionary organizations such as IMDELA, JUCUM, CPC, and Etno (Bertuzzi, 2001).

Mexico expressed some of the same needs as the other national movements, but also exhibited maturity in strategic thinking. The Mexican network committed to intentionally seek, screen and train missionary candidates through local churches and to send thousands of them to the unreached people groups in Mexico and around the world (Bertuzzi, 2001). Puerto Rican leaders celebrated the awakening of missionary fervor in the country, committed to helping churches increase the financial support of missions, and identified *Centro Puertorriqueño de Misiones Mundiales* [Puerto Rican Center for World Missions] (CPMM), and declared their objective of establishing indigenous and autonomous churches in the missionary enterprise (Bertuzzi, 2001).

Venezuelan national leaders confessed their deep concern for the conditions of poverty, injustice, spiritual oppression, violence and insecurity among their population (Bertuzzi, 2001). A state of disunity in the Venezuelan evangelical church and a lack of missionary vision among its leaders accompanied these contextual challenges. Yet, the Venezuelan national movement possessed one of the clearest strategies. Missionary work consisted of simultaneously reaching indigenous people groups in Venezuela; the large cities; the marginalized, namely the poor, orphans, prisoners and children in the streets; and unreached people groups (Bertuzzi, 2001). As Venezuelan leaders rejoiced in the 100 missionaries who were currently serving, they vowed to keep sending more missionaries to the 10/40 Window. Subsequently the Venezuelan network established the following bold goals: (a) increase the involvement of churches in the missionary task from 10% to 50%, (b) double the amount of missionaries sent in five years, (c) establish five additional missionary training centers, (d) establish at least three more missionary agencies which would focus on Venezuela indigenous people groups and/or on the unreached people groups of the 10/40 window, (e) strengthen and develop the Venezuelan Association of Missionary Churches and Agencies to facilitate greater efforts in the missionary enterprise (Bertuzzi, 2001). These idealistic goals betrayed an enormous passion for the missionary cause on behalf of Venezuelan national leaders.

The Less Mature National Mission Movements

A few of the national networks struggled to sustain the missionary vision and mobilization. The national mission movements in Canada, Colombia, the Dominican Republic, Ecuador, Honduras and Paraguay made relatively little progress after the Sao Paulo congress.

The national network in Canada reported that only two percent of its churches were sending missionaries and that the percentage that was actually going cross-cultural was less (Bertuzzi, 2001). Canadian national leaders complained about the indifference of churches and called for COMHINA, the COMIBAM expression in North America, to increase its efforts of informing and mobilizing churches (Bertuzzi, 2001). The Colombian group recognized that churches, pastors and leaders had not been making the missionary mandate a priority and lamented the lack of knowledge and information about missions (Bertuzzi, 2001). Dominican leaders emphasized that evangelicals only accounted for five percent of the country's population (Bertuzzi, 2001). Additionally, according to these leaders, most evangelicals in the Dominican Republic considered that they did not have the resources or the ability to engage the missionary task. In spite of these challenges, missionary conferences in 1995 and 1996 strengthened the catalyzing of the missionary vision in the Dominican Republic. On a positive note, fifteen Dominicans were serving in the mission field, although most of them lacked the support of a local church or missionary organization (Bertuzzi, 2001).

Ecuadorian national leadership underscored administrative challenges in the primary national missionary agency, *Asociación Misionera Evangélica Ecuatoriana* [Ecuadorian Evangelical Missionary Association] (AMEE), aspiring to overcome a narrow denominationalism, a heavy dependency on foreign economical support, and a lack of missionary vision among pastors (Bertuzzi, 2001). The Honduran network gratefully acknowledged the formation of the *Federación Misionera Evangélica de Honduras* [Honduras Evangelical Missionary Federation] (FEMEH) and yet commented on the lack of missionary vision in the country and asked for other national movements to help them (Bertuzzi, 2001).

Nicaraguan national leaders addressed the lack of teaching and motivation about cross-cultural missions, the lack of missionary vision among pastors and denominational leaders, the minimal missionary financial support by churches, the minimal amount of cross-cultural missionaries and the lack of adequate intercessory prayer for world missions (Bertuzzi, 2001). The Paraguay national missions leaders also admitted the challenges of numerical disadvantage, the lack of adequate missionary vision (Bertuzzi, 2001). Notwithstanding, these leaders proactively accepted the responsibility of planting churches among the least reached within their own country, cooperating with others to avoid duplication of efforts, praying for unreached people groups and for the calling out of missionaries from among their churches, and identifying *Comité Nacional de Misiones*

[National Missions Committee] (CONAMI) as the cohesive instrument for missionary mobilization in Paraguay (Bertuzzi, 2001).

Evidently the challenges that national missionary movements faced were many. The willingness of national network leaders to be honest about the progress of mission mobilization revealed maturity in understanding the vision of what could be. Additionally, the fact that leaders could identify the specific needs to address in order to improve mission mobilization in their own countries displayed a significant measure of progress.

The reports of the national mission movements at the Acapulco congress proved very informative. Many of these national networks shared similar concerns and challenges. Not all of the countries moved at the same pace. While perhaps vision and enthusiasm waned in some of the regions, yet, more training centers, more mission agencies, and more churches were cooperating than ever before in sending more missionaries around the world.

COMIBAM Meetings Between Congresses

The Acapulco congress marked a significant milestone for the COMIBAM movement. An important contribution of the congress was that it identified issues of concern that required follow up. These issues included a need for more missiological reflection, the pastoral care of missionaries, the inclusion of the national movements in the COMIBAM process, and the strategy for reaching the unreached people groups. The year 2000 produced four significant meetings to address these issues. The FTL sponsored CLADE IV and invited COMIBAM leaders to participate. COMIBAM convened its First Consultation on the Pastoral Care of Missionaries and the First

COMIBAM General Assembly. The same year the Reach a People Group committee met to evaluate and refine its strategy. Each of these meetings contributed significantly to the development of the movement.

CLADE IV

The Fourth Latin American Congress for Evangelization (CLADE IV) took place with the participation of approximately one hundred evangelical leaders, September 2-8, 2000, in Quito, Ecuador. The purpose of this meeting was a reflection on the cross-cultural mission from a Latin American context (Amado, 2006). Out of concern for an over dependence upon the influence of North American missionary practice, and to avoid any paternalistic control on the newly developing Latin American missionary movement, the FTL sponsored this congress (Amado, 2006). The FTL invited COMIBAM and *Pueblos Musulmanes* [Muslim Peoples] (PM) International leaders to this discussion forum including: David Ruíz of COMIBAM; Paul Davies; Tito Paredes of the FTL; Federico Bertuzzi, a leader in COMIBAM and PM; and Pablo Carrillo of PM (Bertuzzi, 2006c). The meeting raised serious questions: How could the holistic mission model relate to the cross-cultural emphasis? What was the basis and the nature of the cross-cultural mission from Latin America? How would the North relate to the South in the advancement of the mission? David Ruíz, Paul Davies, Tito Paredes and Federico Bertuzzi addressed these questions at CLADE IV, providing dialogue and a rich diversity of viewpoints

David Ruíz (2006a), COMIBAM president at the time of CLADE IV, advocated the legitimacy of the cross-cultural mission. Ruíz (2006a) argued that the nature of the cross-cultural mission was connected to the historical origin of multiple cultures and languages (Genesis11:7-8), the cross-cultural nature of Israel's call (Genesis 12:1-3; Exodus 19:5-6; 1 Kings 8:42-43), the incarnational model of Jesus Christ (Hebrews 1:2), and the four-fold mandate to the church in the Gospels (Matthew 28:18-20; Mark 16:15; Luke 24:27 and John 20:21-23. Thus, on primarily biblical bases, Ruíz asserted convincingly that the cross-cultural mission of Christianity is unique in that it possesses a timeless message for the nations and which is translatable to every culture and people.

Pablo Davies (2006) presented the Old Testament bases for cross-cultural mission. He proposed that God's mission of saving all nations is the unifying element of its thirty-nine books. Davies (2006) provided four segments of this unifying element. First, God's ideal (Genesis 1-2) was that man would relate personally to Him, live in community, and live in a harmonious environment. Secondly, the arrival of sin (Genesis 3-11) brought about disobedience, fear and shame in regard to God, affected man's ability to live in community, and introduced a curse on creation, namely the environment. Thirdly, God's provision to man's problem was the selection of one nation that would be a blessing to all nations (Genesis 12:1-3, 18:17-21; Exodus 19:5-6; Deuteronomy 4:5-8). Fourthly, the mission of the Old Testament prophets consisted of returning Israel to its covenantal relationship so that the nations would know that the Lord was God (Psalm 33; Ezekiel 36:18-30). Davies (2006) concluded that the Old Testament demonstrates that mission is both cross-cultural and holistic, and that to focus on one dimension only it is to be either colonialist or selfish, respectively. Davies successfully established a case for the cross-cultural nature of the mission in the Old Testament. His acknowledgment that the mission is both cross-cultural and holistic reveals a thoughtful approach to merge missiological models.

Tito Paredes (2006), of the FTL, presented the New Testament basis for the cross-cultural mission at CLAVE IV. Paredes (2006) introduced the incarnation of Christ as the paradigmatic model for the cross-cultural mission (John 1:1-2; Philippians 2:6-7). He built his case primarily from the book of Acts. Referring to the Day of Pentecost (Acts 2), the conflict between the Hebrew-speaking and the Greek-speaking widows (Acts 6:1-7), the proclamation of the gospel to the Gentiles by the scattered believers (Acts 8:4—12:25), the encounter of Peter and Cornelius (Acts 10), and the Jerusalem Council (Acts 15), Paredes offers several conclusions. These seven statements offered sound missiological principles to the Ibero American movement:

1. The gospel of Jesus Christ is not the monopoly of one people but it has been everything to all peoples of the earth.

2. All the church of Jesus Christ in all the world is called to participate in the cross-cultural mission.

3. Getting rid of our cultural ethnocentrism is a fundamental step in the cross-cultural mission.

4. A deep love for people and their culture is crucial to the cross-cultural mission.

5. We should develop the willingness to see the grace and general revelation at work in other cultures.

6. We should assume a servant not a bossy or know-it-all attitude.

7. The cross-cultural mission implies that the whole church takes the whole gospel to all the peoples (pp. 52-53).

Thus, Paredes capably provided the basis for the cross-cultural mission within the framework of a holistic mission paradigm.

Bertuzzi (2006c) addressed the issue of the cooperation between U.S. missionary agencies and the Latin American mission. This matter greatly concerned leaders in the Ibero American movement. The cross-cultural mission included also the cross-cultural collaboration between missionaries and missionary agencies from different parts of the world. The tension that existed between some North American missionaries and Latin American leaders was an underlying theme of the COMIBAM dialogue. Few of the leaders discussed the issue as overtly as Federico Bertuzzi did. At CLADE IV, the COMIBAM leader from Argentina referred to this tension as the "Internationalization or the anglicizing of the mission" (Bertuzzi, 2006c, pp. 55-56). While Bertuzzi (2006c) expressed gratitude for the North American missionaries who pioneered evangelical missions in Latin America since the late nineteenth century, he questioned the role of newly arrived missionary agencies. Furthermore, he acknowledged the contributions made by the North American missionaries, namely Bible translation, church planting, numerous construction projects, and the establishment of Christian institutions for various purposes, but he also lamented that these same missionaries did not adequately teach Latin Americans financial stewardship, or engagement in cross-cultural mission, or civic participation. In regard to the resurgence of North American missionary agencies in Latin America, Bertuzzi classified them as to their level of collaboration with Latin Americans. He called the first group the Anglo-affiliation model because the North American organization simply opens a branch in the South. The second model he designated participative because the North American organization establishes a partnership of sorts with Latin Americans. The third one Bertuzzi (2006c) calls the servant model because the North American organization makes itself available to the leadership of local pastors and leaders. The preferred model is this third one. Bertuzzi (2006c) identified two negative factors that run counter to this kind of desired cooperation: North American paternalism and Latin American opportunism. In essence, this Argentine pastor and leader invited North American missionaries and Latin American leaders to recognize the cross-cultural challenges of working together, the immense disparity in power and resources, and the need to work together with mutual respect. The willingness to address this elephant-in-the-room demonstrated the readiness and the earnestness of Latin American leaders to take their proper role in the global mission task.

The COMIBAM and FTL leaders who met at CLADE IV arrived at several practical conclusions after the close of their meeting. These recommendations included recasting the vision of the missionary nature of the church it is own context and to all nations, the developing of curricula at missionary training centers that can reconcile theological reflection and missiological praxis, the close cooperation of missionary agency as servants of the local church, the holistic mission of the church which includes all the elements of *missio Dei,* and the cooperation between missionary agencies from North America and Latin American mission leaders (Bertuzzi, 2006c). Thus, CLADE IV stands as a defining moment for the development of a Latin American model of cross-cultural mission. Thirteen years after the first congress, the missionary mobilization movement in Latin America had reached a new stage of maturity.

First COMIBAM Consultation on the Pastoral Care of Missionaries

As the mission sending movement from Ibero America matured, leaders perceptively identified new needs. COMIBAM leaders took these discoveries seriously and followed through with consultations to understand the issues better and also to develop action plans to address them. One of the significant issues that had preoccupied the mission mobilization networks was the pastoral care of missionaries. In the year 2000, three years after the Acapulco congress, COMIBAM held its first consultation on the pastoral care of missionaries in Lima, Peru (Ekström, 2006; Tostes, 2006). The movement had focused on inspiring, training and sending missionaries but now it recognized a new need. This new challenge consisted of keeping those missionaries on the field and ensuring their holistic health (Matamoros, 2006). The COMIBAM '97 congress identified this need (Tostes, 2006). At this same congress COMIBAM leaders decided to assign a team for the development of missionary pastoral care (Tostes, 2006). The First Consultation on the Pastoral Care of Missionaries listed the following areas of need regarding missionaries on the field: emotional support, presence of leaders, situational conflict resolution training, inter-personal conflict resolution training, decision-making skills under difficult circumstances, and greater personal security (Tostes, 2006). The COMIBAM movement, which had not focused on this area at the onset, responsibly developed programs and resources to address this important need during the second decade of its existence. The pastoral care of missionaries remained a priority for the network during this period and beyond the third congress.

First COMIBAM General Assembly

The COMIBAM movement needed a venue to include grassroots leaders and a process for making decisions in order to have sustainability as a network. The General Assembly became the avenue for this aspect of the COMIBAM work. The able leadership of David Ruiz and Bertil Ekström guided the network to organize a meeting of national network leaders. In conjunction with the consultation on the pastoral care of the missionary, COMIBAM held its First General Assembly. This meeting took place November 13-18, 2000 in Lima, Peru (Ekström, 2006). General Assemblies were different in nature and in constituency than the Congresses. Congresses were mass meetings that sought to cast vision and to inspire large groups of people. In contrast, this first general assembly, which consisted of 125 delegates from 25 countries, sought to describe COMIBAM's identity, to open up decision making and leader selection to national representatives, and to identify the challenges for the future (Ekström, 2006). This assembly featured topics such as the COMIBAM spirit, the viability of the Reach a People Group program, the pastoral care of the missionary, the identity and location of missionaries, and the role of pastors and churches in the missionary task. The presenters at this meeting included Bertil Ekström, Hugo C. Morales, Jesús Londoño, Marcia Tostes, Allan Matamoros and David Ruíz (Ekström, 2006). At the opening session of the assembly, Bertil Ekström (2006) remarked on the historical significance of such a meeting particularly because of the shift in philosophy toward being a grass-roots movement that would have greater participation from the national missionary movements. This significant step in organizational leadership secured greater ownership of the movement by national leaders and provided sustainability for the network.

There was a sense of optimism at this first general assembly. Morales (2006) rejoiced in the great number of missionaries that had been sent from Latin America, the people groups that were being reached, and the strengthening of the sending/supporting base. Referring to the increasing amount of missionary zeal and activity taking place, Matamoros (2006) said, "Missions today is bubbling over like boiling water in many parts of our continent" (p. 49). The same presenter reported that the significant growth of missionary sending had also opened the way for research projects, networks, partnerships and missiological discussions, including the nature of the desired relationship between North and South. According to Morales (2006) Latin American missionaries found that it was to their advantage that they were seen as politically neutral and because they were themselves economically poor it was easier to identify in the least-reached mission fields. This optimism was mixed with realism.

One of the presenters analyzed where Latin American missionaries were serving at the time. Using Limpic's (1997) statistical report, Matamoros (2006) highlighted that (a) the twelve countries with the greatest representation of Latin cross-cultural missionaries were in Ibero America; (b) more than seventy-five percent of all Latin missionaries (approximately 3,000) were serving in these twelve countries; (c) the eleven percent of the Latin missionaries that were serving in the 10/40 window were mostly in Morocco, Senegal, India, China and Japan; (d) there was a significant presence of Latin missionaries in Eastern Europe, Russia, and Sub-Saharan Africa; and (e) while most of the missionaries had been sent by Latin American organizations or organizations with Latin American leaders, the receiving missionary agencies, especially in the unreached parts of the world, were not Latin American. For the presenter these realities were reasons for celebrating and cues to the opportunities that lay ahead for the Latin American missionary movement.

This first assembly was also an opportunity to deal with two themes that had developed interest at the COMIBAM level: Reach a People Group and the pastoral care of missionaries. The Reach a People Group concept was a developing program of the movement by the time of the first general assembly. The presentation on the topic given at this assembly was an attempt to establish a biblical and spiritual rationale for the program, either in response to criticism or in an effort to contextualize this foreign concept for Ibero America. Jesús Londoño (2006a) argued for the need to start with a biblical basis for the missionary task. Londoño (2006a) referenced Genesis 1-11,12; John 4:32-35; Acts 1:8, 2:1-21, 37-47; and 1 Peter 1:20 to present God's redemptive purpose for the world. While the presenter succeeded in providing biblical support for the concept that God's salvific purpose for the world has been eternal, he did not provide specific support for the Adopt a People Group program. Additionally, Londoño (2006a) acknowledged the need for spirituality in advancing the mission in order to keep the church from mere activism. In treating the biblical and spiritual bases for the mission like this, Londoño effectively provides a moderate alternative of the Reach a People Group concept, in contrast with a purely pragmatic approach.

The pastoral care of missionaries discussion included a list of the needs that had been identified at the first consultation on the subject and the list of projects which program leaders set out to develop: communication, connections, training, publications, resource network and regional/national consultations (Tostes, 2006). From his close observation of *Federación Evangélica Misionera de Costa Rica* [Evangelical Missionary Federation of Costa Rica] (FEDEMEC), Matamoros (2006) noted that missionaries on the field were experiencing difficulty in inter-personal relationships, and lacked pastoral care and spiritual vibrancy. These two programmatic developments, Reach a People Group and the pastoral care of missionaries, demonstrated both the strategic direction of COMIBAM and that the movement continued to mature.

In addition to the relevant reflections offered by Londoño, Tostes and Matamoros, the first general assembly counted on another significant contribution to missiological development. David Ruíz, COMIBAM's president during that period, offered a healthy and holistic missiological posture. First, Ruíz (2006b) proposed that obedience to the mission was not only obedience to the Great Commission but to personal transformation, a call for believers to shine as examples of transformed lives who point to Christ as the only hope. Secondly, Ruíz (2006b) spoke of a paradigm shift in his own thinking where the motivation of the church for mission is not primarily the need of the world but the justification for the church's own existence on earth. This was a move toward an understanding of the *missio Dei,* in other words, that the mission belongs to God not to the church. Thirdly, as COMIBAM's president, Ruíz suggested that missionary vision has a dual dimension: a vertical one that sees God's holiness as the transforming power and a horizontal that demonstrates God's love to humanity by means of acts of service and the testimony of a transformed life (Ruíz, 2006b). Fourthly, Ruíz (2006b) insisted on the centrality of the local church and the importance of pastoral leadership for the advancement of the mission. These statements demonstrated a healthy and holistic missiological posture. There was not a narrow focus on numerical growth and the efficiency of the mission but a genuine concern for discipleship, spirituality and love as the conduits of the mission. Ruíz's treatment of the centrality of the local church for mission was more in line with a holistic missiology than with an agency-driven paradigm of mission.

The First General Assembly advanced the movement organizationally as a network. The gathering offered decision-making participation to national network leaders. In addition, leaders dealt with program development and continued to reflect on issues of missiological significance. The content of the presentations at this general assembly provided further evidence that, although COMIBAM identified itself as a mobilization network, the COMIBAM agenda included missiological reflection.

Reach-a-People-Group Committee Strategy Meeting

In the year 2000, the COMIBAM Reach a People Group committee met in Guatemala (Londoño, 2006b). The Reach-a-People-Group program was originally named Adopt-a-People. The committee included national missionary movement directors, COMIBAM International leaders and Reach a People Group coordinators. This group evaluated the program and developed new strategies for its implementation. Londoño traced the development of the Reach a People Group program along several COMIBAM-related meetings after the First Congress. The COMIBAM-related meetings after the First Congress where the Reach a People Group program was progressively developed are shown in Table 6.

COMIBAM had made a commitment in San Jose, Costa Rica to Adopt-a-People group strategy shortly after its first congress (Bertuzzi, 2006a). The San Jose Declaration, shown in Appendix A, manifested the commitment of Ibero American leaders to the Adopt-a-People strategy (Londoño, 2006b).

Table 6

Development of COMIBAM's Adopt-a-People-Group program (Londoño, 2006b)

Meeting	Development
CLAME '90 (Orlando, Florida)	Focus on unreached people groups with special emphasis on Muslims.
First Ibero American Consultation on Adopt a People (San Jose, Costa Rica), 1992	The cross-cultural missionary task for Ibero America was defined as the adoption of unreached people groups and made a commitment to adopt 3,000 of the 11,000 unreached people groups.
First Ibero American Consultation on Missionary Agencies and Churches (Panama), 1994	The unreached people groups became an objective of the cooperation between agencies and churches.
COMIBAM '97 (Acapulco, Mexico)	Conducted an evaluation of the processes and methods being used to reach the unreached.
Reach a People Group Committee Strategy Meeting (Guatemala) 2000	Evaluation of the Reach a People Group program and development of new strategies for its implementation.

The Adopt-a-People consultation was a joint effort of COMIBAM and the *Confraternidad Evangélica Latinoamericana* [Latin American Evangelical Fellowship] (CONELA), bringing together 75 researchers, national leaders of various evangelical and missionary networks from 21 countries to develop a strategy for adopting unreached people groups (Bertuzzi, 2006a). CONELA had close relationships with the Billy Graham Evangelistic Association, the World Evangelical Fellowship, and the Luís Palau Evangelistic Association. The consultation resulted in a continental commitment to adopt 3,000 unreached people groups (Londoño, 2006b). This covenant included the proportionate distribution among Spanish and Portuguese-speaking countries of the 3,000 unreached people groups. The distribution for each of the countries is listed in Appendix B. Later, in an effort to emphasize the urgency of the task, COMIBAM changed the name of the program to Reach a People Group (Londoño, 2006b).

COMIBAM demonstrated its commitment to the Reach a People program by disseminating the ten-step strategy that the Reach a People committee developed. The strategic focus had changed from assigning a proportionate number of people groups per Ibero American country to urging and equipping local churches to reach one unreached people group. COMIBAM leaders correctly recognized by the second decade of the movement that the local church and her leadership were the key for implementing the strategy. The ten steps outlined for local churches to reach a people group were: (a) cast the vision about the unreached; (b) teach the local church her responsibility in regard to the unreached; (c) identify a profile for a people group to be considered; (d) intercede for the unreached; (e) train the church to pray, give and listen regularly for God's call; (f) decide upon an unreached people group to adopt with an appropriate church ceremony; (g) select and train the candidate(s) that fit the profile for the unreached people group to be reached; (h) seek cooperation with existing organizations that relate to the adopted people group; (i) send the cross-cultural missionary out; and (j) reach the people group by evangelizing, discipling and establishing an indigenous church (Londoño, 2006b). These ten steps communicated with clarity and thoroughness the Reach a People Group strategy to churches and national missionary movements. Beyond casting the vision about the unreached world, this process provided a quantifiable way to measure progress for the local church, the national networks and the Ibero American movement in general.

Shortly after the Acapulco congress, COMIBAM leaders managed to address most of the identified concerns. The CLADE IV, the First Consultation on the Pastoral Care of Missionaries, the First COMIBAM General Assembly and the Reach a People Group Committee strategy meeting attained a clearer biblical-theological foundation for the cross-cultural mission, closer participation by national leaders in the COMIBAM process, and developing programs for the pastoral care of missionaries and for reaching the unreached people groups. The leadership of COMIBAM during this era proved to be decisive and proactive.

Leaders and Leadership

A roll call of the continental leaders of the COMIBAM movement during this era includes David Ruíz, Bertil Ekström, Rudy Girón, Jonathan Lewis, Edison Queiroz, Federico Bertuzzi, and Jesús Londoño among many others. As Luís Bush expanded his leadership to the global missions movement, he distanced himself from direct COMIBAM leadership. Most of the continental leaders of this era were pastors who were enthusiastic about mission mobilization. They displayed a commitment to the Bible, a concern for applied missiology, a readiness for reflection and dialogue, and an ability to adapt missiological concepts to the Ibero American context. COMIBAM leaders encouraged the training of local church leaders and missionaries, facilitated consultations that would address relevant issues, opened pathways for participation in the process and created a network of networks. Along the way they developed a missiological hybrid that included the best practices of the U.S. missionary model and Latin American reflection.

Organizational Development by Leaders

COMIBAM succeeded in carrying out many of its tasks because of important organizational developments. Bertuzzi (2006a) proposed three stages for the development of the missionary movement: missionary awareness, including congresses and consultations; missionary training including local church efforts and seminaries; and channeling of resources including the use of mission agencies and networks. To a large measure these three stages took place during the first years of the COMIBAM movement. After its second congress, the movement needed to evaluate the progress of these stages and to find ways to be more effective. The Acapulco congress and the various consultations that followed served the purpose of evaluating the progress of the first decade and of identifying strategic points for the future.

In order to remain effective, COMIBAM needed to reorganize its leadership structure. COMIBAM leaders, including David Ruíz, Rudy Girón, Bertil Ekström and the board of directors, wisely decided to write by-laws that would give national missionary movements more participation in the process and that would ensure the organization's longevity beyond the charisma of a particular individual (Ekström, 2006). COMIBAM leadership accomplished the division of top leadership into two distinct roles: that of president, or chairman, and that of executive director. Immediately before the Acapulco congress, David Ruíz accepted the invitation to fill the executive director role while Rudy Girón continued to fill the presidency (Ekström, 2006). Since Girón had announced his intention to go serve in Russia, the newly named COMIBAM board of directors elected Bertil Ekström to be its third president the day before the Acapulco congress (Ekström, 2006). Thus, by its second congress, COMIBAM had moved from the personality-driven leadership of Luís Bush and Rudy Girón to the organizational leadership of David Ruíz and Bertil Ekström. Bush and Girón provided a catalyst-type of leadership for the birth of the movement. They cast the vision throughout the continent and the Iberian Peninsula fanning the mission mobilization flames. Ruíz and Ekström built on this foundation and secured sustainability and longevity for the movement. The new COMIBAM leadership was committed to structural changes that would give greater participation to the national missionary movements and to the strengthening of those national networks. The First General Assembly provided the first opportunity for national leaders to participate in the new organizational structure.

Luís Bush: Leadership from COMIBAM to AD2000

During COMIBAM's second decade the significance of Luís Bush's leadership consisted of his involvement in the AD2000 movement. Bush's leadership of the AD2000 & Beyond Movement possesses relevance to the study of COMIBAM primarily for two reasons: A Latin American missions leader becomes a global missions leader, and the AD2000 & Beyond Movement developed after the COMIBAM model. The global missions movement received representation from Ibero American evangelicals through the leadership of Luís Bush.

The COMIBAM congress and the extensive travel that Bush accomplished in preparation for it demonstrated his vision and leadership to other global missions leaders. In March of 1986, while Bush was leading consultations in Central America in preparation for COMIBAM '87, Ralph Winter, founder and director of the U.S. Center for World Mission, featured Bush on the cover of the *Missions Frontiers* magazine (Bush, 2001b; Winter, 1986). As Winter presented the historical significance of the

COMIBAM '87 congress, he pointed to Bush as God's man for God's time, describing Bush's unique biographical profile and arguing that largely due to Bush "Latin Americans evangelicals may very well become some of the great mission mobilizers of the world and take the lead…in the final countdown to the end of history" (Winter, 1986). During the COMIBAM '87 congress in Sao Paulo, Chinese-born Thomas Wang, then international director for the Lausanne Committee for World Evangelization (LCWE), invited Bush to write an article about the principles for world evangelization by the year 2000 (Bush, 2001b). Earlier that year Wang proposed that the year 2000 possessed significance for the completion of the Great Commission (Wang, 1987). Wang and Bush eventually conceptualized and gave leadership to the AD2000 Movement (Bush, 2001b; Bush 2002; Coote, 2000). As Bush moved from leading an Ibero American network to leading the AD2000 worldwide network, he conceptualized the 10/40 Window strategy and contributed to the launching of the Joshua Project 2000 (Bush, 2001b; Bush, 2002; Coote, 2000). AD2000 sponsored two meetings that revealed the huge scope of this partnership mobilization network. The Global Consultation on World Evangelization (GCOWE) '95 met May 1995 in Seoul, Korea drawing 4,000 participants from 186 countries (Bush, 2001b). GCOWE '97 convened in Pretoria, South Africa June 30-July 5 1997 with 4,000 participants from 130 countries (Bush, 2001b). The Argentine-born mobilizer of the Ibero American world had found a much larger arena for missions mobilization and partnership.

The COMIBAM principles and organizational structure served as a model for the AD2000 movement. Bush (2001b) testified,

The week following (COMIBAM '87) I wrote the article based on the principles found in the mobilization of the Exodus and the eight principles that COMIBAM was based on...The vision of AD2000 was ignited in my heart at that time. The basic principles were the ones used during the AD2000 process as follows: the principle of spiritual movement, indigenization, consultation, involvement of every population segment, research of the harvest field and the harvest force, the principle of order and cooperation, encouragement, major event focal point. (pp. 15-16)

Not only did Bush utilize the same principles for AD2000 that he had developed for COMIBAM but the participation and sponsorship of AD2000 came primarily from the majority world. In fact, John Stott (1995) argued that missions mobilization from the Majority World provided the attainability of completing the Great Commission by the year 2000. Endorsing the AD2000 & Beyond goals and referring to the majority world, Stott (1995) wrote: "These may under God not only take the Gospel to the ends of the earth but also revitalize the tired churches of the West" (p. 56). Bush (2002) celebrated the coming of age of the majority world's missionary movement when he wrote:

Indeed, much of the leadership of AD2000, and a majority of its funding, emerged from this Two-Thirds world missionary movement. The biggest financial challenge in the decade was GCOWE 95, held in Seoul, Korea...The Two-Thirds world Christian church demonstrated its full partnership, if not primary initiative, in the cause of world evangelization. Since each delegate was expected to raise his or her own travel costs, the vision was at a fundamental level, grass rooted. In addition, more than seventy percent of the consultation's funding came from

Africa, Asia and Latin America. Not only did the Korean church take up the largest share of any country, but they were also the first to financially support and commit to the primary global thrust proceeding from GCOWE 95, called Joshua Project 2000. (p. 133)

The motifs of COMIBAM '87 echoed less than a decade later in the wider arena of the Majority World.

COMIBAM also modeled for the AD2000 movement its grass-roots network organization. Bush (2002) stated, "The AD2000 organizational structure was essentially a flat network, fastened somewhat elastically together by common purpose and vision, rather than a hierarchical arrangement" (p. 145). Both COMIBAM and AD2000 maintained a flat network structure and a commitment to the grass roots movements. They each recognized the vital role of the local church and of national movements in the task of global missions mobilization. Surely the development of Bush's leadership from local church pastor to international leader of AD2000 & Beyond contributed greatly to his commitment to the local church and the national movements. Bush began his ministerial career as pastor of *Iglesia Nazaret* in San Salvador from 1978 to 1984, a church that planted seven other churches and supported over 35 missionaries (Bush, 2001b; Bush, 2002; Coote, 2000; Winter, 1986). With this missions mobilization experience Bush and his Salvadorian church organized and hosted *Misión 84*, a missions conference with the participation of 1,000 individuals from eleven Latin American countries (Bush, 2001b). After founding the first Salvadorian cross-cultural missionary agency, Bush became the regional coordinator of Christian Nationals, which is now called Partners International. While continuing to pastor *Iglesia Nazaret* and work with

Christian Nationals, Bush accepted the leadership of the nascent COMIBAM movement. The year after COMIBAM '87 Bush became CEO of Partners International and began to develop the strategy for the AD2000 & Beyond Movement. Bush dedicated the decade of the 90s to his leadership of the AD2000 & Beyond Movement. Having participated in missions mobilization at the local church, national, Central American, Ibero American, Majority World and world-wide levels, Bush undoubtedly maintained an appreciation for the bases of the mobilization movement: the local church and national networks.

Luís Bush's absence from the everyday leadership of COMIBAM during its second decade did not mean that either Bush or COMIBAM had lost significance. On the contrary, the Ibero American church had shared the torch of missions mobilization from the majority world with the rest of the world.

Partnership with Local Churches and Pastors

While COMIBAM leaders recognized the important role of national network leaders, they also believed in pastoral leadership. Bertuzzi (2006a) wrote,

> If God's servant has a missionary spirit, his church will too. I do not know of a missionary church that does not have a pastor with missionary passion. As goes the pastor, so goes the church. (p. 53)

Similarly, David Ruíz (2006b) stated that, since the local church was central to the advancement of the mission, the pastor was the key to the missionary enterprise (p. 63). Thus, COMIBAM leaders believed in the importance of collaboration between pastors, local churches, missionary training centers and sending agencies. These elements guided organizational developments and leadership emphases.

Other Missiological Issues

This chapter examined the missiological developments of the COMIBAM movement during the era of the second congress. The topics of discussion at the Acapulco congress, the publications related to COMIBAM during that era, and the continental meetings that took place after the congress reveal the themes of their concern. These themes included the biblical bases for the mission, the nature of the mission, the relationship of the mission to eschatology, pastoral care of the missionaries, spiritual warfare, unreached people groups, the establishment of indigenous churches, cross-cultural evangelism, concern for the influence of North America, and a holistic mission. As the COMIBAM movement matured, it developed a hybrid missiology that included aspects of U.S. missionary models such as the focus on unreached people groups, the use of sending agencies, and the establishment of cross-cultural evangelism but adapted these emphases to the Ibero American context. This hybrid missiology maintained a strong biblical basis, a high regard for the local church and for pastors, and a holistic outlook in regard to meeting human needs. Two of the missiological issues that merit additional treatment are the concerns for North American influence on the Ibero American movement and for the spiritual vibrancy of the mission.

Latin American leaders were concerned about the influence from North America. As the Latin American evangelical church came of age, it was eager to become a truly indigenous movement. COMIBAM leaders desired to demonstrate that they were capable of leading the mobilization movement. The two areas of discussion in regard to North American influence on the Ibero American missionary mobilization consisted of a willingness to critique North American models and how to define the working relationship between the North and the South. Latin Americans evangelicals sought to be partners on the same level with other key players in the global mission. They carefully guarded against the pulling of strings from the North in either ideology or leadership.

There was a general recognition of the positive contribution that both European and North American missionaries made to the advancement of mission in Latin America. This gratitude was mixed with a critical caution about repeating all of the patterns of mission that were brought from the North. Latin Americans were ready to "take the torch which was passed to them" in the missionary enterprise (Bertuzzi, 2006a, p. 112). Escobar (2002) spoke of the urgency of developing an evangelical missiological reflection that was willing to be critical of the way mission had been carried out in the 20th century by Europe and the United States. The reason, Escobar (2002) argued, that the post-World War II evangelical missionary movement was unwilling to reflect on the biblical social implications of the gospel were its Dispensationalism tendency, the delayed effects of the liberal-fundamentalist debates, and its close alignment with a Cold War mentality, where social criticism was regarded as subversive, or even Communist. From Escobar's perspective objective reflection on missionary practice in the Latin American context required the removal of some of these obstacles.

COMIBAM leaders were very concerned with the nature of the relationship between North and South. They cried out for a leveled playing field where the different players brought with them their respective resources and shared them with each other. They longed for true partnership to replace all traces of paternalism. This sentiment is illustrated by the way Federico Bertuzzi classified the mission-sending models of Latin America. He listed them as (a) the God bless you model where the sending church does no more than give their blessing to the missionary; (b) the Anglo-Saxon model where the missionary works in isolation of others because of financial security; (c) the Mestizo model where there is a partnership between resources from the North and from the South; (d) the franchise model where multinational organizations find expression in the Latin American context; and (e) the our-way model where there is creativity, enthusiasm and a church-driven process (Bertuzzi, 2006a). COMIBAM leaders were optimistic that progress was made in the direction of true partnership. Morales (2006) reported that the significant growth of missionary sending had also opened the way for research projects, networks, partnerships and missiological discussions, including the nature of the desired relationship between North and South. Matamoros (2006) hoped that the COMIBAM Missionary Agencies and Sending Structures Network would become a forum for dialoguing with the mission organizations in the North about respective roles, work projects, and for the development of mutual respect. Bertuzzi (2006a) recognized that the nature of interdependent relationships is complex, especially when the relationships are between organizations. Latin American leaders needed to be vigilant and diligent in order to have a seat at the global table of missionary partnerships. The issue of possible influence from North America on the Ibero American mobilization movement was an underlying concern in much of the dialogue that took place during that period.

Spirituality constituted another area of concern among COMIBAM leaders. They called for prayer and spiritual vitality as key components of mission advancement (Bertuzzi, 2006a). The concern for spirituality encompassed both the local church setting and the missionary field. Not only did the church need spiritual vitality for the mission but the mission also fueled spirituality. Londoño (2006a) declared:

> What keeps a church alive, revitalized and full of spirituality is the preaching of the gospel to the ends of the earth. When the church faces new challenges in the mission, it feels the need to get closer to God, to review its doctrine, to evaluate its testimony and to change for the sake of His love. (p. 41)

The spirituality of the missionary held equal importance. Matamoros (2006) suggested that one of the greatest needs of the Latin American missionary movement at the turn of the 21st century was to cultivate an individual and collective life-style spiritual vibrancy on the mission field. David Ruíz agreed about the immensity of the need. He expressed that the same lack of spiritual vibrancy Andrew Murray identified at the 1900 World Missionary Convention was true one hundred years later (Ruíz, 2006b). Londoño (2006a) described the nature of this spirituality:

> In light of God's Word, spirituality is a life style; a way of thinking and acting that is consistent with the model of Christ. It has to do with what we are and not with what we do. It is living for the fulfillment of the purpose of God. (p. 39)

The mission, then, would primarily flow from the nature of discipleship. COMIBAM leaders sought integrity between the character of believers and the task of sharing the good news. Matamoros (2006) proposed that missionary training and preparation should include character and spiritual formation as a priority. The COMIBAM movement began in large part by calling Latin American evangelicals throughout the continent to form prayer groups. The concern for prayer and spiritual vitality continued to provide impetus for the movement during the second decade of its existence.

The Ibero American movement critically considered the missiological thinking from its Northern partners and adapted to its own situation after careful reflection.

Through the leadership of Luís Bush, Ibero America also contributed to the Anglo-Saxon missiological thinking. COMIBAM leaders were eager to demonstrate that they were capable of leading the missionary mobilization from Latin America without the control of North American missionaries or agencies. Above all, they were motivated to engage the missionary enterprise with spiritual vibrancy and with the objective of glorifying God.

COMIBAM Missionaries

A missions mobilization movement by its very nature vindicates itself by the ability to send and keep missionaries on the field. Ultimately, the issues of missiology, leadership and strategy are relevant only to the extent that they result in deploying and maintaining of missionaries throughout the world. To what extent was the COMIBAM movement successful in mobilizing Ibero America to send cross-cultural missionaries during its second decade? How did the sending of missionaries from Latin America relate to the sending efforts of other parts of the world? Where were Latin American missionaries serving and how long did they stay on the field?

In the discussion of Ibero American missionaries, this study will use the term Majority World to refer to the population of Africa, Asia and Latin America, and the term Northern Hemisphere to refer primarily to North America and Europe. Some authors use the term The North or the Anglo-Saxon World for North America and Europe. Various writers and publications use the terms South, Non-Western, Third World, Four-Fifths World, Two-Thirds World, Global South, and Majority World to refer to essentially the same population. Of these, the most antiquated is the label Third World since it referred to the Cold War. Furthermore, terms such as Third World and Developing World imply a solely economic optic for categorizing, thereby betraying a Northern Hemisphere bias.

The term Majority World is more accurate and it should have a longer shelf life than those terms which utilize specific fractions.

Ibero American Missionaries: Identity and Geography

During the second decade of the COMIBAM movement, Ibero American missionaries were generally married couples, many of them young, from various denominations serving in every major part of the world. Limpic (2002) reported that in 2002, 73% of the 5,900 Ibero American missionaries were married, 15% were single women, and 12% were single men. Bertuzzi (2006a) declared that young age characterized the Ibero American missionaries. The sheer number of new missionaries sent by Ibero American evangelicals is admirable.

The leadership of COMIBAM labored to develop a strategy for sending missionaries to the unreached world, specifically to the 10/40 window and the Muslim world. Yet, the deployment of Ibero American missionaries revealed a less centralized strategy. In their reports COMIBAM leaders provided anecdotal information about the places where missionaries from Latin America were serving. Bertuzzi (2006a) related encountering Brazilians serving in Bangalore, Costa Ricans serving in Cambodia, Argentines serving in Uzbekistan, and many others serving in North Africa and the Middle East among Muslims. Matamoros (2006) rejoiced that Latin missionaries were serving in countries beyond Ibero America such as Morocco, Senegal, India, China, Japan, Mali, Turkey, Egypt, Uzbekistan, Eastern Europe, Russia and Sub-Saharan Africa. The presence of Latin American missionaries in so many of these countries in the second decade of the COMIBAM movement is quite remarkable. The percentage of missionaries in the various regions of the world affords greater resolution to the picture of mobilization. Limpic (2002) reported that 39% of Ibero American missionaries were serving in South America, 17% were serving in Europe, 12% in Africa, 11% in Mexico and Central America, 8% in North America, 5% in Asia and the rest in the Caribbean, Eastern Europe and Oceania. While these percentages paint the picture of the continents where Latin Americans served, a slightly different set of categories reflects the categories that relate to the unreached world. For example, 39% of Ibero American missionaries were serving in a country other than their own within Ibero America, 20% were serving within their own country, 14% were serving in the 10/40 window, and 27% in the rest of the world (Limpic, 2002). Undeniably, Ibero American evangelicals managed to deploy their own to multiple mission fields throughout the world. These missionaries took the torch and continued running the race of world evangelization.

These categories do not directly address the proportion of Ibero American missionaries who were engaging unreached people groups. Matamoros (2006) acknowledged that a significant number of cross-cultural missionaries was working with indigenous people groups and the mega cities of the Americas but he did not quantify it this involvement. Bertuzzi (2006a) asserted that a significant portion of Ibero American missionaries felt called to the Muslim world resulting in deployment to Spain, Morocco, Eastern Europe and Central Asia. Nevertheless, according to the official COMIBAM statistics, only 14% were serving in the 10/40 Window, which was an area of priority for the movement. Two questions emerge from this information: Did the majority of missionaries and/or sending organizations share the sense of priority about the 10/40 Window? What were the factors that prevented a greater proportion of involvement in the 10/40 Window?

Ibero American Missionaries: The Challenges They Faced

During a decade of great numerical and geographical missionary advance, the Ibero American movement faced multiple challenges. Bertuzzi (2006a) identified a high rate of missionary attrition, lack of financial resources, and minimal networking relationships with Africa and Asia. In regard to missionary attrition, Limpic (2002) reported that by 2002 only 50% of missionaries were staying on the field over three years, 37% were staying between one and three years, and 13% were staying less than a year. The COMIBAM movement had created excitement and fueled the mobilization of Ibero American evangelicals to the mission field. Yet, the movement lacked the infrastructure and the resources to keep missionaries on the field. Even so, the young movement, with scarcity of resources managed to keep 87% of the missionaries on the field for at least three years. Given the variables, this retention rate was significant. Matamoros' (2006) assessment shed light on probable contributing factors to the attrition challenge. He listed (a) difficulties in inter-personal relationships and team development; (b) lack of planning, goal-setting and strategizing; (c) the need for greater spirituality among missionaries; (d) the lack of pastoral care; (e) the need to strengthen sending and receiving missionary agencies. Not surprisingly, COMIBAM gave much attention to the issue of holistic and comprehensive pastoral care for missionaries after these discoveries were made.

COMIBAM, the Majority World and the World Christian Movement

The evangelical church in Latin America came of age as the COMIBAM movement fanned the missionary sending flames. The number of missionaries, the countries and denominations that sent them, and the places where these missionaries served exhibited great progress in the cross-cultural mission from Ibero America. Of course, the number of missionaries reported by COMIBAM does not tell the whole story. Escobar (2002) stated that the conservative estimates of Latin American missionaries did not include many spontaneous movements nor did they include migrants who are not tied to a missionary agency. Yet, as Spanish and Portuguese-speaking evangelicals advanced this cross-cultural mission, they also became important players in mission sending from the Majority World and in the worldwide Christian movement.

The rate of growth in the sending of missionaries, as compared to the Northern Hemisphere, was remarkable. In 1989, Bertuzzi (2006a) optimistically joined Pate in projecting that the amount of missionaries sent from the Southern Hemisphere would surpass those sent from the Northern Hemisphere by the year 2000.

Table 7

Projection of missionary sending shift from the North to the South according to Pate (Bertuzzi, 2006a; Pate, 1989)

	1988	1995	2000
Northern Hemisphere	85,000	100,000	120,000
Southern Hemisphere	36,000	85,000	160,000
Total	121,000	185,000	280,000

The projection did not become a reality by 2000. The numbers, nevertheless, betrayed the high enthusiasm that Ibero American leaders possessed. Bertuzzi (2006a) poetically wrote, "It would seem that the Holy Spirit is working as the 'travel' agent of the Most Holy Trinity, whom has been pleased to pour out now his rich blessing on this Southern part of the world, hungry for the Word of God, which includes, obviously our Latin

America" (p. 84). More significant than the actual number of missionaries sent from the Southern Hemisphere is the rate of growth in missionary sending. The tables below help illustrate this.

Michael Jaffarian (2004) utilized three comparative tables of figures to plot the sending of missionaries. These tables reveal significant progress in the mission sending movement from Latin America and from the Majority World.

Table 8

Christian foreign missionaries in A.D. 2000 according to Barrett (as cited in Jaffarian, 2004)

Global region	Foreign missionaries	Missionaries per million Christians
Four-Fifths World	83,454	
Africa	17,406	51.9
Asia	24,504	79.7
Latin America	41,544	87.3
Western World	336,070	
Europe	192,346	358.3
Northern America	135,222	637.3
Oceania	8,502	397.8
Total	419,524	222.2

Table 8 shows the Christian foreign missionaries sent from various parts of the world in the year 2000. When including Roman Catholics, Table 9 shows that the number of missionaries sent in the year 2000 by the Majority World, labeled Four-Fifths World, in the table, is significantly less than those sent by the Northern Hemisphere, labeled Western World in the table. Latin America sent the most Christian, both Catholic and Protestant, missionaries in the Majority World category, sending 41,544.

Table 9 provides figures for Protestant missionaries sent in the year 2000. When considering only Protestant missionaries, Asia takes the lead in missionaries sent by the Majority World, labeled Four-Fifths World in the table. In terms of number of churches per missionary sent, Latin America takes second place among the Majority World continents.

Table 9

Protestant, Independent, and Anglican missionaries in A.D. 2000 according to Operation World (as cited in Jaffarian, 2004)

Global region	Total national missionaries	Missionaries serving abroad	Churches per missionary sent
Four-Fifths World	91,837	20,570	
Africa	12,442	3,126	48.4
Asia	69,203	13,607	11.3
Latin America	10,192	3,837	30.3
Western World	103,437	70,323	
Europe	22,897	16,077	6.2
Northern America	71,088	50,720	7.2
Pacific	9,452	3,526	6.1
Total	195,274	90,893	11.8

Table 10 provides the most remarkable data about the Ibero American and the Majority World sending movement. The growth rate between the years 1990 and 2000 in the Majority World, labeled Four-Fifths World in the table, was 210% compared to 12%

in the Northern Hemisphere, labeled Western World in the table. Additionally, the categories used in Table 10 present a difficulty in regard to missionary strategy. Jaffarian (2004) corrected Pate's predictions based on foreign and domestic missionary classification. He stated, "To arrive at a fair conclusion, Pate should have compared the same kind of missionaries—either foreign only or both foreign and domestic—for both regions of the world. He did not, however, and thus…the comparison is not valid" (p. 131). This assertion ignores the COMIBAM movement's understanding of cross-cultural missionary sending.

Table 10

Protestant/PIA foreign missionaries in A.D. 1990 and 2000 according to Operation World (as cited in Jaffarian, 2004, p. 132)

Global region	Missionaries in 1990	Missionaries in 2000	Growth rate (%)
Four-Fifths World	6,634	20,570	210
Africa	1,669	3,126	87
Asia	3,476	13,607	291
Latin America	1,489	3,837	158
Western World	62,927	70,323	12
Europe	15,701	16,077	2
Northern America	43,554	50,720	16
Pacific	3,672	3,526	-4
Total	69,561	90,893	31

COMIBAM focused on People Groups, many of which are indigenous tribal groups within their own country's border. This paradigm requires different criteria for cross-cultural missionary sending than foreign and domestic. The problem lies on the extent to which the Northern Hemisphere and the Majority World utilize the same categories for cross-cultural missionary sending so that the comparisons can be valid.

While Asia led the entire globe with a growth rate of 291%, Latin America occupied the second place in the global sending movement with an astonishing growth rate of 158%. In fact, the growth rate of each continent in the Majority World, labeled Four-Fifths World in the table, surpassed that of all the continents together in the Northern Hemisphere, labeled Western World in the table. Together, these three tables demonstrate that the growth rate of missionaries from Latin America increased significantly.

Summary and Conclusions

COMIBAM's second decade produced important meetings, numerous publications, and the increase of missions mobilization in Ibero America. By its second congress in Acapulco, COMIBAM had proven to be a continental movement that continued to march forward. By the year 2002, Ibero America had sent 5,900 missionaries cross-culturally. Various denominational and missionary agencies sent these missionaries. The financial support for these missionary deployments came primarily from Ibero America with secondary but significant support from their Northern partners. Many leaders throughout the continent dialogued and reflected on the nature of cross-cultural mission through venues such as the Acapulco congress, national missionary congresses and consultations, CLADE IV and other continental meetings. COMIBAM published several books to cast the vision and to share the strategy with churches and leaders. The meetings and the publications facilitated the development of a missiological hybrid that included the best missiological thinking from the United States and indigenous Latin American reflection. COMIBAM identified itself as a mobilization network and refused to think of itself as a theological reflection institution. Nevertheless, a significant amount of reflection took place during these years. To be sure, it was a missiology *del camino* [on the road] but it had strong biblical bases and the stamp of Latin American ownership. The national mission movements had varying degrees of success in the mobilization task. Together these networks provided a synergy in Ibero America that resulted in greater mobilization, training and sending of missionaries. The Pastoral Care of the Missionary and the Reach a People Group programs became the primary emphases of COMIBAM International. COMIBAM leaders shifted the organizational structure in a timely manner to provide sustainability and longevity beyond its vision casting days. The Ibero American missionary sending movement joined Asia, Africa and the Northern Hemisphere as a contributing member. COMIBAM had reached young adulthood by the second decade after the Sao Paulo congress.

CHAPTER 5. CONCLUSION

The current study developed a history of the beginnings of the *Cooperación Misionera Ibero Americana* [Ibero American Missionary Cooperation] (COMIBAM). The COMIBAM network mobilized evangelicals in Latin America and the Iberian Peninsula for global mission. The birth, growth and development of this missionary network have demonstrated the manner in which the evangelical church in Latin America and in the Iberian Peninsula came of age as it rose to become a global missionary force. The current study has told the story of COMIBAM during its first sixteen years, namely 1984 to 2000, and presented historical documentation in order to provide a baseline for further research. The time period between 1984 and 2000 saw the stunning growth of the number of missionaries in the field from Latin America and a corresponding growth among sending organizations indigenous to Ibero America.

The thesis of the current study posited that COMIBAM as a missionary network from the Majority World represents an indigenous movement which has made a significant impact on the global missionary advance. Visionary indigenous leadership, a context of ecumenism, missionary fervor, and changes in the Latin American landscape have given COMIBAM International the impetus of a movement. This is a case study of the right leadership in the right context producing an effective missionary network. The historical research conducted supports this thesis.

Chapter 2 of the current study identified precursors and organizations that contributed to the formation of COMIBAM. Chapter 3 traced the birth of COMIBAM from its first continental congress, COMIBAM '87, and examined its development into a network of networks, assessed its leadership, and reviewed the missiological reflection that took place during that period. Chapter 4 described the early development of COMIBAM as it celebrated its second continental congress, COMIBAM '97, and other important meetings and publications which demonstrated the vibrancy of the movement. Common threads emerged in the analysis of these chapters in terms of numerical growth, missiological reflection, leadership and development of the organization.

This conclusion will provide an assessment of COMIBAM in the twentieth century, offer implications of the study, and present recommendations for future research.

Assessment of COMIBAM in the Twentieth Century

COMIBAM's success and longevity establishes the organization as a significant force among Latin American and Iberian evangelicals. The COMIBAM movement also illustrates how the global missionary sending force is shifting to the Majority World. COMIBAM evidenced its success in multiple ways even while the organization also faced challenges. Many factors contributed to the success of COMIBAM.

Remarkable Success and Nominal Challenges

The current study demonstrated that COMIBAM International was a successful missionary network in the twentieth century in regard to the broadening scope of its outreach, the increased number of missionaries sent, the growth in number of missionary training and sending agencies that were formed, and the longevity of the organization. COMIBAM successfully cast a vision that fanned the flames of missionary fervor throughout Latin America resulting in missionary sending. This lists represents remarkable accomplishments by COMIBAM.

COMIBAM faced at least two challenges, which the leadership identified and addressed. COMIBAM did not initially provide an infrastructure that would sustain the missionary sending task long-term. Chapter 4 treated this topic under the section First COMIBAM Consultation on the Pastoral Care of Missionaries. Secondly, COMIBAM leaders initially struggled to identify the role of missiological reflection in the work of the organization. Both of these challenges relate to the nature of COMIBAM. COMIBAM was intended to be a mobilization network, not a missionary sending agency or a theological institution. While these challenges lay outside the scope of the organization's purpose, COMIBAM leaders addressed them because of their concern for the success of the movement beyond the organization.

Extensive reach and numerical success. COMIBAM successfully networked evangelicals along two fronts. This network rallied evangelicals of diverse denominations for missionary mobilization. COMIBAM also brought together evangelicals from multiple countries for the same purpose of mobilization. COMIBAM brought together evangelicals from diverse denominations and from multiple countries for more than two decades. This is a remarkable accomplishment.

The strength of the movement was evident since its first continental congress. COMIBAM '87 surfaced as a breakthrough event in the history of both the Latin American church and global missions. As stated in chapter 3, 3,100 delegates representing 25 Ibero American countries attended COMIBAM '87, making it the largest international Latin American evangelical event until then. In addition to the delegates from Ibero America, 59 other countries were also represented at this watershed event. The effects of this extraordinary congress rippled through the next several years.

As COMIBAM International entered its second decade of work, Ted Limpic (2002) reported that there were approximately 5,900 missionaries sent cross-culturally from Ibero America. This represented nearly a quadrupled growth from the estimated 1,600 cross-cultural missionaries sent in 1987 (*"¿Qué Es COMIBAM?"*, n.d.). As stated in Chapter 4, Limpic's (2002) report revealed that Latin American missionaries were largely sent by agencies, the missionaries sent out were overwhelmingly Ibero Americans, and the funding was mainly Ibero American, and there was diversity in the denominational affiliation of those being sent with a disproportionate amount of Pentecostals among them. Additionally, the movement was indeed continentally Ibero American not only in its vision, its leaders, its organizational structure but also in the actual engagement reflected in the country of origin for missionaries.

A decade after COMIBAM '87, the second congress revealed the progress and sustained vision of the movement. Reports of the national mission movements at the Acapulco congress demonstrate the scope of the COMIBAM impact. These reports were summarized in chapter 4 of the current study under the National Mission Movements section. Many national networks shared similar concerns and challenges, but not all of the countries moved at the same pace. While perhaps vision and enthusiasm were stronger in some regions than others, yet more training centers, more mission agencies, and more churches from Ibero America were cooperating than ever before in sending missionaries around the world. By the year 2000, COMIBAM had demonstrated success in cross-denominational reach, broad participation from the various Ibero American countries, and numerical growth of training centers, mission agencies and missionaries sent.

The challenge of missionary attrition and pastoral care of missionaries. During the decade of great numerical and geographical missionary advance, the Ibero

American movement faced multiple challenges. As noted in Chapter 4, this second decade saw a high rate of missionary attrition, lack of financial resources, and limited networking relationships with Africa and Asia. Only half of Ibero American missionaries were staying on the field longer than three years while a small number returned home before one year. Missionary attrition caused the mission mobilization network to become concerned about the pastoral care of missionaries. Missionary attrition and the pastoral care of missionaries were clearly the great challenges of the movement during its first sixteen years.

The COMIBAM '97 congress assigned a team to address the great need of the pastoral care of missionaries (Tostes, 2006). Subsequently, in the year 2000, COMIBAM held its first consultation on the pastoral care of missionaries. The movement succeeded in inspiring, training and sending missionaries, but as leaders discovered that many of the missionaries were returning from the field too soon for lack of holistic care, they decided to address the issue adequately. The First Consultation on the Pastoral Care of Missionaries identified the various needs of missionaries on the field (Tostes, 2006). COMIBAM addressed the needs responsibly by developing programs and resources to meet this important need during the second decade of its existence. The pastoral care of missionaries remained a priority for the network from that point forward.

The Third Ibero American Congress in Granada, Spain (2006) again demonstrated concern for the adequate care of missionaries on the field. One of the presenters at the Granada Congress, COMIBAM 2006, lamented the lack of financial support and of pastoral care for missionaries (Zapata, 2006). A research report presented at the Granada Congress, COMIBAM 2006, provided hard data about difficulties faced by missionaries on the field in key areas such as financial support, selection of mission field and ministry, fringe benefits, such as health insurance and retirement, vacation, and continued financial support during stateside (DeCarvalho, Jiménez, Gonzáles and Guerrero 2006). This third congress and report lie outside the scope of the present research. It is acknowledged here to demonstrate sustained concern for the issue of the pastoral care of missionaries. COMIBAM leaders such as David Ruíz, Jesús Londoño and Carlos Scott secured an evaluation and self-critique agenda for both COMIBAM '97 and COMIBAM 2006. While the responsibility for the pastoral care of missionaries depends on the local church and the missionary agencies, COMIBAM acted responsibly in evaluating this need and continuing the conversation until the problem was addressed.

Missiological Reflection: Strength or Weakness? The current study acknowledged the critique made by others in regard to COMIBAM's missiological reflection. Historical documents yield evidence that COMIBAM leaders recognized the importance of missiological reflection. The movement engaged in meaningful reflection although its objective was mobilization, not reflection. COMIBAM leaders and influencers did not conduct missiological reflection in a systematic manner; rather they demonstrated adaptability and flexibility in the process. COMIBAM, thus, did not suffer from a lack of missiological reflection. The network's biggest challenge in this regard consisted of defining the role of missiological reflection in the work of the organization. Eventually leaders determined that COMIBAM's objective was mobilization while missiological reflection played an important and supporting role.

The research conducted examined three areas of the COMIBAM missionary movement to determine the extent to which COMIBAM is truly indigenous: leadership, financing, and missiology. Who runs it? From where do the funds come? Whose ideas are implemented? The issue of missiological reflection holds relevance because from its beginning COMIBAM leadership desired missiological reflection to inform the process, and because a contextualized missiology is directly related to the full autonomy of a missionary movement. Although the movement received criticism for lack of indigenous missiological reflection and was accused of uncritically adopting a missiology from North America, the COMIBAM process engaged in missiological discussion through newsletters, national conferences, the plenary sessions of the continental congresses and the Ibero American theological conference. Chapter 2 analyzed these developments under the section Missiological Reflection. The COMIBAM network chose to become an Ibero American movement with a hybrid missiology, adapting insights for setting strategy from numerous sources. COMIBAM advanced as a mobilization network while it undergirded a hybrid missiology from its beginning stages and through its second decade.

Chapter 4 of the current study treated this subject in the Missiological Currents in Latin America. COMIBAM's missiology was indigenous to the extent that it refused to accept uncritically the missionary strategies suggested elsewhere, thus balancing a middle ground between U.S. and Latin American missiological models. The primary objective of the COMIBAM movement dictated the missiological outcome. COMIBAM leadership focused attention primarily on missionary mobilization and secondarily on missiological reflection. Interestingly, at least one Latin American missions leader, Luis Bush, reciprocally influenced U.S. missiology in important ways. Luis Bush's influence on the UPG missiology was treated in chapter 4 of the current study.

Beyond COMIBAM '87 and COMIBAM '97 the movement continued to mature in missiological reflection. CLADE IV proved to be of great significance in the missiological development of COMIBAM. CLADE IV took place in Quito, Ecuador in the year 2000. The meeting intended to reflect on the cross-cultural mission from Latin American context. The FTL, consistent with its concern for an over-dependence upon the influence of North American missionary practice, and to avoid any paternalistic control of the newly developing Latin American missionary enterprise, sponsored this congress (Amado, 2006, p. 6). The FTL invited COMIBAM and PM international leaders to this discussion forum. The COMIBAM and FTL leaders who met at CLADE IV arrived at several practical conclusions and made some important recommendations (Bertuzzi, 2006c). CLADE IV represented a significant turning point for the development of a Latin American model of cross-cultural mission. The missionary mobilization movement in Latin America had reached a new stage of maturity in regard to missiological reflection. While COMIBAM never embraced missiological reflection without practical application, the continued diligence in dialogue proved to be a strength of the movement.

COMIBAM 2006 Research Project

Although by its date COMIBAM 2006 lies outside the scope of the current research, the fact that the congress focused on self-assessment of past activities merits mention. Hopefully, other researchers can continue the study of COMIBAM's history after the year 2000. COMIBAM sought to assess the movement in three phases: Phase I: missionaries on the field to be conducted in 2006; Phase II: sending entities to be conducted in 2007; Phase III: field results and models (DeCarvalho, Jiménez, González, and Guerrero, 2006). For phase I an independent team of missionaries consisting of Dr. Levi DeCarvalho of Brazil, Ninette Jiménez of El Salvador, Carlos González of Spain, and Samuel Guerrero of Mexico conducted a research project with the intent of obtaining hard data about missionaries on the field. The team administered an extensive questionnaire and interviews to 428 Ibero American evangelical missionaries on the field representing each of the mega spheres, multiple ministries, diverse theological positions, and various sending options. The topics of the research covered the missionary's calling, training, sending and field work. The conclusions of the study were given for each of these topics. The publication *Strengths and Weaknesses of the Ibero American Missionary* (2006) by DeCarvalho, Jiménez, González and Guerrero provided the results and conclusions of the study. The serious way in which COMIBAM leaders conducted self-assessment and their demonstrated concern for the missionaries on the field evidenced the movement's commitment and high sense of responsibility to both the Ibero American church and to those sent out.

Contributing Factors to the Success of COMIBAM

Numerous factors contributed to the success of COMIBAM. It was the right time in Latin America for such a movement. Missionary fervor, an openness to work across denominational lines, awareness among Latin Americans of the world missionary movement, growth of the church in Latin America, the development of indigenous theology, and spiritual renewal in the churches all evidenced that it was God's time for such a movement. National and continental leadership seized the moment by casting the vision and mobilizing the church in Ibero America. Inspired by multiple missionary congresses at global and national levels, the first COMIBAM congress in 1987 proved to be pivotal in launching a movement. The COMIBAM leadership skillfully provided a multi-faceted vision and direction for the congress and what followed. Enthusiastic leaders stepped up to give direction to the movement at the right time, masterfully transitioning leadership from the vision casting and launching stage to the organizational stage. The grass-roots nature of this missionary network of networks contributed much to its sustainability, success and longevity.

The right time in Latin America for a missionary movement. The rise of the Ibero American missionary movement, known as COMIBAM, owes much to the leaders' ability to read the times and seize the moment. Those who gave birth to the COMIBAM movement definitely displayed the ability to recognize the *kairos* moment, anticipate, and act with forethought and vision in order to seize the God-given opportunity. God orchestrated the growth of the church, the development of indigenous theology, missionary fervor, cross-denominational cooperation and spiritual renewal in Latin America. Visionary leaders identified the right time for the launching of a missions mobilization movement and acted on it. Chapter 3, The Process for the Conceptualization of the Congress, provided evidence that the conceptualization and organization of the first congress came simultaneously from multiple leaders and organizations. COMIBAM leaders seized the moment by determining both the timing and the nature of the first congress.

A momentous first continental missionary congress. As chapter 2, Congresses on World Evangelization, demonstrated, a multitude of missionary congresses and conferences that advanced the ideal of accomplishing world evangelization by cross-denominational cooperation took place during the twentieth century. COMIBAM took its rightful place participating in this line of important missionary congresses. COMIBAM leadership understood the impact of global mission conferences on world evangelization. As the Edinburg Missionary Conference in 1910 is considered by Knoll (2000) the turning point of Christianity at the beginning of 20th century, so COMIBAM '87 was the turning point for the Latin American evangelical church at the end of the 20th century. COMIBAM '87 was the first congress of its kind and it held historical significance in the development of a native missionary vision within the Latin American church. COMIBAM '87 informed future congresses and retreats, shaped the formation of missionary agencies, and ultimately contributed to the sending of Latin Americans on cross-cultural missions (Bertuzzi, 2006; Ekström, 2006; Escobar, 2002). COMIBAM '87 was undoubtedly pivotal in the launching of this missionary sending movement.

Long-term vision and action for the eventual network. Chapter 3, The Congress Becomes a Cooperation: COMIBAM International, demonstrated that the COMIBAM '87 leadership planned for the establishing of an entity beyond the congress itself. Throughout the preparation and execution stages of the congress leaders announced their intention of catalyzing a process beyond the event itself. Eventually COMIBAM became a network of networks. The new leaders who followed the founders carried the visionary torch and developed the implementation of the cooperation stage.

COMIBAM leaders between congresses displayed high discipline. COMIBAM leadership exercised high discipline by constantly casting its vision, creating a grassroots-based structure, by being inclusive in its dialogues and conferences, and producing publications that communicated the values and strategies of the movement. COMIBAM leaders demonstrated great discernment in choosing a network model for their organization. Grassroots groups could find channels of expression through this network. This organizational structure was innovative. It is remarkable that COMIBAM did not follow the pattern of other missionary organizations in Ibero America. The longevity of the movement, including three international congresses, gives evidence of highly disciplined leadership.

The grassroots participation of leaders in making decisions which gave COMIBAM the sustainability as a network was secured by the concept of the International General Assembly. International General Assemblies, in contrast to Continental Congresses, sought to engage national network leaders securing delegates from each of the countries, thus opening up decision making and leader selection to national representatives (Ekström, 2006). The establishing of International General Assemblies advanced the movement organizationally as a true network.

The right leaders at the right time. COMIBAM created a cooperation of adaptive and visionary leaders. Undoubtedly a great deal of COMIBAM's success depended on its founding leader and those who succeeded him. Luís Bush was definitely the *paladín* [champion] of the COMIBAM movement at its inception. Bush possessed a leadership drive, charisma and vision that were unique and timely. As it is evidenced throughout chapter 3, Bush exercised his leadership through extensive communication, travel, and vision development. This kind of leadership contributed to the success of the first congress and to the visibility of COMIBAM. Yet, the movement continued beyond its infancy due to successful leadership transitions. The succession of COMIBAM's leaders skillfully shepherded the transitions from vision to congress to a sustainable movement, by transitioning from a personality-driven leadership to a more shared leadership approach. Alexandre Araéujo, Edison Queiróz, Rudy Girón, David Ruíz, Bertil Ekström, and Jonathan Lewis take their rightful place in the history of COMIBAM International as those who took the torch from Bush and shaped the movement between the first two congresses.

Implications of the Study

The study of COMIBAM as a missionary network from the Majority World has implications for the global missionary task. As missionary sending from the Majority World continues to grow, COMIBAM offers encouragement and a valid model to imitate. The church in the northern hemisphere would do well to partner with networks like COMIBAM in order to effectively fulfill the Great Commission. Mobilization of Hispanic evangelicals in the United States remains an issue of great relevance for the task of world evangelization. Latino leaders, and other Majority World leaders, should continue developing a missiology in Latin America in order to contribute to a relevant twenty-first century missiology.

COMIBAM and Missionary Sending from the Majority World

Missionary sending from the Majority World has increased at an extraordinary rate. Jaffarian (2004) cited statistics that indicated a growth rate in Majority World sending in the years between 1990 and 2000 of 210% compared to that of 12% in the Northern Hemisphere. In fact, the growth rate of each continent in the Majority World surpassed that of all the continents together in the Northern Hemisphere. As this trend continues, the greater number of missionaries sent cross-culturally will come from the Majority World instead of from the Northern Hemisphere. Missionary movements like COMIBAM are playing an increasingly vital role in world evangelization. Missionary senders from the Majority World should encourage each other and must learn from each other if the Great Commission is to be accomplished effectively.

Furthermore, the kind of missionaries and the kind of churches Ibero Americans will plant will change the face of global Christianity. Escobar (2000) stated that the church in the Southern Hemisphere "is marked by the culture of poverty: an oral liturgy, narrative preaching, uninhibited emotionalism, maximum participation in prayer and worship, dreams and visions, faith healing, and an intense search for community and belonging" (p. 27). Jenkins (2002) rightly stated, "the center of gravity in the Christian world has shifted inexorably southward, to Africa, Asia, and Latin America" (p. 2). If the Majority World maintains the increased rate of missionary sending, the center of gravity may move closer to the equator. The implication of these two factors becomes not only where will the greatest concentration of Christians be on the globe but the increased degree to which Christians around the world reflect Southern Hemisphere characteristics.

The Church in the Northern Hemisphere and Majority World Missionary Sending

Given the growth of missionary sending from the Majority World, the church in the Northern Hemisphere needs to partner with the church in Majority World, and to learn from its methods. On a practical level, partnership in the missionary enterprise between the church in the North and in the South is the best stewardship of resources. Escobar (2003) rightly declared, "Global partnership of churches will be indispensable for mission in the twenty-first century" (p. 164). The imperative of true global partnership also has a biblical and theological basis. At the COMIBAM 2006 congress in Granada, Spain, Carlos Scott (2006), who served as president of COMIBAM at that time, implored,

> Passion for the gospel should lead us to participate, cooperate, and share (Philippians 1:5) not compete…We should be one with the Father's plans (Luke 6:27-31). This oneness speaks to us about a same attitude and agreement (Philippians 2:1-11)…We should enrich the dialogue among the entire body of Christ: the global church. There is no North or South, East or West, but instead only one body. (pp. 74-75)

Additionally, Scott (2004) stated that mission partnership was based on *missio Dei* and declared with realistic enthusiasm that when the North and the South decide to do mission together Satan would be defeated, but it would require the power of the Holy Spirit. This biblical and theological conviction needs to exist in twenty-first century church leaders of both hemispheres. Cuevas (2011) shared this conviction and offered similar theological reasoning,

> Theologically speaking, partnership in mission could be described as the sovereign act of God giving the opportunity to poor countries in Latin America and other continents to empower God's kingdom to accomplish the Christological mandate which include the participation of the whole Church, both rich and poor. (p. 2)

Thus, for practical, biblical and theological reasons the church in the North must take seriously the church in the South as they both partner in advancing the mission of God.

COMIBAM as a missionary network, in addition to contributing to the advance of missionary sending from the Majority World, also offers a workable model for partnership beyond Ibero America. In his analysis of partnership in mission, Cuevas (2011) identified three current models: traditional partnership, which is the partnership between mission societies and churches; innovative networking partnership, which is the partnerships between mission societies in a non-territorial way; and emergent partnership, which is the partnership between local churches and indigenous mission societies. Furthermore he presents COMIBAM as a classic case of innovative networking partnership. This demonstrably effective model of partnership is built into the DNA, the core design and ethos, of COMIBAM. In fact, a COMIBAM leader co-authored a book on the subject: *Alianzas Estratégicas para la Misión de la Iglesia* [Strategic Partnerships for the Mission of the Church] (Rickett & Gava, 2005). The global church would benefit from similar networks and from network-type partnerships among these networks.

Mobilization of Hispanic Evangelicals in the U.S.

The Hispanic population in the U.S. is in a state of growth. Dr. Daniel Sanchez (2006) reported that between 1970 and 2005 the Hispanic population in the U.S. grew by 33.1 million and that by 2050 there will be 102.6 million Hispanics living in the U.S. The potential for an explosive growth of the Hispanic evangelical church in the U.S. is very real. Additionally, the migration of Latinos into and from the United States necessitates a study of the Latino Church's present involvement in the global mission. Commenting on the fifty million Hispanics that lived in the U.S. in 2010, and on the fact that the majority of Hispanics are U.S. born, Rodriguez (2011) stated that Hispanic church leaders need to reexamine ministry paradigms. Furthermore, alluding to New Testament Diaspora Jews, Rodriguez argued, "Hellenists make great cross-cultural missionaries" meaning that U.S. Latinos can be effective "agents of mission" (p. 175). The growth of the Hispanic population and the potential growth of the Hispanic church in the U.S. necessitate an intense and focused strategy to mobilize Hispanic evangelicals for cross-cultural missions.

This current study identified COMIBAM's intentional efforts to mobilize Hispanics in North America through COMHINA. The growing opportunity for mobilizing Hispanics in the U.S for cross-cultural mission requires an assessment of the current progress, the greater engagement of networks such as COMHINA, and the developing of an inclusive strategy. COMIBAM's model and resources are relevant to a portion of the Hispanic population in the U.S. However, because U.S. Latinos represent a diverse cultural context that is not identical to the rest of Latin America, the model for mobilizing them needs to be contextualized.

Lastly, the value of ministry preparation institutions that specialize on preparing Hispanics for ministry and mission must be affirmed. One example of such an institution is the Baptist University of the Americas (BUA) in San Antonio affiliated with the Baptist General Convention of Texas, which serves primarily Hispanic students and prepares them for cross-cultural ministry (Reyes, 2009). The Rio Grande Bible College (RGBC) in Edinburg, Texas, a nondenominational Bible college, also prepares Latinos for international ministry and missions (Dick, 2011). Institutions like BUA and RGBI, providing theologically moderate and very conservative alternatives respectively, will play a vital role in the cross-cultural mobilization of Hispanics.

Development of a Latin American/Majority World Missiology

The present study determined that COMIBAM developed a hybrid missiology that adjusted U.S. models with indigenous reflection. While mobilization networks like COMIBAM must continue to focus on the mission praxis, their continued effectiveness will depend in part by a more fully developed Latin American/Majority World missiology. This responsibility falls on organizations like the FTL, seminaries, missionary training centers and pastors. Nevertheless the dialogue between these entities and missionary mobilization leaders needs to continue.

Escobar's (2003) warning merits serious attention in the 21st century. Referring to concepts such as unreached peoples, homogenous units, the 10-40 window or adopt-a-people, Escobar (2003) wrote,

> These concepts and techniques need the correction that comes from a biblical view of people. What I am seeing in the application of these concepts in the mission field is that missionaries "depersonalize" people into "unreached targets," making them objects of hit-and-run efforts to get decisions that may be reported…The difficult task of discipleship and building the body of Christ are by-passed in the name of managerial goals that seemed to be designed to give their missionary center in the United States an aura of success. (p. 167)

While missionary entities in the North offer valid best practices and research, these practices need to be critiqued and applied using a biblical optic. The FTL and others have made progress in this field. An example of a recent effort in this direction was the Mission for the Third Millennium conference held in London (2002) where John Stott, Paulo Branco, John Nicholls, David Evans, Carlos Scott, Emmanuel Buch, David Hulford, Abel Morales, Alex Ross, John Corrie, Debora Chapman, Andrew Kirk, Samuel Cueva, Federico Bertuzzi and David Ruíz offered reflections on building two-way missionary bridges (Cueva, 2004). Yet, much work remains to be done in developing a Latin American missiology.

Recommendations for Future Research

The current study provided a general historical analysis of COMIBAM International from 1984 to 2000. As such the research examined the continental congresses, the continental leadership and organization, and the missiological currents in Latin America. The predetermined scope of the current study recognized that this is the first complete historical account of the COMIBAM phenomenon and so its documentation was intended to provide a baseline for further research. There are multiple areas that merit further research. The following recommendations are given as a starting point and by no means are exhaustive.

Future research will benefit from access to the COMIBAM/Bertuzzi collection. It is recommendable to house this collection in a responsible institutional library. This researcher began the process of digitizing several of the archive documents. Since then Federico Bertuzzi has continued to scan and upload several of these documents to a public website: recursosmisioneros.com. Completing the process of digitizing the entire archive is a desirable objective.

National and Regional Missionary Movements

The current study presented only a panoramic view of the national missionary movements. Future research projects could focus on an in-depth study of COMIBAM's work in one of the countries of Ibero America and/or a group of countries. Also COMIBAM has subdivided its international assignments into continental regions such as the South Cone, the Iberian Peninsula, North America, the Caribbean, Central America, the Andes, Mexico, and Brazil. An in-depth study of each of these regions would be helpful in assessing the movement's impact throughout the continent.

A 35-Year Assessment

COMIBAM leaders began a self-assessment process after approximately 25 years of existence (COMIBAM 2006). By taking some of those same topics and categories a follow-up assessment at the 35-year mark would provide helpful data. The 35-year mark is significant because it represents a generation of leaders. The young adult pastors and missionaries who were highly invested in missions mobilization in the mid to late 80s will moving toward senior adulthood in the year 2017. How have they continued to be involved? How has their zeal and their experience changed? How successful have they been in passing on the vision to the new generation? What are the goals of current leaders in the movement?

Organizational Developments from Inception to Present Day

The current study examined the transition from the first Ibero American congress to the network structure established by the year 2000. Based on the research report that COMIBAM received in Granada 2006, the Fourth COMIBAM International Assembly meeting in Bogota, Colombia, 2009, proposed constitutional and structural changes (COMIBAM International, 2009). This researcher had the opportunity to attend this meeting and learn first hand about the changes that were to be implemented. The COMIBAM leadership in 2009, namely its president, Carlos Scott and its executive director, Jesús Londoño, reported that the original vision and mission that had been formulated twenty years previously had now been fulfilled and they proposed new vision and mission statements along with organizational changes. Further research that would examine the types of organizational changes that were implemented and the impact they have had is recommended.

Missionary Training Organizations in Latin America

COMIBAM's self-assessment in 2006, called for research into the lives of missionaries on the field, the effectiveness of sending entities, and the missionary results on the field. Further research into the missionary training organizations in Ibero America as to their curricula and their methods would be useful. Additionally, how are traditional seminaries and theological schools addressing missionary training and missiological reflection?

A History of Latin American Missionaries

A history of missionaries sent from Ibero America both previous to the COMIBAM movement and since the first continental congress could provide insightful information about the experiences, models and success of Ibero American missionaries in contrast with those of missionaries from the North. The lives and efforts of these mostly unknown servants of Christ can provide inspiration and helpful information to future missionary efforts.

Conclusion

The missionary network known as the Ibero American Missionary Cooperation (COMIBAM) successfully launched and sustained a movement that cast a missionary vision throughout Ibero America, mobilized churches and agencies to train and send missionaries, and has made a significant impact through those missionaries to world evangelization. This success is demonstrated in the broad participation of evangelicals from multiple denominations and countries, the number of missionaries sent, the number of missionary training and sending agencies established, and the development of a missiological paradigm that has resulted in mobilization.

Evangelical leaders mobilized the church in Ibero American for cross-cultural mission in an unprecedented way between 1984 and 2000 because it was God's timing for such an enterprise, visionary leadership seized God's moment by launching a successful continental missionary congress, and because disciplined leadership transitioned the movement from its vision-casting stage to the grassroots network stage.

The study of COMIBAM as a missionary network from the Majority World yields practical insights for the advancement of mission in the twenty-first century. These implications include the impact of missionary sending from the Majority World on the global church, the need for the church in the northern hemisphere and the church in the southern hemisphere to partner in order to effectively fulfill the Great Commission, the urgency of reexamining the mobilization of Hispanic evangelicals in the United States, and the need for the continued development of a Latin American missiology in the twenty-first century.

REFERENCES

Allen, R. (1962). *Missionary methods: St. Paul's or ours? A study of the church in the four provinces* (2nd ed.). Grand Rapids, MI: Wm. B. Eerdmans.

Allen, R. (1997). *The spontanous expansion of the church: And the causes that hinder it.* Eugene, OR: Wipf & Stock Publishers.

Amado, M. (2006). Prologue. In F.A. Bertuzzi (Ed.), *Misión Transcultural* [Cross-cultural mission] (3rd ed.) (pp. 5-6). Miami, FL: Editorial Patmos.

Anabalón, F. (1987, November). *La oración y las misiones* [Prayer and missions]. Plenary session presented at the First Ibero American Missionary Congress, Sao Paulo, Brazil.

Anderson, J. C. (2005). *An evangelical saga: Baptists and their precursors in Latin America.* Xulon Press.

Avila, M. (1996). *Towards a Latin American contextual hermeneutics: A critical examination of the contextual hermeneutics of the Fraternidad Teológica Latinoamericana.* (Doctoral dissertation). Retrieved from ProQuest Dissertations and Theses. (UMI No. 9634677)

Baptists in Latin America and their theological contributions. Retrieved from http://www.encycolpedia.com/doc/1G1-94160932.html

Barrientos, A. (1987, November). *La realidad Iberoamericana y las misiones* [The Ibero-American reality and missions]. Plenary session presented at the First Ibero American Missionary Congress, Sao Paulo, Brazil.

Bertuzzi, F. A., del Pino, C., Girón, R., Grellert, M., Nuñez, E. A., Paredes, P., Rey, V., & Steuernagel, V. (1995, April). *Encuentro Fraternidad Teológica Latinoamericana y COMIBAM Internacional* [Meeting of the Latin American Theological Fraternity and COMIBAM International]. Miami, Florida. Retrieved from http://www.recursosmisioneros.com/resources/Misiones_latinas_siglo_XXI.pdf

Bertuzzi, F. A. (Ed.). (2001). *Las misiones Latinas para el siglo XXI: Compendio de COMIBAM 97, el Segundo Congreso Misionero Iberoamericano, Acapulco, México, 27 al 31 de octubre de 1997* [Latin missions for the 21st century: Handbook of the COMIBAM 1997, 2nd Ibero American Missionary Congress, Acapulco, Mexico, October 27 through 31, 1997] (2nd ed.). Retrieved from http://www.recursosmisioneros.com/resources/Misiones_latinas_siglo_XXI.pdf

Bertuzzi, F. A. (2006a). *El despertar de las misiones* [The awakening of missions] (2nd ed.). Barcelona, Spain: Editorial CLIE.

Bertuzzi, F. A. (2006b). *Internacionalización o anglonización de la misión* [Internationalization or anglonization of the mission]. In F. A. Bertuzzi (Ed.), *Misión Transcultural* [Cross-cultural mission] (3rd ed.) (pp. 55-64). Miami, FL: Editorial Patmos.

Bertuzzi, F. A. (2006c). *Misión transcultural* [Cross-cultural mission] (3rd ed.). Miami, FL: Editorial Patmos, (ISBN: 1588023850).

Bertuzzi, F. A. (2007). *Los inicios de un movimiento* [The beginnings of a movement]. Granada, Spain: Publidisa.

Bertuzzi, F. & Girón, R. (1999). *La iglesia Latina en misión mundial: Una orientación práctica para iglesias y agencias misioneras* [The Latino church on world mission: A practical orientation for missionary churches and agencies]. Cooperación Misionera Iberoamericana [Ibero American Missionary Cooperation], Confraternidad Evangélica Latinoamericana [Latin American Evangelical Fellowship], COMIBAM Internacional.

Bibliografía misionera [Missionary bibliography] (rev. 2008, July 19). Retrieved from www.comibam.org/docs/bibliografia.pdf

Blackaby, H. & Blackaby, R. (2001). *Spiritual leadership: Moving people on to God's agenda.* Nashville, TN: Broadman & Holman Publishers.

Bolman, L. G. & Deal T. E. (2003). *Reframing organizations: Artistry, choice, and leadership.* San Francisco, CA: Jossey Bass.

Bosch, D. J. (1991). *Transforming mission: Paradigm shifts in theology of mission.* Maryknoll, NY: Orbis Books.

Burns, J. M. (1979). *Leadership.* New York, NY: Harper & Row, Publishers.

Bush, L. K. (1985, October). *Primer congreso de misiones a nivel Latinoamericano* [First missions congress at the Latin American level]. *COMIBAM informa [COMIBAM informs]*, *1* (1), pp. 3-4.

Bush, L. K. (Ed.). (1986). *Manual de intercesión misionera* [Missionary intercession manual] (1st ed.). Guatemala, Guatemala: COMIBAM Internacional.

Bush, L. K. (Ed.). (1986, June 2-4), *La misión de la iglesia y las misiones mundiales* [The mission of the church and world missions]. First Ibero American Theological Conference, Antigua, Guatemala.

Bush, L. K. (1986, July). *Consulta teológica Iberoamericana* [Ibero American theological conference]. (C. Calderón, Ed.) *COMIBAM informa [COMIBAM informs]*, *1* (6), pp. 2-3.

Bush, L. K. (1986, November). *En medio de la crisis nace la visión* [In the midst of crisis The vision is born]. (C. Calderón, Ed.) *COMIBAM informa [COMIBAM informs]*, *1* (7), pp. 4-5.

Bush, L. K. (1987, November). *Luz para las naciones* [Light for the nations]. Plenary session presented at the First Ibero American Missionary Congress, Sao Paulo, Brazil.

Bush, L. K. (1987, March-April). *COMIBAM e nosso* [COMIBAM is ours]. (C. Calderón, Ed.) *COMIBAM Informa* (9), pp. 3, 7.

Bush, L. K. (1990). *Getting to the core of the core: the 10/40 window.* San Jose, CA: Partners International.

Bush, L. K. (2001a). *La globalización del movimiento misionero y los nuevos paradigmas* [The globalization of the missionary movement and new paradigms]. In F.A. Bertuzzi (Ed.), *Las misiones latinas para el siglo XXI: Compendio de COMIBAM 97, el segundo Congreso Misionero Iberoamericano, Acapulco, México* [Latin missions for the 21st century: Handbook of the COMIBAM 1997, 2nd Ibero American Missionary Congress, Acapulco, Mexico] (2nd ed.) (pp. 107-123). Retrieved from http://www.recursosmisioneros.com/resouces/Misiones_latinas_siglo_XXI.pdf

Bush, L. K. (2001b). *Grace at work: A personal case study.* (Unpublished term paper, School of World Mission, Fuller Theological Seminary, Pasadena, CA).

Bush, L. K. (2002). *Catalysts of world evangelization* (Doctoral dissertation). Retrieved From ProQuest, UMI Dissertations Publishing. (DAI-A 63/04)

Bustamante, C. (2006). *Consejos para el cuidado del misionero* [Advice for missionary care]. Miami, FL: Editorial Patmos.

Calderón, C. (1986, September). Editorial. (C. Calderón, Ed.) *COMIBAM informa [COMIBAM informs]*, *1* (6), p. 2.

Calderón, C. (1986, November). Editorial. (C. Calderón, Ed.) *COMIBAM informa [COMIBAM informs]*, *1* (7), p. 2.

Carlisle, J. (2006). *Plantando iglesias pioneras* [Planting pioneer churches]. In L. DeCarvalho (Ed.), *Visión por las naciones* [Vision for the nations] (2nd ed.) (pp. 109-116). Miami, FL: Editorial Patmos.

Carpio, J. (2006a). *Cuatro hombres, tres eras* [Four men, three eras]. In L. DeCarvalho (Ed.), *Visión por las naciones* [Vision for the nations] (2nd ed.) (pp. 49-54). Miami, FL: Editorial Patmos.

Carpio, J. (2006b). *El reino contraataca* [The kingdom strikes back]. In L. DeCarvalho (Ed.), *Visión por las naciones* [Vision for the nations] (2nd ed.) (pp. 39-48). Miami, FL: Editorial Patmos.

Carrillo, P. (2006). *Misioneros latinos ¿Hijos del postmodernismo?* [Latin missionaries: Children of postmodernity]. In F. A. Bertuzzi (Ed.), *Misión Transcultural* [Cross-cultural mission] (3rd ed.) (pp. 65-73). Miami, FL: Editorial Patmos.

Castillo, M. (2001). *La realidad de Asia* [The Asia reality]. In F.A. Bertuzzi (Ed.), *Las misiones latinas para el siglo XXI: Compendio de COMIBAM 97, el segundo Congreso Misionero Iberoamericano, Acapulco, México, 27 al 31 de octubre de 1997* [Latin missions for the 21st century: Handbook of the COMIBAM 1997, 2nd Ibero American Missionary Congress, Acapulco, Mexico, October 27 through 31, 1997] (2nd ed.) (pp. 55-63). Retrieved from http://www.recursosmisioneros.com/resouces/Misiones_latinas_siglo_XXI.pdf

Castro, E. (1985). *Llamados a liberar: Misión y unidad en la perspectiva del reino de Dios* [Called to liberate: Mission and unity in the perspective of the kingdom of God]. Buenos Aires, Argentina: Ediciones la Aurora.

Catálogo de las Organizaciones Misioneras de Argentina [Catalog of Argentina's Missionary Organizations] (2006). Retrieved from http://www.comibam.org/catalogo2006/index.htm

Collins, J. (2001). *Good to great: Why some companies make the leap and others don't.* New York, NY: Harper Business.

COMIBAM. (1985, December). *COMIBAM informa [COMIBAM informs], 1* (2).

COMIBAM. (1986a, February). *COMIBAM informa [COMIBAM informs], 1* (3).

COMIBAM. (1986b, February). *Selección e involucramiento* [Selection and involvement]. *COMIBAM informa [COMIBAM informs], 1*(3), p. 6.

COMIBAM. (1986, April). (F. Mazariegos, Ed.) *COMIBAM informa [COMIBAM informs], 1* (4).

COMIBAM. (1986, July). (C. Calderón, Ed.) *COMIBAM informa [COMIBAM informs], 1* (5).

COMIBAM. (1986, November). (C. Calderón, Ed.) *COMIBAM informa [COMIBAM informs], 1* (7).

COMIBAM. (1987, March-April). (C. Calderón, Ed.) *COMIBAM informa [COMIBAM informs], 1* (9).

COMIBAM. (1987, May-June). (C. Calderón, Ed.) *COMIBAM informa [COMIBAM informs], 1* (10).

COMIBAM/Bertuzzi Archive. Documents related to the COMIBAM network in Ibero America. Santa Fe, Argentina.

COMIBAM International (n.d.). *¿Qué es COMIBAM?* [What is COMIBAM?]. Retrieved from

http://www.comibam.org/que-es-comibam/

COMIBAM International. (1996). *Organizaciones misioneras Argentina (Resumen numérico: 1996)* [Argentina missionary organizations (Numerical summary)]. Retrieved from

http://www.comibam.org/catalogo2006/esp/consulta-1996/arg/_resum.htm

COMIBAM International. (2002, October 28) *Los evangélicos y los misioneros Ibero-americanos* [Evangelicals and Ibero American missionaries]. Retrieved from http://www.comibam.org/Estadisworld01/Ibero-America.htm

COMIBAM International. (2005, September 1). *Informe, Santiago del Estero: Encuentro de la mesa coordinadora y colaboradores 2005* [Report of the Santiago de Estero: Summit of the coordinating board and partners 2005]. Retrieved from http://www.comibam.org/docs/rcc_encuentro_st_esteros.pdf

COMIBAM International (2006a). *Definiciones e información adicional* [Definitions and additional information]. Retrieved from http://www.comibam.org/catalogo2006/Misc/def_es.htm

COMIBAM International. (2006b). *Organizaciones misioneras Argentina (Resumen numérico: 2006)* [Argentina missionary organizations (Numerical summary)]. Retrieved from http://www.comibam.org/catalogo2006/esp/consulta-2006/arg/_resum.htm

COMIBAM International. (2006c). *Organizaciones misioneras de Iberoamérica* [Ibero America missionary organizations]. Retrieved from http://www.comibam.org/catalogo2006/Esp/consulta-2006/Ibe/_agencias.htm

COMIBAM International. (2006d). *Países donde misioneros Ibero-Americanos están trabajando* [Countries where Ibero American missionaries are working]. Retrieved from http://www.comibam.org/catalogo2006/Esp/consulta-2006/Ibe/Campos_res.htm

COMIBAM International. (2006e). *Reporte general del III Congreso Misionero Iberoamericano, Noviembre 13 al 17 de 2006, Granada, España* [General report of the Third Ibero American Missionary Congress, November 13 through 17, 2006, Granada, Spain]. Retrieved from http://www.comibam.org/docs/reporte_comibamIII_es.pdf

Conclusiones: Consideraciones bíblicas. (2000, October). CLADE IV, Quito, Ecuador. Retrieved from http://www.comibam.org/ponencias/CladeIV/index.htm

Coote, R. T. (2000). AD 2000 and the 10/40 Window: A preliminary assessment. *International Bulletin of Missionary Research, 24*(4), 160.

Corbett, S. & Fikkert B. (2009). *When helping hurts: How to alleviate poverty without Hurting the poor…and yourself.* Chicago, IL: Moody Publishers.

Covey, S. (1991). *Principle-centered leadership.* New York, NY: Simon & Schuster.

Coy, T. F. (1999). *Incarnation and the kingdom of God: The political ideologies of Orlando Costas, C. René Padilla and Samuel Escobar.* (Doctoral dissertation). Retrieved from ProQuest Dissertations and Theses. (Order No. 9952586)

Cueva, S. (Ed.). (2004). *Misión para el tercer milenio: Construyendo puentes misioneros de doble vía, una serie de conferencias* [Mission for the third millennium: Building two-way missionary bridges, a series of conferences]. Barcelona, Spain: Editorial CLIE.

Cueva, S. (2011). *Partnership in mission in creative tension: An analysis of the relationships in mission within the Evangelical Movement with special reference to Peru and Britain 1987-2006* (Unpublished doctoral dissertation). University of Wales, Trinity Saint David.

Davies, P. (2006). *Base Veterotestamentaria de la misión transcultural, integral y profética* [Old Testament basis for cross-cultural, holistic and prophetic mission]. In F. A. Bertuzzi (Ed.), *Misión Transcultural* [Cross-cultural mission] (3rd ed.) (pp. 23-39). Miami, FL: Editorial Patmos.

DeCarvalho, L. (Ed.). (2006). *Visión por las naciones* [Vision for the nations]. Miami, FL: Editorial Patmos.

DeCarvalho, L. (2007). COMIBAM III: Research project--phase I. *Connections: The journal of the WEA mission commission, 6,* 20-24.

DeCarvalho, L., Jiménez, N., González, C, and Guerrero, S. (2006). *Strengths and Weaknesses of the Ibero American Missionary.* COMIBAM III: Research project—phase I. Granada, Spain: COMIBAM International. Retrieved from http://www.recursosmisioneros.com/resources/Fortalezas_debilidades.pdf

Departamento de investigación [Research department]. (n.d.). Retrieved from http://www.comibam.org/depart/investigacion/indice.htm

Departamento de publicaciones [Publication department]. (n.d.). Retrieved from http://www.comibam.org/depart/public/objectivos.htm

Dick, L. (2011). God's global plan: God unveils the fourth era of His plan to reach the world with the message of His love. *Rio Grande Magazine 18,* 4-5.

Diguero, R. (2006). *La conexión de Abraham* [The Abraham Connection]. In L. DeCarvalho (Ed.), *Visión por las naciones* [Vision for the nations] (2nd ed.) (pp. 11-19). Miami, FL: Editorial Patmos.

Directorio de COMIBAM [COMIBAM directory]. (n.d.). Retrieved from http://www.comibam.org/equipo.htm

Dos Santos, J. (1987, May-June). *Movimientos misioneros en América* [Missionary Movements in America]. (C. Calderón, Ed.) *COMIBAM informa [COMIBAM informs]*, *1* (10), pp. 5-6.

Eby, J. (2007). *World impacting churches: 10 essential characteristics for changing the world and finishing the great commission.* Mustang, OK: Tate Publishing & Enterprises.

Ekström, B. (Ed.). (2006a). *El espíritu de COMIBAM* [The COMIBAM spirit]. Miami, FL: Editorial Patmos.

Ekström, B. (2006b). *El espíritu de COMIBAM* [The COMIBAM spirit]. In B. Ekström (Ed.), *El espíritu de COMIBAM* [The COMIBAM spirit] (2nd ed.) (pp. 5-23). Miami, FL: Editorial Patmos.

Ekström, B. (2007). From my corner. *Connections: The journal of the WEA mission commission 6*, 3.

Entre nos (1984, December). *1* (3), 3.

Escobar, S. (1987). *La fe evangélica y las teologías de la liberación* [Evangelical faith and liberation theologies]. El Paso, TX: Casa Bautista de Publicaciones.

Escobar, S. (1998). *De la misión a la teología* [From mission to theology]. Buenos Aires, Argentina: Kairos Ediciones.

Escobar, S. (1999). *Tiempo de misión: América latina y la misión cristiana hoy* [Changing tides: Latin America and world missions today]. Bogota, Colombia: Clara Ediciones.

Escobar, S. (2002). *Changing tides: Latin America and world mission today.* Maryknoll, NY: Orbis Books.

Escobar, S. (2003). *The new global mission: The gospel from everywhere to everyone.* Downers Grove, IL: Intervarsity Press.

Escobar, S. (2005, April). *Protestantismo latinoamericano en el contexto de una iglesia global* [Latin American Protestantism in the context of global church]. *Revista electrónica Espacio de Diálogo* [Room for Dialogue, Electronic Journal] (Fraternidad Teológica Latinoamericana). Retrieved from http://www.cenpromex.org.mx/revista_ftl/ftl/textos/ samuel_escobar.html

Escobar, S. (2007). COMIBAM III: A personal perspective. *Connections: The journal of the WEA mission commission 6*, 25-26.

Eshleman, P. (2010). World evangelization in the 21st century: Prioritizing the essential Elements of the Great Commission. Cape Town 2010 Advance Paper. Retrieved from http://conversation.lausanne.org/en/conversations/detail/10522

Etnia a etnia...Esta generación. (n.d.). Retrieved from http://www.comibam.org/docs/etniaaetnia_boletindeprens_1.pdf

Fabio, C. (1987, November). *Apocalipsis, la revelación del reino* [Revelation, the revelation of the kingdom]. Plenary session presented at the First Ibero American Missionary Congress, Sao Paulo, Brazil.

Finley, N. (1986, September). *Australia, campo necesitado* [Australia, needy field]. (C. Calderón, Ed.) *COMIBAM informa [COMIBAM informs]*, *1* (6), p. 7.

Friedman, T. L. (2006). *The world is flat: A brief history of the twenty-first century*. New York, NY: Farrar, Straus and Giroux.

Frizen, E. (1992). *75 years of IFMA, 1917-1992: The nondenominational missions movement*. Pasadena, CA: William Carey Library.

Gava, O. (2007, July 3-6). *Consulta de capacitación región México (COMIMEX— COMIBAM Internacional)* [Mexico region training consultation (COMIMEX— COMIBAM International)]. Mexico. Retrieved from http://www.comibam.org/docs/rcc_consulta_mexico.pdf

Gava, O. (2005, February). *Proyecto (Red de centros de capacitación)* [Project (Training Centers network)]. Retrieved from http://www.comibam.org/docs/rcc_description.pdf

Girón, R. (1987, November). *Espíritu Santo en la misión del pueblo de Dios* [The Holy Spirit in the mission of the people of God]. Plenary session presented at the First Ibero American Missionary Congress, Sao Paulo, Brazil.

Girón, R. (2000). The Latin-American missionary movement: A new paradigm in missions. Celebrate Messiah 2000 Convergence Presentation. Retrieved from http://www.ad2000.org/celebrate/giron.htm

Girón, R. (2001). *El movimiento misionero hacia el siglo XXI* [The missionary movement toward the 21st century]. In F.A. Bertuzzi (Ed.), *Las misiones latinas para el siglo XXI: Compendio de COMIBAM 97, el segundo Congreso Misionero Iberoamericano, Acapulco, México, 27 al 31 de octubre de 1997* [Latin missions for the 21st century: Handbook of the COMIBAM 1997, 2nd Ibero American Missionary Congress, Acapulco, Mexico, October 27 through 31, 1997] (2nd ed.) (pp. 217-235). Retrieved from http://www.recursosmisioneros.com/resouces/Misiones_latinas_siglo_XXI.pdf

Gonzalez, J. (1990). *Mañana: Christian theology from a Hispanic perspective.* Nashville, TN: Abingdon Press.

Gonzalez, J. (2007, March). *The challenge to the church at large.* Lecture at the 2007 Rollins Lectures; The Latino church: Converting challenges to opportunities at the Baptist University of the Americas, San Antonio, Texas.

Gonzalez, S. (2006). *El propósito inalterable de Dios* [The unchangeable purpose of God]. In L. DeCarvalho (Ed.), *Visión por las naciones* [Vision for the nations] (2nd ed.) (pp. 23-27). Miami, FL: Editorial Patmos.

Greenleaf, R. K. (1977). *Servant leadership: A journey into the nature of legitimate power and greatness.* New York, NY: Paulist Press.

Guarneri, J. (2009). COMIBAM: Calling Latin Americans to the global challenge. *Missions from the majority world: Progress, challenges and case studies.* EMS, 17, Pasadena, CA: William Carey Library, 221-262.

Guder, D. L. (1998). *Missional church: A vision for the sending of the church in North America.* Grand Rapids, MI: William B. Eerdmans.

Hatch, R. (1987, November). *Lecciones y modelos* [Lessons and models]. Plenary session presented at the First Ibero American Missionary Congress, Sao Paulo, Brazil.

Hawthorne, S. C. (2009). The story of His glory. In R. D. Winter & S. C. Hawthorne (Eds.). *Perspectives on the world Christian movement* (4th ed.) (pp. 49-63). Pasadena, CA: William Carey Library.

Hesselgrave, D. (2006). *Paradigms in conflict: 10 key questions in Christian missions today.* Grand Rapids, MI: Kregel Publications.

Impressions of III COMIBAM Missionary Congress. (2007). *Connections: The journal of The WEA mission commission 6,* 29-34.

Jaffarian, M. (2004). Are there more non-Western missionaries than Western missionaries? *International Bulletin of Missionary Research, 28*(3), 131-132. Retrieved from http://web.ebscohost.com.library.dbu.edu:2048/ehost/pdfviewer/pdfviewer?sid=69cc6666-3b03-4434-8064-c00c588199a6%40sessionmgr111&vid=13&hid=121

Jenkins, P. (2002). *The Next Christendom: The coming of global Christianity.* New York, NY: Oxford University Press.

Jimenez, O. (2006). *Terminando la tarea, el cuadro completo* [Finishing the task, the complete picture]. In L. DeCarvalho (Ed.), *Visión por las naciones* [Vision for the nations] (2nd ed.) (pp. 97-106). Miami, FL: Editorial Patmos.

John R. Mott: The Noble Peace Prize 1946; Biography. (1946). Retrieved from http://nobelprize.org/nobel_prizes/peace/laureates/1946/mott-bio.html

Johnstone, P., & Mandryk, J. (2001). *Operation world: When we pray God works* (6th ed.). Carlisle, England: Paternoster Lifestyle.

Joshua, P. (2001*).* *La cruz, la guerra espiritual y las misiones mundiales* [The cross, spiritual warfare and world missions]. In F.A. Bertuzzi (Ed.), *Las misiones latinas para el siglo XXI: Compendio de COMIBAM 97, el segundo Congreso Misionero Iberoamericano, Acapulco, México, 27 al 31 de octubre de 1997* [Latin missions for the 21st century: Handbook of the COMIBAM 1997, 2nd Ibero American Missionary Congress, Acapulco, Mexico, October 27 through 31, 1997] (2nd ed.) (pp. 161-179). Retrieved from http://www.recursosmisioneros.com/resouces/Misiones_latinas_siglo_XXI.pdf

Kerr, D. & Ross, K. (Ed.). (2009). *Edinburgh 2010: Mission then and now.* Pasadena, CA: William Carey International University Press.

Knell, B. (2006). Who owns Mission? *Evangel*, 24(3), i-iv.

Knospe, D. L. (2001). *Eurasia: Un desafío misionero* [Eastern Europe: A missionary challenge]. In F.A. Bertuzzi (Ed.), *Las misiones latinas para el siglo XXI: Compendio de COMIBAM 97, el segundo Congreso Misionero Iberoamericano, Acapulco, México, 27 al 31 de octubre de 1997* [Latin missions for the 21st century: Handbook of the COMIBAM 1997, 2nd Ibero American Missionary Congress, Acapulco, Mexico, October 27 through 31, 1997] (2nd ed.) (pp. 145-159). Retrieved from http://www.recursosmisioneros.com/resouces/Misiones_latinas_siglo_XXI.pdf

Lane, D. (2006). *Administración eficaz de una agencia misionera: Un manual elaborado desde y para el tercer mundo, indispensable para la creación y la administración de estructuras de envío misionero* [Effective administration of a missionary agency: A manual prepared from and for the third world, required for the creation and administration of missionary sending organizations]. Barcelona, Spain: Editorial CLIE.

Lanier, S. A. (2000). *Foreign to familiar: A guide to understanding hot- and cold-climate cultures.* Hagerstown, MD: McDougal Publisher.

Latin American Division of the U.S. Center for World Mission. (2006). *La última frontera* [The last frontier]. In L. DeCarvalho (Ed.), *Visión por las naciones* [Vision for the nations] (2nd ed.) (pp. 57-66). Miami, FL: Editorial Patmos.

Lausanne 1974: Historical background. (n.d.). Retrieved from http://www.lausanne.org/lausanne-1974/lausanne-1974-historical-background.html

The Lausanne covenant. (1974, July). Retrieved from

http://www.lausanne.org/all-documents/lausanne-covenant.html

Lausanne occasional paper 2: The Willowbank report: Consultation on gospel and culture. (1978). Retrieved from

http://www.lausanne.org/all-documents/lop-2.html

Lausanne occasional paper 21: Evangelism and social responsibility: An evangelical commitment. (1982). Retrieved from

http://www.lausanne.org/grand-rapids-1982/lop-21.html

Lee, D. T. W. (2001). *El pastoreo y la supervisión de los misioneros* [The pastoral care and supervision of missionaries]. In F.A. Bertuzzi (Ed.), *Las misiones latinas para el siglo XXI: Compendio de COMIBAM 97, el segundo Congreso Misionero Iberoamericano, Acapulco, México, 27 al 31 de octubre de 1997* [Latin missions for the 21st century: Handbook of the COMIBAM 1997, 2nd Ibero American Missionary Congress, Acapulco, Mexico, October 27 through 31, 1997] (2nd ed.) (pp. 181-193). Retrieved from

http://www.recursosmisioneros.com/resouces/Misiones_latinas_siglo_XXI.pdf

Lewis, J. P. (1990a). *Misión mundial: Un análisis del movimiento cristiano mundial: Las bases bíblicas e históricas; Vol. 1* [World mission: An analysis of the world Christian movement: Biblical and historical bases; Vol. 1]. Miami, FL: Editorial Unilit.

Lewis, J. P. (1990b). *Misión mundial: Un análisis del movimiento cristiano mundial: La dimensión estratégica; Vol. 2* [World mission: An analysis of the world Christian movement: the strategic dimension]. Miami, FL: Editorial Unilit.

Lewis, J. P. (1990c). *Misión mundial: Un análisis del movimiento cristiano mundial: Consideraciones transculturales; Vol. 3* [World mission: An analysis of the world Christian movement: Cross-cultural considerations; Vol. 3] Miami, FL: Editorial Unilit.

Lewis, J. P. (1995). *Trabajando tu llamado a las naciones: Una guía para el misionero biocupacional* [Working your call to the nations: A guide for the bivocational missionary] (2nd ed.). COMIBAM Internacional/Editorial Unilit.

Lewis, J. P.(2003, November). *El perfil del misionero frente un mundo turbulento* [The profile of the missionary confronting a turbulent world]. Presentation given at II Asamblea Internacional, San Salvador [COMIBAM's second international assembly, San Salvador]. Retrieved from http://www.comibam.org/ponencias/IIAsamblea/EPM.htm

Limpic, T. (Ed.). (1997). *Catálogo de organizaciones misioneras Iberoamericanas: II Congreso Iberoamericano. Acapulco, México, 27 al 31 de octubre, 1997* [Catalog of Ibero American missionary organizations: 2nd Ibero American congress, Acapulco, Mexico, October 27 through 31, 1997]. Sao Paulo, Brazil: COMIBAM.

Limpic, T. (Ed.). (2002). *Estadísticas misioneras* [Missionary statistics]. Retrieved from http://www.slideshare.net/libroscristianospdf/estadisticas-misioneras

Limpic, T. (Ed.). (2006). *Catálogo de las organizaciones misioneras de Iberoamérica 2006: COMIBAM* [2006 Iberoamerican missionary organizations catalog: COMIBAM]. Retrieved from http://recursosmisioneros.com/resources/Catalogo_organizaciones.pdf

Londoño, J. (2002, November). *La misión de Cristo: Modelos del pasado, presente y Futuro* [The mission of Christ: Models of the past, present and future]. Presentation given at *Cumbre de Liderazgo*, 2002 [COMIBAM's 2002 Leadership Summit] Madrid, Spain. Retrieved from http://www.comibam.org/ponencias/cumpliespa/Palabra.htm

Londoño, J. (Ed.). (2003). *Manual de estructuras de envío: Conclusiones de la consulta Continental de estructuras de envío. Ciudad de Panamá, febrero 11, 12 y 13 de 2003* [Sending mechanisms, Panama City, Panama, February 11, 12 & 13, 2003]. Retrieved from http://www.recursosmisioneros.com/resources/Manual_estructuras_envio.pdf

Londoño, J. (2003, November). *Cambios teológicos en la fuerza misionera* [Theological changes in the missionary force]. Presentation given at II Asamblea Internacional, San Salvador [COMIBAM's second international assembly, San Salvador]. Retrieved from http://www.comibam.org/ponencias/IIAsamblea/CTEFM.htm

Londoño, J. (2006a). *Alcance una etnia* [Reach a people group]. (2nd ed.). Miami, FL: Editorial Patmos.

Londoño, J. (2006b). *Alcance una etnia, un programa viable* [Reach a people group, a viable program]. In B. Ekström (Ed.), *El espíritu de COMIBAM* [The COMIBAM spirit] (2nd ed.) (pp. 35-42). Miami, FL: Editorial Patmos.

Londoño, J. (2007). General report of the III Ibero American missions congress. *Connections: The journal of the WEA mission commission 6*, 11-13.

Loss, M. (1996). *Choque transcultural* [Cross-cultural shock]. New York, NY: Ballantine Books.

The Manila Manifesto. (1989, July). Retrieved from http://www.lausanne.org/manila-1989/the-manila-manifesto.html

Manual del Congreso [Congress Manual]. (2006, November 13-17). III Congreso Ibero-Americano [Third Ibero American Congress]. COMIBAM International. Retrieved from http://www.comibam.org/docs/manual_es.pdf

Marroquín, S. (1986, November). *Discipulado con visión misionera* [Discipleship with missionary vision]. (C. Calderón, Ed.) *COMIBAM informa [COMIBAM informs]*, *1* (7), p. 3.

Matamoros, A. (2006). *Misioneros latinos ¿Quiénes son? ¿Dónde están?* [Latin Missionaries: Who are they? Where are they?]. In B. Ekström (Ed.), *El espíritu de COMIBAM* [The COMIBAM spirit] (2nd ed.) (pp. 49-56). Miami, FL: Editorial Patmos.

Mead, L. B. (1991). *The once and future church: Reinventing the congregation for a new mission frontier*. Herndon, VA: Alban Institute, Inc.

Miller, D. (Ed.). (1994). *Coming of age: Protestantism in contemporary Latin America*. Lanham, MD: University Press of America.

Minatrea, M. (2004). *Shaped by God's heart: The passion and practices of missional churches*. San Francisco, CA: John Wiley & Sons, Inc.

Morales, H. C. (2006). *Adelphos, sunergos o sustratiotes* [*Adelphos, sunergos or sustratiotes*]. In B. Ekström (Ed.), *El espíritu de COMIBAM* [The COMIBAM spirit] (2nd ed.) (pp. 25-33). Miami, FL: Editorial Patmos.

Morales, I. (1987, March-April). *Pedid pues, al Padre que envíe obreros a su mies* [Ask, then the Father to send workers to his harvest]. (C. Calderón, Ed.) *COMIBAM informa [COMIBAM informs], 1* (9), p. 6.

Moreno, P.P. (2001). *Baptists in Latin America and their theological contributions.* Baptist History and Heritage Society. Retrieved from http://www.encyclopedia.com/doc/1G1-94160932.html.

Noll, M. A. (2000). *Turning points: Decisive moments in the history of Christianity.* Grand Rapids, MI: Baker Academic.

Nuñez, E. A. (1997). *Hacia una misionlogía evangélica Latinoamericana: Bases bíblicas de la misión (Antiguo Testamento)* [Toward a Latin American Evangelical missiology: Biblical bases for the mission (Old Testament)] [PDF version]. Retrieved from http://www.recursosmisioneros.com/resources/Hacia_misionologia_latinoamericana.pdf

Nuñez, E. A. & Taylor, W. (1996). *Crisis and hope in Latin America: An evangelical perspective.* Pasadena, CA: William Carey Library.

O'Donnell, K. (2006). *El cuidado integral del misionero: Perspectivas y prácticas alrededor del mundo* [Doing member care well: perspectives and practices from around the world]. Colombia: COMIBAM Internacional.

Ott, C. & Netland, H. (Ed.). (2006). *Globalizing theology: Belief and practice in an era of world Christianity.* Grand Rapids, MI: Baker Academic.

Padilla, C. R. (1986). *Misión integral: Ensayos sobre el reino y la iglesia* [Holistic mission: Essays on the kingdom and the church]. Grand Rapids, MI: Nueva Creación.

Padilla, C. R. (2006, March 10). What Is Integral Mission? *Integral Mission Newsletter*. Retrieved from http://www.integral-mission.org/PDF_files/Rene-What_is_integral_mission.pdf

Padilla, C. R. (2007). *Evangelical theology in a Latin American context*. Retrieved from http://integral- mission.org/PDF_files/Evangelical_Theology_in_LA_context.pdf

Palau, L. (Speaker). (1982). *Una vision evangelística y misionera* [An evangelistic and missionary vision]. (Audio file). Congreso de pastores 1982 [Pastors Congress 1982], Villa Giardino, Córdoba, Argentina. Retrieved from http://www.mensajescristianos.com.ar/?p=735

Palau, L. (1987, November). *Sueña grandes sueños* [Dream big dreams]. Plenary session presented at the First Ibero American Missionary Congress, Sao Paulo, Brazil.

Paredes, T. (2006). *Base Neotestamentaria de la misión transcultural* [New Testament basis for cross-cultural mission]. In F. A. Bertuzzi (Ed.), *Misión Transcultural* [Cross-cultural mission] (3rd ed.) (pp. 41-53). Miami, FL: Editorial Patmos.

Parks, S. K. & Scott, J. (2010). Missing peoples: The unserved "one-fourth" world: Especially Buddhists, Hindus & Muslims. Cape Town 2010 Advance Paper. Retrieved from http://conversation.lausanne.org/en/conversations/detail/10535

Pate, L. D. (1987). *Misionología: Nuestro cometido transcultural* [Missiology: Our cross-cultural commitment]. Miami FL: Editoral Vida.

Pate, L. D. (1989). *From every people: A handbook of two-thirds world missions, with directory/history/analysis.* Morovia, CA: MARC.

Penyak, L. & Petry, W. (Ed.). (2006). *Religion in Latin America: A documentary history.* Maryknoll, NY: Orbis Books.

Peralta, A. (1986, September). *Testimonio* [Testimony]. (C. Calderón, Ed.) *COMIBAM informa [COMIBAM informs], 1* (6), pp. 6-7.

Peralta, A. (pseudonym). (2007). Message to the church in Ibero America: A COMIBAM congress plenary. *Connections: The journal of the WEA mission commission 6*, 14-16.

Pickett, R. C. & Hawthorne S. C. (1981). Helping others help themselves: Christian Community development in *Perspectives on the world Christian movement,* translated by Jonathan Lewis (1990) in *Misión mundial* [World mission], vol. 2. Miami: Editorial Unilit.

Plou, D. S. (2004). Ecumenical history of Latin America. *A History of the Ecumenical Movement.* WCC Publications. Retrieved from http://overcomingviolence.org/en/new-and-events/archive/past-annual-foci/2006-latin-america.html

Pocock, M., Van Rheenen, G. & McConnell, D. (2005). *Changing face of world missions: The engaging contemporary issues and trends.* Grand Rapids, MI: Baker Academic.

Porter, R. (2007). Global Mission and local church. *Evangel*, 25(1), i-iv.

Prado, O. (2001). *El envío de misioneros desde América Latina* [Missionary sending from Latin America]. In F.A. Bertuzzi (Ed.), *Las misiones latinas para el siglo XXI: Compendio de COMIBAM 97, el segundo Congreso Misionero Iberoamericano, Acapulco, México, 27 al 31 de octubre de 1997* [Latin missions for the 21st century: Handbook of the COMIBAM 1997, 2nd Ibero American Missionary Congress, Acapulco, Mexico, October 27 through 31, 1997] (2nd ed.) (pp. 125-143). Retrieved from http://www.recursosmisioneros.com/resouces/Misiones_latinas_siglo_XXI pdf

Queiróz, E. (1987, November). *La iglesia y las misiones* [The church and missions]. Plenary session presented at the First Ibero American Missionary Congress, Sao Paulo, Brazil.

Queiróz, E. (2006). *Batalla espiritual y misión, estrategia misionera desde la iglesia Local* [Spiritual warfare and mission, mission strategy from the local church]. In L. DeCarvalho (Ed.), *Visión por las naciones* [Vision for the nations] (2nd ed.) (pp. 119-128). Miami, FL: Editorial Patmos.

Quicaña, F. (2001). *La realidad de las sociedades indígenas* [The reality of tribal communities]. In F.A. Bertuzzi (Ed.), *Las misiones latinas para el siglo XXI: Compendio de COMIBAM 97, el segundo Congreso Misionero Iberoamericano, Acapulco, México, 27 al 31 de octubre de 1997* [Latin missions for the 21st century: Handbook of the COMIBAM 1997, 2nd Ibero American Missionary Congress, Acapulco, Mexico, October 27 through 31, 1997] (2nd ed.) (pp. 195-215). Retrieved from http://www.recursosmisioneros.com/resouces/Misiones_latinas_siglo_XXI.pdf

Rance, D. (2006). *Comunicando el evangelio en otra cultura* [Communicating the gospel in another culture]. In L. DeCarvalho (Ed.), *Visión por las naciones* [Vision for the nations] (2nd ed.) (pp. 69-79). Miami: Editorial Patmos.

Reyes, A. L. (2009). *Intercultural relationships in organizational transformation: A single case-study of Baptist University of the Americas* (Doctoral dissertation). Andrews University, Berrien Springs, MI.

Risk, M. (2001). *La realidad de los evangélicos en el Medio Oriente árabe* [The reality of Evangelicals in the Arabic Middle East]. In F.A. Bertuzzi (Ed.), *Las misiones latinas para el siglo XXI: Compendio de COMIBAM 97, el segundo Congreso Misionero Iberoamericano, Acapulco, México, 27 al 31 de octubre de 1997* [Latin missions for the 21st century: Handbook of the COMIBAM 1997, 2nd Ibero American Missionary Congress, Acapulco, Mexico, October 27 through 31, 1997] (2nd ed.) (pp. 101-105). Retrieved from http://www.recursosmisioneros.com/resouces/Misiones_latinas_siglo_XXI.pdf

Rivera, E. (2006). *Jesús, el Mesías para todas las naciones* [Jesus, the Messiah for all nations]. In L. DeCarvalho (Ed.), *Visión por las naciones* [Vision for the nations] (2nd ed.) (pp. 31-38). Miami, FL: Editorial Patmos.

Robb, J. (1989). *¡Foco! El poder del pensamiento puesto en el grupo humano: Un Manual práctico para planear estrategias que nos permitan alcanzar a los no alcanzados* [Focus! The power of people group thinking: A practical manual for strategy planning to reach the unreached]. Monrovia, CA: MARC.

Robert, A. (2004). *Conciencia misionera* [Missionary awareness]. Barcelona, Spain: Editorial CLIE.

Robert, D. (2009). *Christian mission: How Christianity became a world religion.* San Francisco, CA: Wiley-Blackwell.

Rodriguez, D. A. (2011). *A future for the Latino Church: Models for multilingual, multigenerational Hispanic congregations.* Downers Grove, IL: IVP Academic.

Rodríguez, J. & Gava, O. (2005, September 26). *Rumbo a la excelencia en la capacitación misionera* [Toward excellency in missionary training]. Report at the Consulta de Centros de Capacitación Misionera de Centro América (COMCA) [Central America missionary training centers consultation]. Retrieved from http://www.comibam.org/docs/rcc_consulta_centroamerica.pdf

Ruiz, D. D. (n.d.). *COMIBAM as a process leading to a congress.* Retrieved from http://www.comibam.org/docs/COMIBAM_process.pdf

Ruiz, D. D. (Ed.). (1997). *Guía para los movimientos misioneros nacionales: Una orientación para su formación y fortalecimiento* [Guide for the national missions movements: An orientation for their formation and strengthening]. Retrieved from http://www.recursosmisioneros.com/resources/Guia_movimientos_nacionales.pdf

Ruiz, D. D. (2000, October). *La singularidad de nuestra misión transcultural* [The uniqueness of our cross-cultural mission]. Presentation made at CLADE IV, October 2000; Quito, Ecuador. Retrieved from http://www.comibam.org/ponencias/CladeIV/ponencia4.htm

Ruíz, D. D. (2001a). *La selección del misionero* [The selection of the missionary]. In F.A. Bertuzzi (Ed.), *Las misiones latinas para el siglo XXI: Compendio de COMIBAM 97, el segundo Congreso Misionero Iberoamericano, Acapulco, México* [Latin missions for the 21st century: Handbook of the COMIBAM 1997, 2nd Ibero American Missionary Congress, Acapulco, Mexico] (2nd ed.) (pp. 27-39). Retrieved from http://www.recursosmisioneros.com/resouces/Misiones_latinas_siglo_XXI.pdf

Ruíz, D. D. (2001b). Prologue. In F.A. Bertuzzi (Ed.), *Las misiones latinas para el siglo XXI: Compendio de COMIBAM 97, el segundo Congreso Misionero Iberoamericano, Acapulco, México* [Latin missions for the 21st century: Handbook of the COMIBAM 1997, 2nd Ibero American Missionary Congress, Acapulco] (2nd ed.) (pp. 81-99). Retrieved from http://www.recursosmisioneros.com/resouces/Misiones_latinas_siglo_XXI.pdf

Ruiz, D. D. (2002a, November). *Identidad, visión y proyección del movimiento misionero Ibero-Americano* [Identity, vision and projection of the Ibero American missionary movement]. Presentation made at the Cumbre de Liderazgo [COMIBAM's leadership summit], Madrid, Spain. Retrieved from http://www.comibam.org/ponencias/cumpliespa/identidad.htm

Ruíz, D. D. (2002b, November). *Tendencias de la iglesia y sus implicaciones en el movimiento misionero Ibero-Americano: Amenazas y desafíos* [Tendencies of the church and their implications to the Ibero American missionary movement: Threats and challenges]. Presentation made at the Cumbre de Liderazgo [COMIBAM's leadership summit], Madrid, Spain. Retrieved from http://www.comibam.org/ponencias/cumpliespa/tendencias.htm

Ruíz, D. D. (2003, November). *Cambios paradigmáticos en el liderazgo global de las misiones* [Paradigm changes in global leadership for missions]. Presentation given at the II Asamblea Internacional [COMIBAM's second international assembly]. Retrieved from http:www.comibam.org/ponencias/IIAsamblea/CPEE.htm

Ruíz, D. D. (2006a). *La singularidad de nuestra misión transcultural* [The singularity of Our cross-cultural mission]. In F. A. Bertuzzi (Ed.), *Misión Transcultural* [Cross-cultural mission] (3rd ed.) (pp. 7-21). Miami, FL: Editorial Patmos.

Ruíz, D. D. (2006b). *Iglesias Fuertes, pastores con visión* [Strong churches, pastors with vision]. In B. Ekström (Ed.), *El espíritu de COMIBAM* [The COMIBAM spirit] (2nd ed.) (pp. 57-69). Miami, FL: Editorial Patmos.

Ruíz, D. D. (2006, November). *Marco histórico: III Congreso misionero Iberoamericano* [Historical framework: Third Ibero American Missionary Congress] *COMIBAM 2006*. Paper presented at COMIBAM 2006, Granada, Spain. Retrieved from http://www.comibam.org/docs/manual_es.pdf

Ruíz, D. D. (2007a). COMIBAM as a process leading to a congress. *Connections: The journal of the WEA mission commission 6*, 8-10.

Ruiz, D. D. (2007b). COMIBAM as a viable regional mission movement. *Connections: The journal of the WEA mission commission 6*, 5-7.

Samuel Escobar, Urbana speaker: Peruvian missiologist and missionary to the US and Spain. Retrieved from http://www.urbana.org/u2003.speakers,samuel.cfm

Sanchez, D. (2006). *Hispanic realities impacting America: Implications for evangelism and Missions*. Fort Worth, TX: Church Starting Network.

Saracco, N. (2000). Mission and missiology from Latin America. In Taylor, W. (Ed.), *Global missiology for the 21st century: The Iguassu dialogue*. Grand Rapids, MI: Baker Academic.

Scott, C. (1999). *De pastor a pastor* [From pastor to pastor]. Miami, FL: Editorial Patmos.

Scott, C. (2002, November). *El representante regional y su ministerio* [The regional representative and his ministry]. Presentation made at the Cumbre de Liderazgo [COMIBAM's leadership summit], Madrid, Spain. Retrieved from http://www.comibam.org/ponencias/cumpliespa/represenregio.htm

Scott, C. (2004). *Las misiones occidentales y su rol para el tercer milenio* [Western missions and their role in the third millennium]. In *Misión para el tercer milenio* [Mission for the third millennium] (pp. 69-80). Barcelona, Spain: Editorial CLIE.

Scott, C. (2006, November). *Un nuevo capítulo de los hechos del Espíritu Santo* [A new chapter of the acts of the Holy Spirit]. Paper presented at COMIBAM 2006, Granada, Spain. Retrieved from http://www.comibam.org/docs/manual_es.pdf

Scott, C. (2007). Projections and challenges for the Ibero American mission movement. *Connections: The journal of the WEA mission commission 6*, 17-19.

Scott, C. & Londoño, J. (2006). *Where is COMIBAM International heading? Strategic Focal points*. Retrieved from http://www.comibam.org/docs/whereiscomibamheading.pdf

Scott, L. (2000, January) Review of the book *Bases bíblicas de la misión: Perspectivas latinoamericanas* [Biblical bases for mission: Latin American perspectives]. *International Bulletin of Missionary Research*, 42-43.

Shenk, W. R. (2000). Venn, Henry. In A. S. Moreau (Ed.), *Evangelical Dictionary of World Missions* (p. 999). Grand Rapids, MI: Baker Books.

Smalley, W. A. (1978). Cultural implications of an indigenous church. In *Readings in Missionary Anthropology II* (pp. 363-372). Pasadena, CA: William Carey Library.

Smith, A.C. (1983). *The Essentials of missiology from the evangelical perspective of the Fraternidad Teológica Latinoamericana*. (Doctoral dissertation). (DAI-A 44/06, Item number1833)

Smith, O. J. (2003). *Pasión por las almas* [The passion for souls]. Terrassa, Spain: Editorial Clie.

Surenian, E. (1999). *Un clamor para las naciones* [A cry for the nations]. Miami, FL: Editorial Patmos.

Steuernagel, V. R. (2001). *¡Quita las sandalias de tus pies!* [Take the sandals off your feet]. In F.A. Bertuzzi (Ed.), *Las misiones latinas para el siglo XXI: Compendio de COMIBAM 97, el segundo Congreso Misionero Iberoamericano, Acapulco, México, 27 al 31 de octubre de 1997* [Latin missions for the 21st century: Handbook of the COMIBAM 1997, 2nd Ibero American Missionary Congress, Acapulco, Mexico, October 27 through 31, 1997] (2nd ed.) (pp. 11-25). Retrieved from http://www.recursosmisioneros.com/resouces/Misiones_latinas_siglo_XXI.pdf

Stott, J. (1995). Twenty years after Lausanne: Some personal reflections. *International Bulletin of Missionary Research, 19*(2), 50.

Taylor, W. D. (1987, November). *El desafío cultural* [The cultural challenge]. Plenary session presented at the First Ibero American Missionary Congress, Sao Paulo, Brazil.

Taylor, W. D. (1994). *Kingdom partnerships for synergy in missions.* Pasadena, CA: William Carey Library.

Taylor, W. D. (Ed.). (2000). *Global missiology for the 21st century: The Iguassu dialogue.* Grand Rapids, MI: Baker Academic.

Taylor, W. D. (2001). *La inminencia escatológica y las misiones* [Eschatological eminence and missions]. In F.A. Bertuzzi (Ed.), *Las misiones latinas para el siglo XXI: Compendio de COMIBAM 97, el segundo Congreso Misionero Iberoamericano, Acapulco, México, 27 al 31 de octubre de 1997* [Latin missions for the 21st century: Handbook of the COMIBAM 1997, 2nd Ibero American Missionary Congress, Acapulco, Mexico, October 27 through 31, 1997] (2nd ed.) (pp. 65-79). Retrieved from http://www.recursosmisioneros.com/resouces/Misiones_latinas_siglo_XXI.pdf

Taylor, W. D. (2007). From the heart and mind of the editor. *Connections: The Journal of the WEA Mission Commission 6*, 4.

Tinsley, W. (2005). *Finding God's vision: Missions and the new realities*. Rockwall, TX: Veritas Publishing.

Tostes, M. (2006). *El cuidado pastoral del misionero* [The pastoral care of the missionary]. In B. Ekström (Ed.), *El espíritu de COMIBAM* [The COMIBAM spirit] (2nd ed.) (pp. 43-47). Miami, FL: Editorial Patmos.

Tucker, R. (2004). *From Jerusalem to Irian Jaya: A biographical history of Christian Missions* (2nd ed.). Grand Rapids, MI: Zondervan.

van Laar, W. (2007). From mission field to missional church: Missionary congress of Latin Americans in Granada. *Connections: The Journal of the WEA Mission Commission 6*, 27-28.

Wagner, P. (1987). Prologue in *Misionología: Nuestro cometido transcultural* [Missiology: Our cross-cultural commitment]. Miami, FL: Editoral Vida.

Wang, T. (1987, May). By the year 2000: Is God trying to tell us something? *Mission Frontiers*. Retrieved from http://www.missionfrontiers.org/oldsite/1987/05/m872.htm

Williams, T. (1987, November). *Finance and missions*. Plenary session presented at the First Ibero American Missionary Congress, Sao Paulo, Brazil.

Winter, R. D. (1981a). The Kingdom strikes back: The ten epochs of redemptive history in *Perspectives on the world Christian movement,* translated by Jonathan Lewis (1990) in *Misión mundial* [World mission], vol. 1. Miami, FL: Editorial Unilit.

Winter, R. D. (1981b). The long look: Eras of mission history in *Perspectives on the World Christian Movement,* translated by Jonathan Lewis (1990) in *Misión mundial* [World mission], vol. 1. Miami, FL: Editorial Unilit.

Winter, R. D. (1986, March). Luis Bush, Latin America, and the End of History. *Mission Frontiers*. Retrieved from http://www.missionfrontiers.org/issue/article/luis-bush-latin-america-and-the-end-of-history

Winter, R. D. (1988, January). Report from Brazil: COMIBAM 87, the meeting of the century. (R. D. Winter, Ed.) *Mission Frontiers*. Retrieved from http://www.missionfrontiers.org/oldsite/1988/01/j883.htm

Winter, R. D. (1990). The warp and the woof of the Christian movement in *The warp and the woof: Organizing for Christian mission,* translated by Jonathan Lewis (1990) in *Misión mundial* [World mission], vol. 2. Miami, FL: Editorial Unilit.

Winter, R. D. (1995). The story of a movement in *Thy Kingdom come*. Pasadena, CA: William Carey Library Publishers.

Winter, R. D. & Hawthorne, S. C. (1981). The task remaining: All humanity in mission perspective in *Perspectives on the World Christian Movement,* translated by Jonathan Lewis (1990) in *Misión mundial* [World mission], vol. 2. Miami, FL: Editorial Unilit.

Winter, R. D. & Hawthorne, S. C. (Eds.). (2009). *Perspectives on the world Christian movement: A reader* (4th ed.). Pasadena, CA: William Carey Library.

Winter, R. D. & Latourette, S. (1970). *The twenty-five unbelievable years, 1945 to 1969* (8th ed.). Pasadena, CA: William Carey Library.

Yates, T. (1994). *Christian mission in the twentieth century.* Cambridge, United Kingdom: Cambridge University Press.

Yukl, G. (2002). *Leadership in organization* (5th ed.). Upper Saddle River, NJ: Prentice Hall.

Zapata, C. (2006, November). *Mensaje a la iglesia: Necesidades y desafíos* [Message to The Church: Needs and challenges]. Paper presented at COMIBAM 2006, Granada, Spain. Retrieved from http://www.comibam.org/docs/manual_es.pdf

Appendix A

Forty-One Documents[4] Published by or about COMIBAM

Given that this dissertation offers the first comprehensive study of COMIBAM. It will be helpful to list published resources in this fashion, if for no other reason than to document that the movement gave rise to a large number of new written resources. While these titles are found in the reference list, there is value in collecting them as directly tied or published by COMIBAM.

Bertuzzi, F. A., del Pino, C., Girón, R., Grellert, M., Nuñez, E. A., Paredes, P., Rey, V., & Steuernagel, V. (1995, April). *Encuentro Fraternidad Teológica Latinoamericana y COMIBAM Internacional* [Meeting of the Latin American Theological Fraternity and COMIBAM International]. Miami, FL. Retrieved from

http://www.recursosmisioneros.com/resources/Misiones_latinas_siglo_XXI.pdf

Bertuzzi, F. A. (2000, October). *Internacionalización o anglonización de la misión* [Internationalization or anglicizing of the mission]. Presentation given at CLADE IV, Quito, Ecuador. Retrieved from

http://www.comibam.org/ponencias/CladeIV/ponencia6.htm

---

[4] Since the initial retrieval by this researcher of many of these documents from the COMIBAM webpage, COMIBAM has compiled and published many of them in booklet form and removed them from the website. The researcher possesses hard copies of these. The reference list includes the most recently published form of the document.

Bertuzzi, F. A. (Ed.). (2001). *Las misiones Latinas para el siglo XXI: Compendio de COMIBAM 97, el Segundo Congreso Misionero Iberoamericano, Acapulco, México, 27 al 31 de octubre de 1997* [Latin missions for the 21st century: Handbook of the COMIBAM 1997, 2nd Ibero American Missionary Congress, Acapulco, Mexico, October 27 through 31, 1997] (2nd ed.). Retrieved from http://www.recursosmisioneros.com/resources/Misiones_latinas_siglo_XXI.pdf

Bibliografía misionera [Missionary bibliography] (rev. 2008, July 19). Retrieved from www.comibam.org/docs/bibliografia.pdf

Catálogo de las Organizaciones Misioneras de Argentina [Catalog of Argentina's Missionary Organizations] (2006). Retrieved from http://www.comibam.org/catalogo2006/index.htm

COMIBAM, International. (1996). *Organizaciones misioneras Argentina (Resumen numérico: 1996)* [Argentina missionary organizations (Numerical summary)]. Retrieved from http://www.comibam.org/catalogo2006/esp/consulta-1996/arg/_resum.htm

COMIBAM, International. (2002, October 28) *Los evangélicos y los misioneros Ibero-americanos* [Evangelicals and Ibero American missionaries]. Retrieved from http://www.comibam.org/Estadisworld01/Ibero-America.htm

COMIBAM, International. (2005, September 1). *Informe, Santiago del Estero: Encuentro de la mesa coordinadora y colaboradores 2005* [Report of the Santiago de Estero: Summit of the coordinating board and partners 2005]. Retrieved from http://www.comibam.org/docs/rcc_encuentro_st_esteros.pdf

COMIBAM International (2006a). *Definiciones e información adicional* [Definitions and additional information]. Retreived from http://www.comibam.org/catalogo2006/Misc/def_es.htm

COMIBAM, International. (2006b). *Organizaciones misioneras Argentina (Resumen numérico: 2006)* [Argentina missionary organizations (Numerical summary)]. Retrieved from http://www.comibam.org/catalogo2006/esp/consulta-2006/arg/_resum.htm

COMIBAM, International. (2006c). *Organizaciones misioneras de Iberoamérica* [Ibero America missionary organizations]. Retrieved from http://www.comibam.org/catalogo2006/Esp/consulta-2006/Ibe/_agencias.htm

COMIBAM, International. (2006d). *Países donde misioneros Ibero-Americanos están trabajando* [Countries where Ibero American missionaries are working]. Retrieved from http://www.comibam.org/catalogo2006/Esp/consulta-2006/Ibe/Campos_res.htm

COMIBAM, International. (n.d.). *¿Qué es COMIBAM?* [What is COMIBAM?]. Retrieved from http://www.comibam.org/queescomi.htm

Conclusiones: Consideraciones bíblicas. (2000, October). CLADE IV, Quito, Ecuador. Retrieved from http://www.comibam.org/ponencias/CladeIV/index.htm

Davies, P. (2000, October). *Las bases bíblicas veterotestamentarias de la misión transcultural: Misión Integral y misión profética* [Old Testament biblical bases for cross-cultural mission: Holistic mission and prophetic mission]. Presentation given at CLADE IV, Quito, Ecuador. Retrieved from http://www.comibam.org/ponencias/CladeIV/ponencia1.htm

Departamento de investigación [Research department]. (n.d.). Retrieved from http://www.comibam.org/depart/investigacion/indice.htm

Departamento de publicaciones [Publication department]. (n.d.). Retrieved from http://www.comibam.org/depart/public/objectivos.htm

Directorio de COMIBAM [COMIBAM directory]. (n.d.). Retrieved from http://www.comibam.org/equipo.htm

Etnia a etnia...Esta generación. (n.d.). Retrieved from http://www.comibam.org/docs/etniaaetnia_boletindeprens_1.pdf

Gava, O. (2007, July 3-6). *Consulta de capacitación región México (COMIMEX—COMIBAM Internacional)* [Mexico region training consultation (COMIMEX—COMIBAM International)]. Mexico. Retrieved from http://www.comibam.org/docs/rcc_consulta_mexico.pdf

Gava, O. (2005, February). *Proyecto (Red de centros de capacitación)* [Project (Training Centers network)]. Retrieved from http://www.comibam.org/docs/rcc_description.pdf

General report of the III Ibero-American missions congress. Granada, Spain. (2006, November). Retrieved from http://www.comibam.org/docs/reporte_comibamIII_es.pdf

Lewis, J. P. (2003, November). *El perfil del misionero frente un mundo turbulento* [The profile of the missionary confronting a turbulent world]. Presentation given at II Asamblea Internacional, San Salvador [COMIBAM's second international assembly, San Salvador]. Retrieved from http://www.comibam.org/ponencias/IIAsamblea/EPM.htm

Limpic, T. (Ed.). (2002). *Estadísticas misioneras* [Missionary statistics]. Retrieved From http://www.slideshare.net/libroscristianospdf/estadisticas-misioneras

Londoño, J. (2002, November). *La misión de Cristo: Modelos del pasado, presente y Futuro* [The mission of Christ: Models of the past, present and future]. Presentation given at Cumbre de Liderazgo, 2002 [COMIBAM's 2002 Leadership Summit] Madrid, Spain. Retrieved from http://www.comibam.org/ponencias/cumpliespa/Palabra.htm[4]

Londoño, J. (Ed.). (2003). *Manual de estructuras de envío: Conclusiones de la consulta Continental de estructuras de envío. Ciudad de Panamá, febrero 11, 12 y 13 de 2003* [Sending mechanisms, Panama City, February 11, 12 & 13, 2003] [PDF version]. Retrieved from http://www.recursosmisioneros.com/resources/Manual_estructuras_envio.pdf

Londoño, J. (2003, November). *Cambios teológicos en la fuerza misionera* [Theological changes in the missionary force]. Presentation given at II Asamblea Internacional, San Salvador [COMIBAM's second international assembly, San Salvador]. Retrieved from http://www.comibam.org/ponencias/IIAsamblea/CTEFM.htm

Manual del Congreso [Congress Manual]. (2006, November 13-17). III Congreso Ibero-Americano [Third Ibero American Congress]. Retrieved from http://www.comibam.org/docs/manual_es.pdf

---

[4] Document no longer available from the www.comibam.org site. Researcher has hard copy.

Matamoros, A. (2000, November). *Misioneros latinos, ¿quiénes son? ¿dónde están?* [Latin missionaries, who are they? Where are they? Presentation given at Asamblea Internacional de COMIBAM [COMIBAM's International Assembly], Lima, Peru. Retrieved from http://www.comibam.org/ponencias/lima/ponencia1.htm

Paredes, T. (2000, October). *Las bases neotestamentarias de la misión transcultural* [The New Testament bases for cross-cultural mission]. Presentation given at CLADE IV, Quito, Ecuador. Retrieved from http://www.comibam.org/ponencias/CladeIV/ponencia5.htm

Rodríguez, J. & Gava, O. (2005, September 26). *Rumbo a la excelencia en la capacitación misionera* [Toward excellency in missionary training]. Report at the Consulta de Centros de Capacitación Misionera de Centro América (COMCA) [Central America missionary training centers consultation]. Retrieved from http://www.comibam.org/docs/rcc_consulta_centroamerica.pdf

Ruiz, D. D. (n.d). *COMIBAM as a process leading to a congress.* Retrieved from http://www.comibam.org/docs/COMIBAM_process.pdf

Ruiz, D. D. (Ed.). (1997). *Guía para los movimientos misioneros nacionales: Una orientación para su formación y fortalecimiento* [Guide for the national missions movements: An orientation for their formation and strengthening] [PDF version]. Retrieved from http://www.recursosmisioneros.com/resources/Guia_movimientos_nacionales.pdf

Ruiz, D. D. (2000, October). *La singularidad de nuestra misión transcultural* [The uniqueness of our cross-cultural mission]. Presentation made at CLADE IV. Retrieved November from http://www.comibam.org/ponencias/CladeIV/ponencia4.htm

Ruiz, D. D. (2002a, November). *Identidad, visión y proyección del movimiento misionero Ibero-Americano* [Identity, vision and projection of the Ibero American missionary movement]. Presentation made at the Cumbre de Liderazgo [COMIBAM's leadership summit], Madrid, Spain. Retrieved from http://www.comibam.org/ponencias/cumpliespa/identidad.htm

Ruiz, D. D. (2002b, November). *Iglesias fuertes, pastores con visión* [Strong churches, pastors with vision]. Presentation made at the Cumbre de Liderazgo [COMIBAM's leadership summit], Madrid, Spain. Retrieved from http://www.comibam.org/ponencias/lima/ponencia3.htm

Ruiz, D. D. (2002c, November). *Tendencias de la iglesia y sus implicaciones en el Movimiento misionero Ibero-Americano: Amenazas y desafíos* [Tendencies of the church and their implications to the Ibero American missionary movement: Threats and challenges]. Presentation made at the Cumbre de Liderazgo [COMIBAM's leadership summit], Madrid, Spain. Retrieved from http://www.comibam.org/ponencias/cumpliespa/tendencias.htm

Ruiz, D. D. (2003, November). *Cambios paradigmáticos en el liderazgo global de las Misiones* [Paradigm changes in global leadership for missions]. Presentation given at the II Asamblea Internacional [COMIBAM's second international assembly]. Retrieved from http:www.comibam.org/ponencias/IIAsamblea/CPEE.htm

Scott, C. (2002, November). *El representante regional y su ministerio* [The regional representative and his ministry]. Presentation made at the *Cumbre de Liderazgo* [COMIBAM's leadership summit], Madrid, Spain. Retrieved from http://www.comibam.org/ponencias/cumpliespa/represenregio.htm

Scott, C. & Londoño, J. (2006). *Where is COMIBAM International heading? Strategic Focal points.* Retrieved from http://www.comibam.org/docs/whereiscomibamheading.pdf

Tostes, M. (2000, November). *Cuidado pastoral del misionero* [Pastoral care for the missionary]. Presentation given at the Asamblea Internacional de COMIBAM [COMIBAM's international assembly]. Retrieved from http://www.comibam.org/ponencias/lima/ponencia6.htm

Appendix B

Twenty-one Books Published by COMIBAM

While Appendix A listed documents published by COMIBAM, Appendix B lists books published.

Bertuzzi, F. A. (2006a). *El despertar de las misiones* [The awakening of missions] (2nd ed.). Barcelona, Spain: Editorial CLIE.

Bertuzzi, F. A. (2006b). *Misión transcultural* [Cross-cultural mission] (3rd ed.). Miami, FL: Editorial Patmos.

Bertuzzi, F. & Girón, R. (1999). *La iglesia Latina en misión mundial: Una orientación práctica para Iglesias y agencias misioneras* [The Latino church on world mission: A practical orientation for missionary churches and agencies]. Cooperación Misionera Iberoamericana [Ibero American Missionary Cooperation], Confraternidad Evangélica Latinoamericana [Latin American Evangelical Fellowship], COMIBAM Internacional.

Bush, L. K. (Ed.). (1986). *Manual de intercesión misionera* [Missionary intercession manual] (1st ed.). Guatemala, Guatemala: COMIBAM Internacional.

Bustamante, C. (2006). *Consejos para el cuidado del misionero* [Advice for missionary care]. Miami, FL: Editorial Patmos.

Cueva, S. (Ed.). (2004). *Misión para el tercer milenio: Construyendo puentes misioneros de doble vía, una serie de conferencias* [Mission for the third millennium: Building two-way missionary bridges, a series of conferences]. Barcelona, Spain: Editorial CLIE.

DeCarvalho, L. (Ed.). (2007). *Visión por las naciones* [Vision for the nations]. Miami, FL: Editorial Patmos.

Ekström, B. (Ed.). (2006). *El espíritu de Comibam* [The Comibam spirit]. Miami, FL: Editorial Patmos.

Lane, D. (2006). *Administración eficáz de una agencia misionera: Un manual elaborado desde y para el tercer mundo, indispensable para la creación y la administración de estructuras de envío misionero* [Effective administration of a missionary agency: A manual prepared from and for the third world, required for the creation and administration of missionary sending organizations]. Barcelona, Spain: Editorial CLIE.

Lewis, J. P. (1990a). *Misión mundial: Un análisis del movimiento cristiano mundial: Las bases bíblicas e históricas; Vol. 1* [World mission: An analysis of the world Christian movement: Biblical and historical bases; Vol. 1]. Miami, FL: Editorial Unilit.

Lewis, J. P. (1990b). *Misión mundial: Un análisis del movimiento cristiano mundial: La Dimension estratégica; Vol. 2* [World mission: An analysis of the world Christian movement: the strategic dimension]. Miami, FL: Editorial Unilit.

Lewis, J. P. (1990c). *Misión mundial: Un análisis del movimiento cristiano mundial: Consideraciones transculturales; Vol. 3* [World mission: An analysis of the world Christian movement: Cross-cultural considerations; Vol. 3] Miami, FL: Editorial Unilit.

Lewis, J. P. (1995). *Trabajando tu llamado a las naciones: Una guía para el misionero biocupacional* [Working your call to the nations: A guide for the bivocational missionary] (2nd ed.). COMIBAM Internacional/Editorial Unilit.

Limpic, T. (Ed.). (1997). *Catálogo de organizaciones misioneras Iberoamericanas: II Congreso Iberoamericano, Acapulco, México, 27 al 31 de octubre, 1997* [Catalog of Ibero American missionary organizations: 2nd Ibero American congress, Acapulco, Mexico, October 27 through 31, 1997]. Sao Paulo, Brazil: COMIBAM.

Londoño, J. (2006). *Alcance una etnia* [Reach an ethnic group] (2nd ed.). Miami, FL: Editorial Patmos.

Loss, M. (1996). *Choque transcultural* [Cross-cultural shock]. New York, NY: Ballantine Books.

O'Donnell, K. (2006). *El cuidado integral del misionero: Perspectivas y prácticas alrededor del mundo* [Doing member care well: perspectives and practices from around the world]. Colombia: COMIBAM Internacional.

Robert, A. (2004). *Conciencia misionera* [Missionary awareness]. Barcelona, Spain: Editorial CLIE.

Scott, C. (1999). *De pastor a pastor* [From pastor to pastor]. Miami, FL: Editorial Patmos.

Smith, O. J. (2003). *Pasión por las almas* [The passion for souls]. Barcelona, Spain: Editorial Clie.

Surenian, E. (1999). *Un clamor para las naciones* [A cry for the nations]. Miami, FL: Editorial Patmos.

Appendix C

Twenty-Four Books and Articles with Direct References to COMIBAM

While appendices A and B list documents and books published by COMIBAM, Appendix C lists book and articles which treat COMIBAM but are published by other entities.

DeCarvalho, L. (2007). COMIBAM III: Research project--phase I. *Connections: The Journal of the WEA Mission Commission, 6*, 20-24.

Dick, L. (2011). God's global plan: God unveils the fourth era of His plan to reach the World with the message of His love. *Rio Grande Magazine 18,* 4-5.

Ekstrom, B. (2007). From my corner. *Connections: The Journal of the WEA Mission Commission 6*, 3 (April-May: 2007).

Escobar, S. (2002). *Changing tides: Latin America and world mission today.* Maryknoll, NY: Orbis Books.

Escobar, S. (2007). COMIBAM III: A personal perspective. *Connections: The Journal of the WEA Mission Commission 6*, 25-26.

Frizen, E. (1992). *75 years of IFMA, 1917-1992: The nondenominational missions movement.* Pasadena, CA: William Carey Library.

Guarneri, J. (2009). COMIBAM: Calling Latin Americans to the global challenge. *Missions from the majority world: Progress, challenges and case studies.* EMS, 17, Pasadena, CA: William Carey Library, 221-262.

Impressions of III COMIBAM Missionary Congress. (2007). Connections: The journal of The WEA mission commission 6, 29-34.

Londoño, J. (2007). General report of the III Ibero-American missions congress. *Connections: The journal of the WEA mission commission 6*, 11-13.

Miller, D. (Ed.). (1994). *Coming of age: Protestantism in contemporary Latin America.* Lanham, MD: University Press of America.

Nuñez, E. & Taylor, W. (1996). *Crisis and hope in Latin America: An evangelical perspective.* Pasadena, CA: William Carey Library.

Peralta, A. (pseudonym). (2007). Message to the church in Ibero America: A COMIBAM congress plenary. *Connections: The Journal of the WEA Mission Commission 6*, 14-16.

Ruiz, D. D. (2007). COMIBAM as a process leading to a congress. *Connections: The Journal of the WEA Mission Commission 6*, 8-10.

Ruiz, D. D. (2007). COMIBAM as a viable regional mission movement. *Connections: The Journal of the WEA Mission Commission 6*, 5-7.

Saracco, N. (2000). Mission and missiology from Latin America. In Taylor, W. (Ed.), *Global missiology for the 21st century: The Iguassu dialogue.* Grand Rapids, MI: Baker Academic.

Scott, C. (2007). Projections and challenges for the Ibero American mission movement. *Connections: The Journal of the WEA Mission Commission 6*, 17-19.

Taylor, W. (1994). *Kingdom partnerships for synergy in missions.* Pasadena, CA: William Carey Library.

Taylor, W. (Ed.). (2000). *Global missiology for the 21st century: The Iguassu dialogue.* Grand Rapids, MI: Baker Academic.

Taylor, W. (2007). From the heart and mind of the editor. *Connections: The Journal of the WEA Mission Commission 6*, 4.

Tucker, R. (2004). *From Jerusalem to Irian Jaya: A biographical history of Christian Missions* (2nd ed.). Grand Rapids, MI: Zondervan.

van Laar, W. (2007). From mission field to missional church: Missionary congress of Latin Americans in Granada. *Connections: The Journal of the WEA Mission Commission 6*, 27-28.

Wagner, P. (1987). Prologue in *Misionología: Nuestro cometido transcultural* [Missiology: Our cross-cultural commitment]. Miami, FL: Editoral Vida.

Winter, R. D. (1986, March). Luis Bush, Latin America, and the End of History. *Mission Frontiers*. Retrieved from http://www.missionfrontiers.org/issue/article/luis-bush-latin-america-and-the-end-of-history

Winter, R. D. (1988, January). Report from Brazil: COMIBAM 87, the meeting of the century. (R. D. Winter, Ed.) *Mission Frontiers*. Retrieved from http://www.missionfrontiers.org/oldsite/1988/01/j883.htm

Appendix D

COMIBAM/Bertuzzi Archive, Santa Fe, Argentina

The relevant documents produced by COMIBAM since its inception are collected in a single repository. The COMIBAM/Bertuzzi archive is a collection of documents stored at a property located on Pedro Zenteno 751, Santa Fe, Argentina. The person designated as responsible for the documents was Federico A. Bertuzzi, a former Baptist pastor in Santa Fe, Argentina, and one of the founders and the first president of *Misiones Mundiales* [World Missions], which is the National Missions Movement in Argentina (Bertuzzi, 2007). Furthermore, Bertuzzi served as COMIBAM's executive director and as publications director (Bertuzzi, 2006a). During this time, he filed and archived letters, e-mails, faxes, brochures, programs, meeting minutes, newsletters and many other documents related to missions mobilization in Latin America, including COMIBAM congresses, consultations, and other COMIBAM International information. He organized these documents in file drawers and boxes and placed them in a storage room of his former home in Santa Fe, Argentina. Bertuzzi currently lives in Granada, Spain (Bertuzzi, 2006c).

The Bertuzzi files that were of most interest came from two file drawers: *EMI (General, Títulos)/COMIBAM Internacional*, and *PERSONAS INTERNACIONAL* (D-Z); and from two cardboard boxes: *CONGRESO COMIBAM '87 CORRESPONDENCIA* and *CONGRESO COMIBAM '97 ACAPULCO*. Listings of these files and how they were organized are given below. The researcher has used the actual names given by Bertuzzi to the files, rather than translating them to English, for retrieval purposes.

Figure 3. Photos of file drawers and cardboard boxes in Bertuzzi archive room

Table 11

Organization of COMIBAM/Bertuzzi Archive, Santa Fe, Argentina

File Drawer:	File Number:	File Names & (No. of Documents)
EMI/COMIBAM INTERNACIONAL	96	**Bibografía (8):** • Brad Walz • Cesar Ramirez • Español • LA Comm IFMA_0001 • P Larson (Mexico) • Portugués Anotada • Puente • Univ Católica Boliv
	100	**COMIBAM Publicaciones (22)**
	171	**AMTB**
	172	**Capacitación Misionera Transcultural (2):** • Boletín • Lista de Recipientes
	181	**COMHINA (23)**
	182	**COMIBAM-Bolivia (5)**
	183	**COMIBAM-Capacitación (1)**
	184	**COMIBAM-Chile (42)**
	185	**COMIBAM-Colombia (28)**
	186	**COMIBAM-Ecuador (5)**
	187	**COMIBAM-España (2)**
	188	**COMIBAM-Honduras (3)**
	189	**COMIBAM-Panamá (1)**
	190	**COMIBAM-Paraguay (26)**
	191	**COMIBAM-Publicaciones (6)**
	192	**COMIBAM-Uruguay (31)**
	193	**COMIBAM-Venezuela (19)**
	194	**COMIBAM (1990-91) (21)**
	197	**COMIBAM Internacional:** • Chile (6) • Costa Rica (3) • Ecuador (10) • EEUU (5) • Paraguay (35) • Paraguay 2 (1) • Sao Paulo (3)
	198	**COMHINA '93 (24)**

	199	Consulta Asunción (22)
	200	Consulta AUP (Costa Rica 1992) (3)
	201	Consulta FTL-COMIBAM (Miami 1995) (8)
	202	Consulta Montevideo (13)
	203	Encuentro de Iglesias y agencias (Panamá '94) (9)
	204	FUNDACOM Internacional (2)
	205	Uruguay '93 (I Congreso Misionero)
PERSONAS INTERNACIONAL (D-Z)	283	Luís Bush (17)
	296	Bertil Ekström (14)
Cardboard Boxes: CONGRESO COMIBAM '87 CORRESPONDENCIA	17	File(s): <ul><li>1985-1986 (63)</li><li>Brasil (21)</li><li>Correspondencia:<ul><li>Cartas Precongreso (14)</li><li>Copias (8)</li><li>Individuos (21)</li><li>Instituciones (12)</li><li>Procesamientos (1)</li><li>Promoción y Seguimiento (13)</li></ul></li><li>Guatemala (Oficina) (50)</li><li>Hatch (10)</li><li>Luís Bush (45)</li><li>Plenarias-Borrador (1)</li></ul>
CONGRESO COMIBAM '97 ACAPULCO	20	• (44)

The COMIBAM/Bertuzzi Archive is listed as one source in the reference list in the following format:

COMIBAM/Bertuzzi Archive. Documents related to the COMIBAM network in Ibero America. Santa Fe, Argentina.

In accordance with the *APA publication manual, sixth edition* (2011) section 7.10, the citation of a particular letter from that collection will be cited in the text as follows:

(Ekström, B. 1994-1999, Ekström to F. A. Bertuzzi, March 21, 1994)

A single document in the collection that is not part of a collection of letters will be listed as follows in the text:

(Bertuzzi, F. ca. 1991, *Gacetilla de prensa* [Press release]. File folder 194. COMIBAM/Bertuzzi Archive, Santa Fe. Argentina)

CARPETAS AMARILLAS

Revisión: 23/05/2010 09:48

No están en existencia

PM INTERNACIONAL

Administración
1. Actas
2. Candidatos
3. Células de intercesión
4. Comité Ejecutivo
5. Consejo Internacional
6. Convenios de representación
7. Copias cartas Proyecto Magreb
8. Curso de Orientación Transcultural (COT)
9. Departamento Consulting Pro Mundis (DCPM)
10. Direcciones varias
11. Estructura (Reglamento)
12. Ex-personal en proceso
13. Folletos
14. Formularios varios (modelos)
15. Gacetillas
16. Granada
17. Informes de viajes (1993-97)
18. Informes de viajes (1998-00)
19. Informes de viajes (2001)
20. Iniciativa Evangélica Transcultural (IET)
21. Junta Directiva
22. Listado de materiales entregados
23. Listado de obreros
24. Manual de la misión
25. Newsletters web
26. Oficina de Brasil
27. Oficina de Coordinación de Am. Latina (OCAL)
28. Oficina Latinoamericana (Santa Fe)
29. Oficina Latinoamericana (Panamá)
30. Operación Tránsito
31. Oportunidades de servicio
32. Plan quinquenal (1991-96)
33. Presupuestos de campos
34. Publicaciones
35. Publicaciones (Presupuestos)
36. Recursos Gráficos
37. Revista: Expansión
38. Seguros Médicos
39. Sitio Web
40. Transacción PMI-AUP
41. Varios

Eventos
42. Clame '90 (Ponencias)
43. Comité Ejecutivo (Granada 1999)
44. Consulta PM I (Rabat)
45. Consulta PM II (Guadalajara)
46. Consulta PM III (Santa Fe)
47. Consulta PM IV (San Pablo)
48. Consulta PM V (Granada)
49. Consulta PM VI (Orlando)
50. Consulta PM VII (Guatemala)
51. Consulta PM VIII (Panamá)
52. Encuentro Misionero PMI (Brasil 2000)
53. Evaluación y Planeamiento (Grx 1996)
54. Gira FAB 1999 (Centroamérica-Andinos)
55. Hacia una teología intergral de misiones (1997)
56. Musulmania (Bolivia)
57. Musulmania (El Salvador 2001)
58. Musulmania (Guatemala 1999)
59. Musulmania (varias)
60. Musulmania '94
61. Musulmania '95
62. Musulmania '96 (gira Andrés Prins)
63. Musulmania '97
64. Representantes (Brasil 1997)
65. Representantes (El Salvador 1997)
66. Retiro de Obreros PMI (España 2000)
67. Seminario Raimundo Lulio (SRL)
68. Seminario Raimundo Lulio II

Países
69. Australia
70. Bolivia
71. Brasil
72. Chile
73. Colombia
74. Costa Rica
75. Cuba
76. Ecuador
77. EE.UU.
78. El Salvador
79. España
80. Guatemala
81. Holanda
82. Honduras
83. Mauritania
84. Mexico
85. Nepal
86. Nicaragua
87. Panamá
88. Paraguay
89. Perú
90. Puerto Rico
91. República Dominicana
92. Uruguay
93. Uzbekistán
94. Venezuela

EDITORIAL MISIONERA IBEROAMERICANA

General
95. Action International
96. Bibliografía
97. Buena Semilla (David Peacock)
98. CLC (Eduardo Nieto)
99. Clie
100. COMIBAM Publicaciones
101. Correcciones NVI
102. Correcciones RVR-95
103. Desarrollo Cristiano/
104. Descoberta
105. Ediciones Hebrón
106. Editora Sepal
107. Editoriales
108. EMI (Estadísticas)
109. ISBN
110. Letra Viva
111. Luz para las Naciones (edic. argentina)
112. Originales de autores (p/artic./boletines, etc.)
113. Propiedad intelectual
114. Unilit (Cartas)
115. Unilit (Facturas)
116. Unilit (Regalías)
117. Vida

Títulos
118. Libro: ¡Foco!
119. Libro: 30 días de oración por musulmanes
120. Libro: 52 tarjetas de oración
121. Libro: Administración eficaz agencia misionera
122. Libro: Alcance Un Pueblo
123. Libro: Argentina en misión mundial
124. Libro: C. T. Studd
125. Libro: Capacitación misionera internacionalizada
126. Libro: Catálogo de organizaciones misioneras
127. Libro: Choque transcultural
128. Libro: COMIBAM '97 (7 títulos)
129. Libro: Comparte con musulmanes amor de Dios
130. Libro: Conciencia misionera
131. Libro: Consulta Iguazú
132. Libro: Cuida tu corona
133. Libro: Demasiado valioso para perderse
134. Libro: Desde lo último de la tierra
135. Libro: Despertar de las misiones
136. Libro: Diccionario de la misión
137. Libro: Disfrute de otra cultura
138. Libro: Entendiendo a los árabes
139. Libro: Esperanza para los musulmanes
140. Libro: Espíritu de Comibam
141. Libro: Finanzas para misiones mundiales
142. Libro: Hacia una misionol. evang. lat.
143. Libro: Humor en las misiones
144. Libro: Iglesia latina en misión mundial
145. Libro: Iglesia local y las misiones
146. Libro: Juntos en tu presencia
147. Libro: Latinos en el mundo islámico
148. Libro: Manual de intercesión misionera
149. Libro: Manual para establecimiento iglesias
150. Libro: Minifaldas, madres, musulmanes
151. Libro: Misión mundial, Guía del tutor, Videos
152. Libro: Misión transcultural
153. Libro: Misiones latinas para el siglo XXI
154. Libro: Misiones Mundiales, 10° aniversario
155. Libro: Misiones mundiales: en 10 lecciones
156. Libro: Misionol. Global P/ Siglo XXI
157. Libro: Movilización misionera de la iglesia local
158. Libro: Musulmanes que encontraron a Cristo
159. Libro: Ocultismo en el islam
160. Libro: Operación Mundo
161. Libro: Pasión por las almas
162. Libro: Perspectivas
163. Libro: Poder empresarial en misión integral
164. Libro: Que hablen los misioneros
165. Libro: Ríos en la soledad
166. Libro: Sirviendo al enviar obreros
167. Libro: Trabajando tu llamado a las naciones
168. Libro: Una iglesia apasionada por las misiones
169. Libro: Una investigación
170. Libro: Uzbekistán

COMIBAM INTERNACIONAL
171. AMTB
172. Capacitación Misionera Transcultural
173. Carey
174. Censo Chile
175. Censo Costa Rica
176. Censo Ecuador
177. Censo EE.UU.
178. Censo Paraguay
179. Censo Sao Paulo
180. Censo Uruguay
181. COMHINA
182. COMIBAM - Bolivia
183. COMIBAM - Capacitación
184. COMIBAM - Chile
185. COMIBAM - Colombia
186. COMIBAM - Ecuador
187. COMIBAM - España
188. COMIBAM - Honduras
189. COMIBAM - Panamá
190. COMIBAM - Paraguay
191. COMIBAM - Publicaciones
192. COMIBAM - Uruguay
193. COMIBAM - Venezuela
194. COMIBAM (1990-91)
195. COMIBAM '87
196. COMIBAM '97
197. COMIBAM Internacional
198. COMINHA '93
199. Consulta Asunción
200. Consulta AUP (Costa Rica 1992)
201. Consulta FTL-COMIBAM (Miami 1995)
202. Consulta Montevideo

203. Encuentro de iglesias y agencias (Panamá '94)
204. FUNDACOM Internacional
205. Uruguay '93 (I Congreso Misionero)

MISIONES MUNDIALES

206. Capacitación misionera
207. COMIBA
208. COMICE
209. Congreso Litoral (Carpeta)
210. Congreso Litoral (Preparativos)
211. Congreso Misionero Bahía Blanca '94
212. Congreso Misionero Bs.As. (COMIBA 1988)
213. Congreso Misionero Centro
214. Congreso Misionero de Misiones (Alem 1990)
215. Congreso Misionero del Norte
216. Congreso Misionero Rosario
217. Congreso Misionero Cuyano
218. Congreso Santa Fe 2002
219. Consulta Centro
220. Consulta Comahue
221. Consulta Cuyo
222. Consulta Docencia Misionológica I
223. Consulta Litoral
224. Consulta Lomas de Zamora
225. Consulta Máximo Paz (Carpeta)
226. Consulta Máximo Paz (Preparativos)
227. Consulta Misiones
228. Consulta Noreste
229. Consulta Noroeste
230. Consulta Profesionales
231. Consulta Rosario
232. Consulta Villa Giardino
233. Curso Básico de capacitación misionera
234. Curso Intensivo de Verano (Crespo 1989)
235. Curso para Movilizadores (V. del Lago, 1998)
236. Misión '98 (Córdoba)
237. MISIÓN '97 (Bs.As.)
238. MISIÓN '99 (Saenz Peña)
239. MISIÓN '86
240. MISIÓN '89
241. Misiones Mundiales (1997-2000)
242. Misiones Mundiales (2001)
243. Misiones Mundiales (copia de cartas)
244. Misiones Mundiales (Estudio Eliezer)
245. Misiones Mundiales (Fundación)
246. Misiones Mundiales (Inventario)
247. Misiones Mundiales (Socios)
248. Seminario Edison Queiroz (1995)
249. Seminario Misión Mundial '87 (Av. Libertador)

PERSONAS

Nacionales
250. Abel Marcelo
251. Acevedo Javier
252. Acevedo Javier (1997)
253. Almonacid Irene
254. Arce Adrián
255. Bianchi Daniel
256. Cabrera Omar
257. Englund Lennart
258. Hurtado Daniel
259. Laffite Marcelo
260. Leguizamón Silvia
261. Libert Samuel O.
262. Malcolm Susana
263. Padilla René
264. Panotto Nicolás
265. Perfetti Luis
266. Perreta Juan C.
267. Proietti, Rubén
268. Somoza Carlos
269. Terranova Juan
270. Walz Brad
271. Zaharadnicek Carlos

Internacionales
272. Acuña Ramiro
273. Amado Marcos
274. Amado Marcos (1987-97)
275. Araujo Gerson
276. Ávila Omar
277. Azzati Adrián
278. Bademian Susana
279. Benson Ian
280. Blaxland Gregory
281. Bloise Carlos
282. Bojorques Oseas
283. Bush Luis
284. Calderón Carlos
285. Calixto Carlos
286. Carrillo Pablo
287. Carrillo Pablo (1980-93)
288. Carrillo Pablo (1994-2001)
289. Carvalho Waldemar
290. Casaccia Ernesto
291. Chavez Carlos
292. Cordón Paz Silvia
293. De Marco Miguel Angel
294. De Prado Fabiana
295. Dekker John
296. Ekström Bertil
297. Escobar Eliseo
298. Falco Gabriel
299. Fallas José
300. Folta Erika
301. Funk Carlos
302. Gallor Jorge
303. Giordano Christian
304. Girón Rudy (1994)
305. Girón Rudy (1995-1996))
306. Giuffré Elizabeth
307. González Julio
308. González Valentin
309. Grau Olin
310. Guerrero Samuel
311. Gularte Fredy
312. Halls Tim
313. Hamra Abdulmassih
314. Hauser Albrecht
315. Hocking Pedro
316. Johnson Esteban
317. Johnstone Patrick
318. Juez Miguel
319. Klassen Siegfried
320. Lewis Jonatán (1991-93)
321. Lewis Jonatán (1994-96)
322. Lima Elizete
323. Limpic Ted
324. Livingstone Greg
325. López José
326. López Moisés
327. Loss Mario
328. Matamorros Allan
329. Mc Curry Don
330. Mehdi Ksara
331. Mejia Moisés
332. Meliá Gladys
333. Mena Eduardo
334. Michel Manuel
335. Milk Thomas
336. Moreno Pedro
337. Muñoz Jairo
338. Murashkin Vladimir
339. Myers Dallas
340. Nöhre Wolfgang
341. Palau Luis
342. Panotto Abel
343. Paredes Patricio
344. Pascual Lázaro
345. Pate Larry
346. Prins Andrès (1984-96)
347. Prins Andrès (1997-2001)
348. Queiroz Edison
349. Quinteros Juan Carlos
350. Reimer Johannes
351. Rendel Jack
352. Rising David
353. Riveiro Junior
354. Rocha Fabio
355. Roop Guillermo
356. Ruiz David
357. Saavedra Sergio
358. Salinas Héctor
359. Sánchez Nèstor
360. Schulz Eduardo
361. Serrano Oscar
362. Sider Bruce
363. Sifontes Pedro
364. Solis Eduardo
365. Sookhdeo Patrick
366. Sotile Gaetano
367. Soto Jonathan
368. Sperger Randy
369. Suter Heinz (1984-93)
370. Suter Heinz (1994-2001)
371. Taylor Bill
372. Thomas Chacko
373. Uchest Ubaldo
374. Verwer George
375. Winter Ralph
376. Zarazaga Eduardo

ORGANIZACIONES

Nacionales
377. ACCRA
378. ACEMAS
379. ACIERA
380. ACIERA Santa Fe
381. AECA
382. Agencia Misionera Argentina (AMA)
383. Agencias Misioneras
384. AMI (CEBA)
385. Argentina en Misión Evangelizadora (AME)
386. Asamblea de Dios
387. ASIT
388. Asoc. Bautista Santa Fe Centro
389. Asociación Evangelística Argentina (AEA)
390. Ayuda Cristiana
391. CEFORMA
392. Centro de Entrenamiento Cristiano (CEC)
393. CIAM (San Juan)
394. CNCE
395. Consejo Pastoral Santa Fe
396. Consejo Pastoral Santa Fe II
397. Consejo Pastoral Santa Fe (Reglamento interno)
398. Cruzada Estudiantil y Prof. para Crsito
399. Ctro. Capac. Misionera Transc. (CCMT)
400. DEM (1988-92)
401. DEM (1993-00)
402. Escuela Bíblica Misionera (Jujuy)
403. Escuela Juan Wycliffe Argentina
404. FELA
405. FLET
406. Iglesia Nordeste
407. Instituto Teológico Bautista de Misiones
408. JUCUM
409. LAPEN
410. MAGE
411. MAIN
412. MEI
413. Misión Austral
414. Movimiento Cristiano Independiente
415. Movimiento Cristiano y Misionero
416. Operación Primavera
417. Plan Provincial Plantación Iglesias
418. RAIM
419. SEIT
420. Sociedades Bíblicas
421. Visión de Futuro

Internacionales
422. AD 2000 (1989-93)
423. AD 2000 (1994-01)
424. Aglow
425. Arab World Ministries (NAM)
426. AWEMA
427. Barnabas
428. Boletín Alturas
429. CAFE
430. Caleb Project
431. Call of Hope (Stuttgart)

432. Call to prayer
433. Center for Ministry to Muslims
434. CenterNet
435. CET Internacional (Bolivia)
436. Christian Aid
437. CONELA
438. Consejo Mundial de Iglesias
439. EFMA
440. El Manarah
441. Fellowship or Failh for Muslims
442. Fraternidad Teológica Latinoamericana (FTL)
443. Friends of Turkey
444. Frontiers
445. Fuller Theological Seminary
446. Global Mapping Proyect
447. Global Roundtable
448. GMU
449. Hilfe für Brüder
450. liBET
451. IMDELA
452. Interdev
453. JUCUM
454. Kairós (Brasil)
455. LAM
456. Latin Link
457. Lausanne
458. Lima al Encuentro con Dios
459. Llamada de Salvación
460. Llamas
461. MECO
462. Middle East Media OM
463. Misiones Internacionales
464. Missao Antioquía
465. Missao Nova Vida
466. Operación Movilización (OM)
467. Operation Abba
468. PAI
469. Partners
470. People International (The Gairdner Ministries)
471. PIN (Peoples Information Network)
472. Programa Alhambra
473. Puertas Abiertas
474. Red Sea Team International
475. Revista Internacional de Misión Mundial (RIMM)
476. Santiago al Encuentro con Dios
477. Servant Fellowship International
478. SETECA
479. Training for cross cultural ministrie
480. TWMA
481. Uzbek Spin
482. Visao Mundial
483. WEC International
484. WEF
485. WEF (Mission Commission)
486. William Carey International University
487. World Horizons
488. World Languages
489. World Mission
490. Wycliffe (USA)
491. Zwemer Institute

EVENTOS

Nacionales
492. CNCE (Buenos Aires 1999)
493. COMLA 6 (Paraná, 1999)
494. Congreso JEBA (Santa Fe 1985)
495. Congreso Evangelización del Litoral 2003
496. Jornadas Iglesias comprometidas (Sta. Fe 1998)
497. MEI (Embalse 1998)
498. Simposio Evangelización (Mar del Plata, 1990)
499. Tent Makers (Horward Norrish, Logos II, 1993)

Internacionales
500. Adopt a People Consultation (Londres '90)
501. Alcance 2000
502. Amsterdam '83
503. Centercon II (Londres '90)
504. Clade III (Ecuador '92)
505. CLADE IV (Ecuador 2000)
506. Conferencia Misionera (Italia '99)
507. Congreso Brasileiro de Missoes
508. Congreso Juvenil de Misiones (Asunción)
509. Expolit '95
510. Feria Latinoamericana de Misiones (Bolivia '91)
511. FTL: Consulta (Chile '96)
512. GCOWE '97 (Pretoria)
513. Global Consultation Singapur '89 (Carpeta)
514. Global Consultation Singapur '89 (Preparativos)
515. IV Conferencia misionera Seteca (1998)
516. Latinoamérica 2000 (Panamá 1996)
517. Lausana II (Manila '89)
518. Llamada '84
519. Misión '83 (Lausana)
520. Misión '84 (San Salvador)
521. Misión '90 (Amsterdam)
522. Misión '93 (Utrecht)
523. Operaçao Mundo '82 (San Pablo)
524. Simposio OC (Málaga 1997)
525. Simposio OC (Panamá 1998)
526. TWMA (Portland 1988)
527. TWMA (Portland 1989)
528. UBLA (Asunción '84)
529. Uruguay '78 con Luis Palau
530. WEF (Manila 1992)
531. Weltkongress Berlin '66

GEOGRÁFICO

Paises
532. Albania
533. Alemania Democrática
534. Alemania Federal
535. Andorra
536. Argelia
537. Argentina
538. Austria
539. Bangladesh
540. Bélgica
541. Bolivia
542. Brasil
543. Bután
544. Canadá
545. Checoslovaquia
546. Chile
547. China
548. Colombia
549. Corea
550. Costa Rica
551. Cuba
552. Dinamarca
553. Djibouti
554. Ecuador
555. EE.UU.
556. Egipto
557. El Salvador
558. Eritrea
559. Escocia
560. España
561. Filipinas
562. Finlandia
563. Ghana
564. Gibraltar
565. Grecia
566. Guatemala
567. Guyana
568. Haití
569. Holanda
570. Hong Kong
571. Hungria
572. India
573. Indonesia
574. Inglaterra
575. Irak
576. Irán
577. Islandia
578. Israel
579. Italia
580. Jamaica
581. Japón
582. Jordania
583. Kampuchea
584. Kenia
585. Líbano
586. Libia
587. Liechtenstein
588. Luxemburgo
589. Magreb
590. Malasia
591. Mali
592. Malta
593. Marruecos
594. Mauritania
595. México
596. Mónaco
597. Mongolia
598. Nepal
599. Nicaragua
600. Nigeria
601. Noruega
602. Pakistán
603. Panamá
604. Papua Nueva Guinea
605. Paraguay
606. Perú
607. Portugal
608. Puerto Rico
609. Rusia
610. San Marino
611. Santo Domingo
612. Singapur
613. Siria
614. Sudáfrica
615. Suiza
616. Swazilandia
617. Tibet
618. Túnez
619. Turquia
620. URSS
621. Uruguay
622. Vaticano
623. Venezuela
624. Yugoslavia

Islámicos
625. Afganistán
626. Asia Central
627. Berèberes
628. Burusho
629. China
630. Cozacos
631. Fulas
632. Islam (varios)
633. Kanuri
634. Kurdos
635. Magreb
636. Mandigos
637. Mozabitas
638. Mujer
639. Saharuis
640. Sahel
641. Shina
642. Tuareg
643. Uighurs
644. Uzbecos

Tribales
645. Alemania
646. Argentina
647. Bolivia
648. Brasil
649. Colombia
650. Ecuador
651. EE.UU.
652. Estadísticas
653. Guatemala
654. Kechuas
655. Makà
656. México
657. Paraguay
658. Perú
659. Tobas
660. Tribus

661. Venezuela

GENERAL

662. Aborto
663. Aconsejamiento
664. Aduana (flete internacional)
665. Apócrifos
666. Argentinos en el exterior, cartas
667. AT Históricos
668. AT Pentateuco
669. AT Poéticos
670. AT Proféticos
671. Audiovisuales
672. Aviación
673. Ayuno
674. Banco de Galicia
675. Bivocacionales
676. Catolicismo
677. Censo Argentina (Antecedentes, '60 y '80)
678. Censo Argentina (Cartas, 1987)
679. Censo Argentina (Organización, 1987)
680. Ciegos
681. Circulares de oración FAB
682. Computación (Comprobantes de compra)
683. Computación (Presupuestos)
684. Comunismo
685. Contactos en el Sur
686. Copias cartas Iglesia Nordeste 1973-1986
687. Copias de cartas
688. Copias de faxes
689. Crecimiento de iglesia
690. Currículos
691. Declaración de Fe
692. Demonología
693. Direcciones internacionales
694. Direcciones nacionales
695. Discipulado
696. Dones
697. Ecumenismo
698. Encuestas
699. Escatología
700. Espíritu Santo
701. Estadísticas – Mapas
702. Estatutos
703. Ética Cristiana
704. Eurail
705. Evangelismo Personal
706. Evidencias Cristianas
707. Fundaciones
708. Gacetillas
709. Historia de la iglesia
710. Homilética
711. Humanismo
712. Ideas para sermones
713. Iglesia – Estado
714. Inmortalidad
715. Introducción Bíblica
716. Judíos
717. Liderazgo
718. Malvinas
719. Monumento a la Biblia
720. Música y culto
721. Niños: visión misionera
722. NT Cartas
723. NT Cartas Paulinas
724. NT Evangelios
725. Películas
726. Profecías
727. Recortes de diario
728. Salud
729. Sanidades
730. Santa Fe (Mapas)
731. Santificación
732. Sectas
733. Universalismo
734. Urbanevangelización
735. Varios
736. Versión Popular
737. Vida Victoriosa

Comunicaciones
738. Comunicaciones (Call Back)
739. Comunicaciones (Gigared)
740. Comunicaciones (Satlink, Advance)
741. Comunicaciones (Servicios varios)
742. Comunicaciones (Sitio Web)
743. Comunicaciones (sobre manila)
744. Comunicaciones (Universidad, Ceride)
745. Encotesa
746. Radio
747. Radio Cristiana
748. Telecom
749. TV

Figure 4. Catalog of file folders compiled by Bertuzzi

CAJAS DE CARTÓN
Oficina Casa San Lucas
Vigencia: 27/12/04.

IGLESIA EVANGÉLICA BAUTISTA NORDESTE
1. CARTAS NUMERADAS AÑOS 1972-83
2. CARTAS NUMERADAS AÑOS 1983-86
3. CARTAS AÑOS 1974-78
4. CARTAS AÑOS 1979-81
5. CARTAS AÑOS 1982-85
6. IGLESIA NORDESTE EVENTOS FAB

MISIONES MUNDIALES
7. CARTAS AÑOS 1983-88
8. CARTAS AÑOS 1989-91
9. CARTAS AÑOS 1992-94
10. CARTAS AÑOS 1995-96
11. CONGRESO MISIÓN '89 MAR DEL PLATA
12. CONGRESO MISIÓN '92 CARLOS PAZ
13. CONGRESO MISIÓN '92 INSCRIPCIONES
14. CONSULTAS AÑOS 1986-88
15. FICHAS INSCRIPCIÓN Y COMPROMISO AÑOS 1986-95
16. ORGANIZACIÓN

COMIBAM INTERNACIONAL
17. CONGRESO COMIBAM '87 CORRESPONDENCIA
18. CONGRESO COMIBAM '87 INSCRIPCIONES
19. CONGRESO COMIBAM '87 MANUALES VARIOS
20. CONGRESO COMIBAM '97 ACAPULCO
21. CONSULTAS COSTA RICA '92 - PANAMÁ '94
22. CORRESPONDENCIA
23. DOCUMENTOS, FUNDACOM ELLOS & NOSOTROS
24. REUNIONES COMITÉ EJECUTIVO

PM INTERNACIONAL
25. CLAME '90
26. CORRESPONDENCIA
27. MUSULMANIA '95
28. PUBLICACIONES PROPIAS
29. TRAMITACIÓN CANDIDATOS - CARTAS NACIONALES

30. RECURSOS GRÁFICOS ISLAM
31. RECORTES SOBRE ISLAM
32. ENSAYOS SOBRE ISLAM
33. ENSAYOS ISLÁMICOS

VARIOS
34. CENSO NACIONAL EVANGÉLICO '87 (ACIERA)
35. CENTRO CAPACITACIÓN TEOLÓGICA (CCT)
36. CURSOS BÍBLICOS
37. DPTO. EVANGELISMO Y MISIONES (CEBA) - ASOCIACIÓN BAUTISTA SANTA FE
38. IGUALDAD RELIGIOSA 1
39. IGUALDAD RELIGIOSA 2

40. INVITACIONES PREDICAR FAB
41. SOSTENEDORES FAB

IMPRENTA E IMPRESOS
42. AFICHES - AUDIOVISUALES
43. IMPRESOS FAB PROPIOS 1
44. IMPRESOS FAB PROPIOS 2
45. IMPRESOS FAB PROPIOS 3
46. IMPRESOS FAB AJENOS 1
47. IMPRESOS FAB AJENOS 2
48. RECORTES DE DIARIOS
49. IMPRESOS FAB HECTOGRÁFICOS

50. RECURSOS GRÁFICOS VARIOS

PAÍSES
51. ALEMANIA
52. ESPAÑA
53. ESTADOS UNIDOS
54. INDIA
55. MARRUECOS
56. UZBEKISTÁN
57. BRASIL

BOXES
58. Carpetas congresos FAB
59. Fundación Misiones Mundiales
60. Iglesia Nordeste

Figure 5. Catalog of cardboard boxes compiled by Bertuzzi

Appendix E

List of Interviews Conducted in Chronological Order

Date	Interviewee	Medium	Place
September 24, 2008	David Ruíz, former COMIBAM president and executive director	In person	Denver, Colorado
September 25, 2008	Jesús Londoño, COMIBAM executive director 2000-2009	Phone	
April 28, 2009	José de Dios, Strategic Partnerships director for COMIBAM	In person	Fort Worth, Texas
May 8, 2009	Daniel Bianchi, Argentine Pastor, national director for COMIBAM Argentina and COMIBAM International officer	In person	Fort Worth, Texas
October 29, 2009	Ted Limpic, director of statistics for COMIBAM	In person	Bogota, Colombia
October 29, 2009	Carlos Scott, COMIBAM president 2006-2009	In person	Bogota, Colombia
October 30, 2009	Federico Bertuzzi, co-founder of *Misiones Mundiales* (Arg.) and director of publications for COMIBAM	In person	Bogota, Colombia
October 30, 2009	Carlos Cordero, COMCA (Central America) leader	In person	Bogota, Colombia
October 31 and November 1, 2009	Rudy Girón, former COMIBAM president	In person	Bogota, Colombia
October 30 and 31, 2009	Jonathan Lewis, former vice-president for COMIBAM	In person	Bogota, Colombia
May 26, 2010	Pablo Bongarrá, pastor and missionary leader in Argentina	In person	Buenos Aires, Argentina

Date	Interviewee	Medium	Place
May 27, 2010	Edgardo Surenian, pastor and missionary leader in Argentina	In person	Buenos Aires, Argentina
May 31, 2010	Pablo Deiros, rector of the Argentine Baptist Seminary	In person	Buenos Aires, Argentina
February 2, 2011	Antonio Amigo, missionary to Portugal and COMIBAM assembly delegate	Skype	
February 2, 2011	Luis Marti, Salvadorian pastor and COMIBAM officer	Skype	
February 4, 2011	Luis Bush, first COMIBAM president	Phone	
February 4, 2011	Dana Wilson, missionary in Bolivia and COMIBAM assembly delegate	Skype	
February 9, 2011	Federico Bertuzzi, co-founder of *Misiones Mundiales* in Argentina and director of publications for COMIBAM	Skype	
February 9, 2011	Bertil Ekström, former COMIBAM president	Skype	
February 18, 2011	Alvaro Fernandez, COMIMEX leader and COMIBAM assembly delegate	Skype	

Appendix F

Interview questions

1. Tell me about your personal involvement with COMIBAM.

2. Describe what COMIBAM is.

3. What are the areas in which COMIBAM is effective? What do you think are the factors that contribute to this effectiveness?

4. What are the areas in which COMIBAM is ineffective? What do you think are the factors that contribute to this ineffectiveness?

5. How has COMIBAM changed throughout the first twenty-five years of existence (1984-2009)? Which of these changes do you consider positive and why? Which of these changes do you consider negative and why?

6. In which ways is COMIBAM a movement? In which ways is it an institution? How do these two aspects relate to each other in the work of COMIBAM?

7. Who have been some of the key leaders of COMIBAM and how have they contributed to it?

8. How have the national and regional missionary movements contributed to the formation and development of COMIBAM? How has COMIBAM contributed to the development of national and regional missionary movements?

9. How is COMIBAM a contributing factor in the missionary sending force from Ibero America?

Appendix G

National Missions Conferences and Congresses Leading to COMIBAM '87

Table 12

National Missions Conferences and Congresses Leading to COMIBAM '87 (Boltodano, R., 1985, November 8. [Letter to Luís Bush]. COMIBAM/Bertuzzi Archive Box 17; Bush, L. K., 1985, April 21. *Informe de actividades* [Report of activities]; 1985, October. *Reporte COMIBAM '87 a* [COMIBAM '87 Report a]; 1986, January 6. [Letter to Federico Bertuzzi]. COMIBAM/Bertuzzi Archive Box 17; Calderón, 1986, September, p. 2; COMIBAM, 1985, December. *Consulta misionera nacional* [National missionary conference]. COMIBAM/Bertuzzi Archive Box 17; COMIBAM, 1985, December; 1986, February; 1986, April; 1986, November; 1987, March-April; 1987, May-June; Moreno, J., 1985, December 2. [Letter to Luís Bush]. COMIBAM/Bertuzzi Archive Box 17; Martínez, M. & Marroquín, S., 1986, January. *Primera consulta nacional misionera hondureña* [First Honduran national missionary conference]. COMIBAM/Bertuzzi Archive Box 17; Mejía, M., 1986. *Primera consulta misionera de la iglesia evangélica en Guatemala* [First missionary conference of the evangelical church in Guatemala]. COMIBAM/Bertuzzi Archive Box 17).

Date	Country/Region	Participation	Committee Chair(s)	Speakers
May 27, 1985	Ecuador (Quito)	26 Pastors & leaders	Roberto Hatch	Colon Altamirano, Dieter Brephol
June 19-20, 1985	Chile	80 Pastors & leaders from 21 denominations & institutions	Carlos San Martin, Hermes Canales	Manuel Carrasco, Luís Pozo, Jose Alfredo Ramirez, Nicolas Piño, Luís Bush, René Arancibia, Ricardo Rodriguez
July 25, 1985	Costa Rica (La Garita Retreat Center)	44 denominations		
November 11, 1985	Bolivia			Luís Bush

Date	Country/ Region	Participation	Committee Chair(s)	Speakers
November 15-19, 1985	Venezuela (Rancho Grande Camp, El Limón)	325 pastors and youth from across the country	FRAMINEV[5], Roberto Hatch, Valetin Vale, Samuel Olson	Edison Queiróz, Luís Magin Alvarez, Calixto Patricio, Bill Boerop, Luís Bush
December 11-12, 1985	Nicaragua[6]			Luís Bush, Agustín Ruíz, Antonio Gallegos, Jorge A. Ponce, Patricia Cortéz, Roger Araica, Gustavo Sevilla, Ignacio Hernández, Feliz Rosales
December 27, 1985	Colombia[57] (Bogota)	37 church leaders	Ruperto Velez, Esteban Aldrich	Luís Bush, Aristóbulo Pórras
January 3, 1986	(Youth) El Salvador	70 youth leaders		Luís Martí, Ninette Jiménez, Roberto Azzatir, Moisés Mejía
January 9-11, 1986	Honduras (Tegucigalpa)	34 leaders from 26 churches and institutions	Saúl Gómez[8]	David Harms, Douglas Livingstone

---

[5] Fraternity of Evangelical Ministers

[6] In a memo from Luís Bush (1986, January 4. *Asuntos varios de COMIBAM '87* [Various matters about COMIBAM '87]. COMIBAM/Bertuzzi Archives Box 17) he reported that the organizing pastors of the Nicaragua conference had been arrested and threatened, and had thus decided to postpone the conference.

[7] This was actually a breakfast sponsored by COMIBAM and SEPAL (Bush, L. K., 1986, January 4. *Asuntos varios de COMIBAM '87* [Various matters about COMIBAM '87]. COMIBAM/Bertuzzi Archive Box 17).

Date	Country/Region	Participation	Committee Chair(s)	Speakers
February 4-5, 1986	Mexico (Oaxtepec)		Vidal Valencia, Samuel Castro	
February 21-23, 1986	Central America & Mexico (Guatemala)	Women	Regina de Broli	Graciela Esparza, Beatríz de Zapata, Esther de Cajas, Otí de Cárcamo
February 21-23, 1986	Central America (Guatemala)	Youth	Uriel Garcia[6]	
February 24-26, 1986	Guatemala (Antigua)	129 leaders from various denominations and national evangelical organizations	Mardoqueo Muñoz[7]	Ralph Winter, Mardoqueo Muñoz, Emilio Antonio Nuñez, Luís Bush
March 14-15, 1986	Spain (Granja)		Juan Gili	Evis Carballosa, Luís Bush, Samuel Pérez Millos
March 21-22, 1986	Portugal		Evis Carballosa, Samuel Pérez, Abel Rodríguez	

---

[8] Other committee members: David Harms, Carlos Hernandez, Belsasar, José María Sandoval, and Mario Vargas.

[6] Other committee members: Benjamin Muñoz, Cesar Ramirez, Silvia Cordon, Carlos Salazar, Miguel Toledo, Abner Paredes, Mario Chamale, María Campos, Vicente Sánchez

[7] Other committee members: Jorge López, Juan José Ajú, Domingo Guitz, Estéban Sywulka, Rudy Girón, Stan Herod, Luís Bush, Emilio Antonio Nuñez

Date	Country/Region	Participation	Committee Chair(s)	Speakers
April 1-3, 1986	Costa Rica (La Garita Retreat Center)		Rafael Baltodano	
April 11-12, 1986	El Salvador (San Salvador)	50 leaders		Luís Bush
June 17-22, 1986	Argentina			Pablo Smith, Bill Boerop
July 21, 1986	Puerto Rico	10 denominational representatives	Víctor Pagán, Pedro Martínez	Rudy Girón
July 23, 1986	Dominican Republic (Santo Domingo)		Braulio Portes	
July 26-28, 1986	Costa Rica	44 denominations and entities represented		
September 23-24, 1986	Nicaragua	33 national leaders from 15 denominations	Félix Rosales, Antonio Gallegos, Jórge Ponce	Moisés Mejía
October 31-November 2, 1986	(Youth) Guatemala (Quezaltenango)	160 youth leaders		

Date	Country/Region	Participation	Committee Chair(s)	Speakers
November 13-15, 1986	Panama	95 people from 20 denominations and other ministries		
November 14, 1986	Peru (Lima)	60 leaders	Alberto Garcés	Pedro Arana, Víctor Laguna, Roberto Hatch, Hector Piña
November 20, 1986	Bolivia (Cochabamba)	110 leaders representing 60 denominations and entities	Ulíses Sánchez, Julián Coronel, José Moreno	Roberto Hatch, Ulíses Sánchez
November 21-23, 1986	Venezuela (Caracas)	80 people	Santiago Montero	Roberto Hatch, Daniel Atari
January 8-11, 1987	Honduras (Siguatepeque)			
March 9-11, 1987	(Youth) Bolivia (Santa Cruz de la Sierra)	150 participants from 15 churches and 13 denominations		David Morales, Dario Suárez, Guillermo Espinoza, Carlos Walter,[8]

---

[8] Other speakers included, Francisco Haggerty, Gustavo Oropeza, Carlos Ramsey, and Ulíses Sánchez

Date	Country/Region	Participation	Committee Chair(s)	Speakers
May 1-3, 1987	Colombia[9] (Bogota)	250 pastors and leaders		Roberto Hatch, Albert Marulanda, Juan Muñoz, Roberto Linthicum, Zacarías Salas

---

[9] A Colombian national consultative committee consisted of Jerónimo Pérez (ACECOL), Gloria de Figueroa (Gospel Recordings), Hector Pardo (CEDEC), David Peacock (Christian Literature Center), Juanita de Bucana (Missionary Orientation Center), Eduardo Gómez (New Covenant Christian Corporation), Joselín Pinilla (JUCUM), Estéban Aldrich (SEPAL), Alfónso Corzo (Biblical Societies), and Zacarías Salas (World Vision).

Appendix H

Definition of Key Missiological Terms Prior to 1986 Conference[10]

The present document is offered to assist the English reader in understanding the glossary of key terms developed in anticipation of the first COMIBAM conference. The translation from Luis Bush's Spanish text is by the author.

Church:	The community of people around the world who have been redeemed by the blood of Jesus Christ, reborn by the Holy Spirit, that have accepted Christ as Savior, and live under His Lordship who gather in local groups with the purpose of serving Him, along with others who have the same commitment (Acts 2:42-47; Colossians 1:24). (Note Evangelical Christians from around the world, in the Lausanne Covenant, declared: "The church more than an institution, is the community of the People of God. The church is not identified with a culture, social or political system, or with a particular human ideology." The nature of the church is to expand, adapting to new contexts. The essence of missions for the church is given by the gifts and roles that God programs for a particular historical moment.

---

[10] Bush, L. K., (1986, February 21). *Terminología; Significado de palabras importantes* [Terminology: Meaning of important words]. COMIBAM/Bertuzzi Archive Box 17.

> The church justifies its presence in the world when it takes the responsibility of evangelizing "all nations").

Evangelism: All activity carried out by the members of the body of Christ with the objective of convincing men and women of accepting Jesus Christ as Lord and Savior and serving Him in the community of the church (Matthew 28:19; Acts 4:4; 18:7-11). (Note: Evangelism represents the activity that challenges men and women to serve Christ by proclaiming the "good news of salvation." By using this term it is important to make a distinction: When evangelism takes place between two or more persons, of the same culture, it is mono-cultural, and it should be distinguished from the term "missions." "Missions" implies doing evangelism and church planting in other cultures).

Mission[11]: The biblical task, trusted to the church, which includes, preaching, fellowship, teaching and service (Ephesians 3:10; 4:11-13; Matthew 25:34-46). (Note: The Commission for the whole church to do the ministry of

---

[11] Bosch (2006) traced the evolution in evangelicalism from a one-mandate strategy (evangelism only) to a two-mandate strategy (evangelism and social responsibility) from the 1966 Wheaton Declaration to the 1966 Berlin Congress and on to Lausanne '74 (p. 404-405). COMIBAM's glossary reflects a slight awareness of the social responsibility aspect of missions but it is, at best, secondary.

God, for herself, for the Body of Christ, and for the whole world. This includes teaching, worship, ministry to the community, as well as evangelism and missions. "Mission" differs from "missions," since the latter refers to the responsibility of the church of doing cross-cultural ministry. Missions is a portion of the whole mission of the church.[12] The Lausanne covenant declares: "In the mission of the sacrificial service of the church, evangelism is primary. World evangelization requires the whole church taking the whole gospel to the whole world. The church is the center of God's cosmic purpose and its primary significance is the preaching of the gospel").

---

[12] Bosch (2006) made a distinction between "mission" and "missions" to refer *missio Dei* and *missiones ecclesiae* respectively, (p. 10). Nevertheless, this initial definition by COMIBAM leadership refers to both "mission" and "missions" as *missiones ecclesiae*; in other words, as belonging to the church. Minatrea (2004) contrasted the traditional view with what he terms the "missional" view as follows, "The mission-minded church perceives mission as *one expression of its ministry;* the missional church perceives mission as *the essence of its existence*, (p. 11). Members of the FTL developed a version of this latter perspective around the time of the first COMIBAM congress.

Missions:	Fulfilling the biblical task trusted to the church in other cultures and/or nations (Matthew 28:19; Acts 1:8; 11:20, 21).
Missionary:	One sent to fulfill the mission of the church by crossing cultural or national boundaries (Romans 11:13; Acts 11:20, 21; 16:6-10). (Note: It is necessary to distinguish among three types of missionaries:
	A. Church Planter. A cross-cultural or cross-national worker, whose primary task is to make disciples and start churches that are able to reproduce themselves primarily within the target people group.
	B. Church Builder. A cross-cultural or trans-national worker that serves in a secondary role, helping churches to establish themselves better in another culture or country; i.e.: teaching ministry, theological education, literature production.
	C. Church Servant. A cross-cultural or trans-national worker that serves to meet the needs of people in the host culture; i.e.: medical work, orphanages and general education).
Missionary Organization:	A denominational or interdenominational entity that serves and encourages the local church in the cross-cultural and cross-national mission. It provides the structure to channel

the funds, the necessary support services, and the supervision of the missionaries work (Acts 1:3; 13:1-3). (Note: It is necessary to categorize missionary agencies according to the type of missionaries that they send, and according to the way they relate to denominations. For example, if an agency becomes known as a church-planting agency, this means that said agency gives priority to church planting missionaries. Another way of classifying missionary agencies is:

A. Denominational. An agency established as part of the ministry of one or more churches of a given denomination.

B. Interdenominational. An agency that relates to various denominations, but is autonomous and independent of the control of a specific denomination).

A People: A human conglomerate that shares a common culture (Acts 2:5-12; Matthew 24:12; Revelation 5:9, 7:9).

Appendix I

1992 San José Declaration: Researcher's Translation of the *Declaración de San José*

(Londoño, 2006b)

The San José declaration is included here because it was a significant agreement reached by leaders of the various Ibero American countries in regard to the "Adopt a People" strategy. The translation to English from Spanish is by the author.

We, the participants of the Ibero American Consultation on "Adopt a People," convened by the Ibero American Missionary Cooperation (COMIBAM International) and with the added participation of the Latin American Evangelical Fraternity (CONELA), held in San Jose, Costa Rica on October 6 through 10, 1992; as representatives of Ibero American national evangelical alliances, national missions committees, and various other church and missionary organizations, affirm that:

The mission of the church is to bless all people groups on the earth with the Good News of the kingdom of God given in Jesus Christ. We understand that God's desire is that humanity, which is represented in all the different peoples of the earth, would relate harmoniously to Him and His creation.

Currently there are approximately 6,000 languages and 24,000 people groups on the earth of which approximately 11,000 have not had any possibility of hearing the Good News of salvation. For this reason, we reaffirm our conviction and commitment to carry the gospel of the kingdom of God to these peoples, with the objective of fulfilling God's commandment to Abraham (Genesis 12:1-3) and of our Lord to His disciples (Acts 1:8). We affirm our dedication to this task with renewed vision and passion and until the Lord comes.

Therefore,

We declare

1. That the church should give priority to the biblical mandate of making disciples of all nations (Matthew 28:18-20). We understand that the phrase "all nations" includes also these people groups that are in our countries and in others who have never had the opportunity of understanding the gospel in their own context (Romans 15:20-21).

2. That the responsibility and the implications of adopting unreached people groups on the part of the church includes prayer, research, information, selection, financial support, specific training and the sending of missionaries to these people groups. We encourage each country in our continent to adopt a proportional number of unreached people groups in order to allow us to fulfill the remaining task of world evangelization[13] (Matthew 24:14).

3. The need for missionary intercession on behalf of the unreached people groups and for the efforts carried it out in this great task.

4. The great importance of research in the adoption of unreached people groups. Through research we can transport our hearts to the various people groups, sensing the urgent need they have of knowing the Lord Jesus Christ and his gospel. That is why we declare our interest in working as one body and we recommend the creation of national and regional centers for missionary research.

5. The need for information dissemination. All knowledge about unreached people groups should be shared with each country, denomination and church through the various means of communication available. At the same time, the church should

---

[13] Appendix J provides a list of the proposed proportional distribution

utilize all of the resources to disseminate to its membership the information on the situation and need of said people groups, with the given clarifications and prudence in the managing of certain data.

6. With reference to the type of organizations and the historical tension between the church and missions, we declare our understanding that within time and space, God has honored and blessed the different ways in which they have organized themselves and have cooperated in order to carry out the missionary task. We affirm that both types of organizations, local churches and missionary agencies, are vital in the process of adoption of unreached people groups, and therefore, they should work in the most efficient manner and with the greatest stewardship of resources.

7. That the missionary task demands a great effort at specific training for those who are going on the mission field and for those that send them. This training should be adequate, balanced and should encompass the spiritual, intellectual and practical aspects. We understand that training should not be limited to an event but it should be extended for the duration of the work life of the missionary. We recommend, in the same manner, that the seminaries and Bible institutes in our continent develop cross-cultural missionary training and equipping programs.

8. That the local church has the primary responsibility of providing finances for missions. In the same manner the church is a responsible party and a partner with the missionary of the various stages of his preparation, sending, staying on the field, return and adaptation to home. Taking into consideration that our countries have the economic capacity to support the missionary task, the sending church should contextualize the need of the missionary with the reality of the assigned mission field.

9. That the spirit of cooperation should characterize all efforts in the missionary task until the gospel is preached to all the nations.

Consistent with these declarations, we accept the challenge of adopting 3,000 of the 11,000 unreached people groups, as part of a world missionary effort.

San José, Costa Rica

October 10, 1992

Appendix J

Assignment of People Groups per Ibero American Country

The San Jose Declaration (Londoño, 2006b, pp. 60-63) encouraged each country in Ibero America to adopt a proportional number of people groups. The table below contains the list of countries with the proportionate (according to the population of Spanish or Portuguese-speaking evangelicals) amount of people groups they could conceivably adopt in order to reach approximately 3,000 people groups as an Ibero American movement.

Table 13

Assignment of people per Ibero American Countries (Londoño, 2006b, p. 64)

Country	People Groups to Adopt
Brazil	1,615
Mexico	312
United States[14]	249
Chile	184
Guatemala	111
Argentina	78
El Salvador	69
Puerto Rico	55
Colombia	51

---

[14] The proportion of people groups assigned to the U.S. is for the Spanish and Portuguese-speaking evangelicals who live there.

Country	People Groups to Adopt
Venezuela	46
Nicaragua	37
Peru	37
Dominican Republic	32
Honduras	25
Bolivia	23
Costa Rica	15
Ecuador	15
Panama	14
Cuba	9
Paraguay	7
Portugal	5
Uruguay	3

www.ingramcontent.com/pod-product-compliance
Lightning Source LLC
Chambersburg PA
CBHW081126170426
43197CB00017B/2761